HURTING
TOO MUCH

HURTING TOO MUCH

SHOCKING STORIES FROM
THE FRONTLINE OF CHILD PROTECTION

HARRY KEEBLE *with*
KRIS HOLLINGTON

**SIMON &
SCHUSTER**

London · New York · Sydney · Toronto · New Delhi

A CBS COMPANY

First published in Great Britain by Simon & Schuster UK Ltd, 2012
A CBS COMPANY

5 7 9 10 8 6

Simon & Schuster UK Ltd
1st Floor
222 Gray's Inn Road
London WC1X 8HB

www.simonandschuster.co.uk

Simon & Schuster Australia, Sydney
Simon & Schuster India, New Delhi

A CIP catalogue record for this book is available
from the British Library.

ISBN: 978-0-85720-848-4

Typeset by M Rules
Printed in Great Britain by CPI Group (UK) Ltd,
Croydon CR0 4YY

Detective Sergeant Harry Keeble has almost twenty years' experience in inner-city proactive policing. He joined the Met after leaving university in 1989. In 1999, Harry joined Haringey drugs squad as a uniformed sergeant and spent the following twelve months planning and leading a hundred raids on fortified crack houses.

Appalled at the number of abused children he encountered, and in particular by the senseless death of Victoria Climbié, Harry joined Hackney's Child Protection Team. He spent the following five years bringing dozens of child abusers to justice, managing several international police investigations related to child abuse across Europe, Africa and the Caribbean. He has prosecuted major drug dealers, rapists and child abusers at the Old Bailey and currently works for Specialist Operations at New Scotland Yard.

Kris Hollington is a freelance journalist, playwright, author and ghost-writer of fourteen books, including the *Sunday Times* bestsellers *Baby X* and *Little Victim*, written with Detective Sergeant Harry Keeble. Kris's articles and books have featured on television and radio (including Channel 4's *Cutting Edge*, ITV1's *Real Crime*, BBC Radio 4's Saturday Play and BBC Drama). He lives in East London.

CONTENTS

AUTHORS' NOTE

It is important to ensure that the details of some of the individuals encountered through my work (witnesses, police officers, social workers, teachers, etc.) are not described in a way that would enable people to recognise them. And of course it is also necessary to protect the identities of children and parents whose stories are detailed in this book. The authors have, with the exception of names that are in the public domain, protected the identities of some people by changing names and altering some background details. Those cases that are a matter of public record are reported in their original detail.

CHAPTER ONE

WEST IS EAST

A sixteen-year-old girl had barricaded herself inside her room.

'She's hysterical,' the manager of the children's home said to me over the phone. 'Police assistance is most definitely required.'

I looked across the office. Rob, our rotund and benevolent boss, was discussing a new child protection policy with the rest of the team. I sighed. I'd have to be briefed later. At least the children's home was nearby and it would probably only take a few minutes to sort out. Kids usually end their protest soon after the police turn up, considering our arrival to be a victory of sorts. Besides, although it hadn't been my case, I'd briefly met this extremely polite and quiet girl once before, and I was surprised to learn that she was responsible for a disturbance like this.

'I'll be right over.'

I emerged from Stoke Newington Police Station into the hot summer's morning, climbed in my grey unmarked police Fiesta and drove for ten minutes to the address. The house was like many in Hackney, a tall Victorian brick building that had long lost its splendour.

It was sandwiched between two B&Bs on a wide and busy road. These were the sort that would never make it on to a

British Tourist Board website. Most of Hackney's B&Bs were populated by homeless families and people claiming asylum. Any tourist here was lost and in need of directions.

I shook the manager's hand. He was in his forties, slightly overweight and wore the stressed expression of a man whose nerves had been wound taut by his troubled residents.

'Is it just you?' he asked with concern, peering over my shoulder.

I smiled. 'Well, yes, we don't usually send the riot squad for a child barricaded in her bedroom, even in Hackney.'

'That's not what I meant.' He was clearly not amused. 'She's on the second floor,' he said, already breathing heavily as we climbed the first set of stairs. 'You know her don't you?'

'Nadeema? Oh yes. Her parents tried to force her into marrying her much older cousin.'

The man paused on the second-floor landing, panting. Once he'd caught his breath he said, 'And needless to say, she disagreed with their choice.'

The white door was made of solid wood, not one that would be easy to kick down. I knocked.

'Nadeema? It's Detective Sergeant Harry Keeble, from Hackney's Child Protection Unit. We met once before. Is everything OK in there?'

Silence. I pressed my ear up against the door. I thought I could hear sobbing.

'What's she got in there?' I asked the manager.

He shrugged.

'Nadeema, I need you to speak to me—'

A sharp, angry voice cut through the door. 'There's nothing you can do, nothing! Go away!'

'What happened?'

'I want to die! I want to die!'

*

Earlier that morning all our phones were off the hook, except for the one belonging to our short but indomitable office manager, Clara. Forty-something Clara was the unit's unofficial aunt; she knew exactly when to be stern or sympathetic and somehow, by using methods that bordered on genius, she kept our over-stretched office in order.

Clara always held the fort during our weekly semi-formal office meeting, which was led by the walking encyclopedia that was Rob, our avuncular and overweight Detective Inspector, aka the Fat Controller. During this meeting all fifteen members of Hackney's Child Protection Unit were able to sound off about anything job related, whether we simply wanted to share infor-mation, or rant about the injustice of a particular case, or complain about the uselessness of a certain policy. You could almost hear the hiss as our frustrations were gradually released under Rob's expert guidance. Once that was done, it was time to digest our latest performance figures while munching Rob's bis-cuits and slurping cups of tea.

Although these figures played an important part of the meet-ing, we never received a dressing-down over their numbers. Unlike the more traditional burglary or robbery squads who were target-driven, we used the figures as they should have been: as a guideline. They were there to highlight where we needed to improve, rather than a sign that crime 'must' come down and that files 'must' be closed.

That we were able to do this was thanks to Rob. 'I don't do figures,' he told me the day we'd first met. 'We do what's right. Detections, if we get them, we get them, if we don't we don't. In child protection they don't count, we do what's best for the kid. I've had lots of flack for it, but I've got twenty-eight years in, so what?' He gave a cheeky smile. Clearly, being promoted to Chief Inspector didn't interest him.

To me, the most shocking figures remain – and I suspect that this always will be the case – those regarding disabled children. They are three times more likely to be abused than non-disabled children, and about one third of all disabled children will suffer some kind of abuse, whether physical, sexual or emotional. The 'clear-up' rates are bad enough to make you cry.

As we talked about these astounding rates of abuse, Rob said, 'The one thing that makes all this at least partly bearable – at least to me – is that when we do find a child in danger, I can say, hand on heart, that money has and never will be an issue when it comes to making them safe, whatever the circumstance. We will always do whatever it takes, whatever our budget, and we should take comfort in that.'

'I bet social services wish they could say the same,' Craig said. Craig was in his early thirties, a rock-solid, baby-faced detective with almost ten years' experience in child protection.

'That's true enough,' I said, my long arm reaching for yet another one of Rob's biscuits. 'Foster care alone costs them tens of thousands every month, but we all know Victoria Climbié didn't die thanks to a lack of resources. She died thanks to a series of bad decisions.'

'Problem is,' Sarah said, 'I don't think we have enough staff due to all the court trials we've got at the moment.'

Sarah was in her mid-twenties. She'd joined our team as a uniformed officer three years earlier. She was passionate, independent and wasn't afraid to tell me – or anyone else – when she thought I was wrong about something. She'd recently earned her detective's status and was now leading her own investigations with speed and determination that put many older and more experienced detectives to shame.

'We've never been so busy,' she continued. 'Even if we had an extra ten million pounds in the budget, if we've only got five officers then we're in trouble – and so are the children we're supposed to be protecting.'

Sarah had just highlighted our one downfall. Being so short-staffed often forced us to make very difficult decisions about which case we needed to take further and when. Choosing one case over another with only a short form from social services to go by could sometimes be a fine art, and sometimes impossible.

For example, do you take the alleged beating of a five-year-old child by his stepfather, or a report from an uncertain teacher regarding the possible sexual abuse of a ten-year-old girl? Choose the girl first and the boy may end up being beaten to death before you get to him. Choose the boy and the girl may suffer a horrendous rape before you get to her. Sometimes, neither case would end up being of any concern.

When we recover pornographic films of children, we have to watch them so that we can collect vital evidence that may help us find the children in the films. Knowing that you can't save these children from the horrific torture you're watching isn't easy to live with. Some cases will haunt you for years, as Rob, the most experienced officer in the game, knew only too well.

Despite this, those few people who made it through the recruitment process didn't leave. No one joins child protection unless they are absolutely sure. It's made very clear what you will have to face, from the questions you will have to ask witnesses, the decisions you will have to make that will affect people's lives forever, and the evidence you will have to look at. There is no covering of the eyes in child protection; that was why we always had a recruitment problem.

We investigated all forms of abuse (whether physical, mental, sexual, as well as kidnappings) carried out against a child by family members, extended family members, main carers, babysitters, youth workers and school workers – because in most cases of child abuse, that is exactly who's responsible.

In Hackney, cases arrived by the truckload each week, covering everything from rape to ritual abuse, from allegations of assault and/or inappropriate sexual behaviour to unacceptable behaviour from doctors, from paedophiles stalking schools to businessmen downloading child pornography from the Internet.

'Well,' Rob said, as he picked up our staff rota folder, 'we're going to be working a lot more closely with social workers on our investigations from now on. For once, the higher-ups have had a good idea. I am fed up with reading about delays in investigations while you wait for discussions with social workers. I know some of you have said that we should share the same office space with social services, so that information and investigations would flow more smoothly. That's not going to happen just yet but this is a definite step in the right direction.'

As Rob scrutinised the rotas, Clara's phone rang. She snatched it up and beckoned me over with the receiver a few seconds later.

I excused myself, got up and strode over.

I really needed Nadeema to open the door. To do this, I needed to build up rapport, but how was I supposed to create a bond with this girl so I could help her?

It might be nothing, or it could be a barricade–suicide. If so, then it would take at least an hour for the crisis management team to arrive with a negotiator. Then I'll be here all day, I thought, and there's a big pile of work waiting on my desk.

Just about all police officers will have to deal with someone on the verge of suicide during their career. It's an extraordinary position to be in. From one moment to the next you're trying to find the words that will stop someone from leaping off a roof. It's not a time to become tongue-tied.

Some suicidal individuals view the police officer that comes to deal with them as their very last opportunity to find help, their last ray of hope. This is one hell of a responsibility and you have to live with those times when the words don't come.

I had no idea what I needed to say to get through to Nadeema, to give her the attention, or reassurance and understanding she needed. I searched my memory. It had been a while. What does one do in this situation? The rulebook says contain the incident, gather intelligence, set up cordons and establish contact with the subject.

Right. Nadeema was in her room, contained. I needed the rest of the building's occupants to keep quiet. Kids can be cruel and in my experience it wasn't uncommon for teenagers to shout encouragement to jumpers, so the last thing I needed was some idiot shouting out a stupid comment.

The manager didn't seem to know much more than what he'd already told me, except that he was certain there was no one else with her in the room. We both knew why she was in care and who her peers were but we had no idea what the catalyst for the present situation was. Without that, progress would be slow.

I had to keep Nadeema talking. Generally, these situations tend to end well if the would-be victim is still talking an hour later.

While people tend to think about suicide for a long time before attempting it, the act itself is usually impulsive, in that victims choose a method based on what's readily available.

Suicidal police officers that have access to them choose guns, as do farmers. These produce terrible crime scenes. When placed under the chin, high-powered weapons will sometimes lift the brain in its entirety out of the skull and send it flying across the room. One officer found an intact brain in a sink. His first thought was that the suicide victim had been the target of a satanic cult. In another case a man's brain lifted out of his skull and landed on the coffee table in front of him.

Doctors prefer to use drugs, usually a much tidier death, while fishermen use the ocean and commuters step out in front of trains. People who live by or hang out on rooftops or bridges jump off them, producing traumatic results that passers-by will never forget.

A sixteen-year-old girl will turn to the leg razor or nail scissors, or perhaps Mummy's sleeping pills.

If Nadeema was planning to commit suicide, then she wanted to show the world how much she was hurting, how much others had hurt her, and how alone and helpless she felt.

My worst enemy now was silence.

'Nadeema, remember I'm a police officer and I'm here to help you. Everything is under control out here. I need to know what's going on in there.'

Silence. I placed my ear as close as I could to the door. I could hear movement inside, pacing perhaps.

'Nadeema, please talk to me, I want to help.'

'My brothers found me!' she sobbed suddenly through the door. 'They want to have me married in Afghanistan or dead. It's no good. I'll never be able to hide from them. They'll never give up. I've had enough.'

I'd dealt with many suicidal people before but nothing like this. It was clear from this statement that the system, for whatever reason, had failed Nadeema and she felt she was in terrible danger.

It was hard to judge her exact state of mind through the door – just how serious was she? There was a huge risk in underestimating someone's suicidal intent. A police officer, in perfectly good faith, once tried to use humour to end a situation because the suicidal man he was dealing with was standing on the ledge of a first-floor hotel room.

'If you were serious,' he said, 'you'd have rented a room higher up.' He was immediately proved wrong when the man jumped headfirst onto the concrete, instantly killing himself.

It pays to take every case seriously but determining when a

dramatic intervention is a necessary risk, considering that lives may be put in danger, is a fine art.

'Have you taken anything?'

'What do you mean?'

'Any pills, medicine, drugs, alcohol.'

'No.'

'Why were your brothers looking for you?'

'Because once I finished my GCSEs, they were going to fly me to Afghanistan to marry a man twenty years older than me.'

Nadeema sobbed for a moment before continuing, almost in a wail.

'I was going to spend a lifetime being raped by someone old enough to be my dad in the middle of nowhere. I wanted to be a doctor, fall in love and marry whoever I wanted.'

'Did you tell your family this?'

'Yes! My brothers punched me in the face. They said I should never speak to them like that, that if I did not do what they said, then I was ruining the family honour and they would be forced to kill me, and that nobody would find out. Now they have found me I know there is no other choice. I am going to save them the trouble of having me killed. I hope they think I will have suffered enough to save the family honour.'

This was not looking good. Expressions of hopelessness and helplessness are very serious suicide clues, the dividing line between depression and the intent to actually commit suicide.

Nadeema wanted it to hurt because she saw herself as guilty for betraying her family; she wanted them to know she had punished herself. Even after all they'd put her through, she still loved them.

'What happened after they beat you?'

'I ran away.'

'Where did you go?'

'To friends.'

'Then what happened?'

Silence.

I was going too fast.

'Don't worry,' I said, 'no one's coming in there and you're not in trouble. After all, nothing has happened, has it? We're just talking about your problems and I'm going to help you solve them. You've done nothing wrong, I'm only going to help.'

The last thing I needed to do was to make demands or start bargaining with her; I wanted her to feel safe but also that I was in charge here. That as long as she was talking to me then everything was stable, under control. Attempting to push her could end in disaster, especially as I could not see what she was up to behind the door.

'You need help and protection. I work in child protection. This is what I do. I will help you. I just need you to talk to me.'

A resounding silence came at me through the door. I could hear movement inside.

'Nadeema?'

After all I'd said, if the Territorial Support Group (the riot squad) had to charge into the room with a battering ram and subdue Nadeema, her sense of helplessness and hopelessness would grow. She would end up more traumatised and it was possible she'd try suicide again in the future, perhaps without giving any warning next time.

'Do you have any sisters?'

I was looking for a way to end the incident, to give Nadeema hope, or find something that she would want to live for, despite everything.

'No. I have a baby brother though.'

'And you love him, right?'

'Yes. I've written him a goodbye note. I've written a note to my parents too.'

'I'd like to hear them,' I said. 'Would you read them out to me?'

'No, they're private.'

'I understand. But I'm sure your little brother needs you. If you come out and talk to me here, you can write other letters to your parents, explaining how you feel.'

'Look, erm – what's your name again?'

'Harry.'

'Harry, everything's OK. Just give me a few more minutes.'

She was telling *me* that everything was OK? Another bad sign. This was not an improvement. Nothing I'd said or done had made her feel any better as far as I could tell.

I'd been crouching at the door with my ear pressed to it. I straightened. It seemed strangely quiet around me. I wondered about calling for assistance. Perhaps the sound of an approaching siren would push her over the edge, or would it perhaps help? Show her we were taking her problems seriously? No doubt, if I asked, police cars would be here shortly and would throw up their cordons, while the citizens of Hackney, well used to such sights, would go about their daily business.

We'd only been talking for a few minutes but I really didn't like that statement. If Nadeema didn't respond to anything I said next, then it would be down to me to kick the door in.

Just then the door clicked.

I tensed.

It opened.

Nadeema was standing there.

Her hands were empty, no knife, razor or pills. Our eyes met; there was such a distance between us, our lives were so different, but in that moment I felt incredibly close to her.

All I wanted to do was help her.

In that instant I looked over Nadeema's shoulder, scanning her room with my policeman's eye. Then I saw it. A five-litre fuel can on the bed. As the air moved from the opening of the door I smelled the tang of petrol.

Jesus Christ.

Setting oneself ablaze is a severe case of malice aforethought.

An extraordinarily painful option, self-immolation is also the most dramatic, a political act that would have guaranteed Nadeema the front page of most English newspapers. She clearly wanted to show the world how much she was hurting, how much others had hurt her, and how alone and helpless she felt.

In her home country of Afghanistan, however, it might well have passed unnoticed outside her immediate family. The Ministry of Women's Affairs in Afghanistan reported that a total of 103 women set themselves on fire between March 2009 and March 2010.[1]

No one knows what the real numbers are, given the difficulty of collecting data. More than 80 per cent of women who set themselves ablaze die and many families, shamed by this terrible act, simply don't tell the authorities. Self-immolation remains both common and poorly understood, with few resources devoted to its prevention. It has long existed as a method by which Afghan women try to escape their abusive marriages. Marriage in Afghanistan today is still more like a trade than a union based on love. Women are exchanged to resolve family disputes or strengthen family bonds. And the male-controlled tribal structures don't side with women in domestic-abuse cases.

I looked back at Nadeema. She was terrified. What kind of childhood was this? She'd spent months worrying and worrying about her future. I might be able to protect her physically but the emotional damage had been overwhelming.

'I want you to help me,' she said, quietly. 'I don't want to die.'

'I'm not the only one,' she told me later. 'I have three friends from school, here in Hackney, that have been forced to marry men that their parents have chosen for them. They did not resist.'

This was extraordinary news to me. I planned to talk to Rob about this as soon as possible.

At least Nadeema was safe. Over the next few months she started to build a new life on her own. She still had hopes of reconciliation, however, and wrote home every week.

Once Nadeema had cleaned up and packed and was on her way to a new safe house in a much more secure location with my promises of help ringing in her ears, I answered my phone, which had been buzzing impatiently for some time. It was Clara.

'Harry, don't forget you have a home visit with Ella from social services.'

I'd forgotten all about it. 'Right, yes. Of course.'

'Everything all right? If something has come up I can cancel it.'

'No, it's no problem. I'll hop in the car and head over now.'

CHAPTER TWO

OPEN HOUSE

I parked in a street on the edge of the large rectangular Kingsmead Estate. I wound up the windows, checked I'd left nothing on the seats and stepped out into the sunshine. Only police officers and gardeners welcome rain. A heatwave signals a crimewave.

It was the summer holidays, a time when, if the sun shines for long enough, even the most dedicated X-Box gladiators eventually pull back the curtains and emerge, squinting into the sunlight, ready for a short dose of reality. Young kids filled the small greens and paths. For once, the high-rise estate, which was surrounded on three sides by parks and a canal, felt alive, happy almost. Against all the odds, there had been improvements.

Any cop who'd worked in this part of town knew the Kingsmead Estate all too well. It was usually mentioned in the same breath as 'urban decay', 'feral gangs' and 'the H-Blocks' (for its prison-like shape).

Kingsmead had been the scene of too many infamous crimes during the past two decades, the worst of which was the murder of Jason Swift in 1985, butchered by paedophile Sidney Cooke, aka 'Hissing Sid'. Cooke, who was in his sixties at the time, displayed evil and cunning beyond belief by setting up his own funfair stall, a children's 'Test Your Strength' machine, at fairgrounds around the country, to trap unsuspecting victims.[1] Dressed in a dirty suit and trilby hat, Cooke – along with his gang – was eventually suspected to be responsible for the deaths of up to nine boys, either underage male prostitutes or children snatched off the streets.

Jason was a fourteen-year-old rent boy from Hackney. Cooke drugged him and, with the help of his friends Robert Oliver, Lennie Smith and Leslie Bailey, he tortured poor Jason to death in Cooke's Kingsmead Estate flat. His body was later found in a shallow grave on the outskirts of London.

Detective Superintendent David Bright described Cooke as 'cocky and arrogant' before he eventually confessed to Jason's killing. Cooke was sent to prison for nineteen years in 1989 for Jason's manslaughter but had his sentence reduced on appeal to sixteen years. Leslie Bailey later named Cooke as one of the killers of seven-year-old Mark Tildesley, who disappeared after visiting a funfair near his home in Wokingham. Cooke lured Mark away to his caravan by promising him a 50p bag of sweets.

In 1991, the Crown Prosecution Service (CPS) decided not to prosecute Cooke for Mark's death as he was already in prison for killing Jason. Cooke later indicated that he knew where Mark's body was buried but refused to tell police or the boy's grieving parents exactly where his grave was.

Other paedophiles hero-worshipped Cooke, partly because of the extent of his depravity and partly because of the lengths to which he went to ensnare his victims. His successes and excesses encouraged other like-minded paedophiles to emulate him.

Incredibly, Cooke was released after nine years, in 1998, even after he refused to attend rehabilitation sessions, saying he would probably offend again. He was right, there is no 'cure' or 'treatment' for paedophilia. It's not a state of mind; it's a state of being.

To add insult to injury, Cooke lived, at his own request, in a suite of three police cells – for his own safety.

He was soon rearrested for a whole host of other sexual offences carried out between 1972 and 1981, many of them uncovered by the Channel 4 programme *Dispatches*. Cooke was convicted and sentenced to two life sentences in 1999 and although he's currently eligible for parole, he remains in Wakefield Prison, aka 'Monster Mansion'.

Cooke has recently made friends with 'Britain's Josef Fritzl', a paedophile who repeatedly raped his two daughters over twenty-five years – starting when they were aged eight and ten years old – fathering nine of his own grandchildren. The 56-year-old man – who can't be named to protect his daughters' identity – was jailed for life in 2008. The two men, both of whom are unrepentant, are said to be 'inseparable'.[2]

'No one with a kid should have to live here,' a single mother, pushchair in front of her, had told reporters upon hearing the news that Cooke had been rearrested, the broken windows behind her emphasising her point.

It was a popular argument in the wake of Cooke's conviction, an argument that also had its roots in the case of five-year-old Daniel Vergauwen, who was punched to death by his stepfather Gerald Dowden in 1989, after three years of being beaten by his mother.

Although placed on the at-risk register at the end of 1988, and despite Dowden's threats to throw a social worker off the balcony the following July, Daniel remained in their care until he was beaten so badly that his stomach ruptured and he died in his bedroom on 8 September. Dowden was sentenced to life while his mother, Leonie, was cleared of manslaughter but convicted of cruelty.[3]

If this sounds familiar, then you'd be right. Baby P (Peter Connelly) suffered a similar fate in the neighbouring borough of

Haringey in 2007. His horrifying case, although exceptional, was not new.

Jason's and Daniel's murders marked Kingsmead as a criminal haven; the rates for burglary, drug-dealing and vandalism shot up over the following years.

But, bit-by-bit, since 2001, things had begun to get better. By the time I parked on the estate that day, the local primary school was thriving, despite the fact that 95 per cent of its pupils were from 46 different countries and spoke English as a second language. It was a remarkable transformation, despite having spent several years languishing in the 'at-risk' category (in that it was failing to provide an acceptable level of education).

That wasn't to say the estate was now a beacon of respectability brimming over with community spirit. There remained a constant underlying threat from some younger people, the sons and daughters of long-term residents. Not all of them saw a future they liked and so they remained an unstable element, ready to explode the moment we, the police, overstepped a certain mark, or the moment a certain crime highlighted societal injustice.

The problem with doing home visits on these most deprived estates during daylight hours – especially sunny ones – is that the arrival of the smartly dressed acts as a loud doorbell signalling the unwelcome presence of authority. Besides the youngsters playing football, riding bikes and chasing one another, older teenagers smoked and drank on balconies, stairwells and on the grass, waiting for something to happen.

Any visiting cop could be that something.

Had I roared up in a car with smoked windows playing loud dubstep, no one would have looked up. As it was, a group by the stairwell watched me, waiting to see what business the cops had on their territory.

After waiting a few minutes for the social worker, who was

running late, I noticed some familiar patterns. A group of boys, the eldest of whom was about fourteen, were bouncing an old leather football around a small courtyard, while a large section of grass between the flats remained bare; a sign that it was 'owned' by a larger, older and stronger gang of boys.

A strange concrete skate park of twisted cement hills and gulleys had been taken over by some men in their early twenties, who sat on a metal bench with a cover, staring at me angrily, waiting for me to go so they could get on with business.

They knew I was probably a cop because – apart from the smart suit – I stared back openly and without fear, a sure giveaway that I was a member of London's biggest gang.

Those younger children who would have made good use of the skate park were cycling up and down the street, jumping the speed bumps on their ghetto bikes.

I checked my watch:15:13. Another two minutes and I'd call the office. But at least the job paid for my car. For social worker Ella, the estate was a winding bus ride away from Hackney Social Services.

It was too hot. Too hot to stay waiting in the car, and too hot for a suit. The start of the summer had been exceptionally dry and, for once, the promised heatwave had arrived.

Kids in school can be challenging enough, but here the fifteen-year-olds were six feet tall and roamed without supervision. They were also diverse, not just culturally, but in terms of their personality. Some were mentally tougher than others, some liked life on the estate while others fought to escape. Some of them would go on to achieve the same as your average middle-class kid from the Home Counties, although they had a much steeper climb.

All too often, dealing with these kids left me with feelings of despair and hope all at once, an emotional cocktail presented to cops and social workers everywhere.

When I was a uniformed constable I was called to deal with a disturbance in a high school not far from the Kingsmead Estate. It had been an unusually long and hot June. The pupils had overrun the school and were totally out of control. While some were simply having fun, others shared more sinister agendas such as settling scores with rivals and stealing school equipment.

Most of the older boys refused to be subdued by our threats of arrest and fought back. A colleague, frustrated beyond reason by the extended taunting, snapped out his Asp, the extendable baton.

Not a good idea.

Police beating a black schoolboy with batons? The inevitable headlines, inquiries and indignation would only fuel distrust and hatred of the police and help to push kids at risk into the arms of drug dealers. Realising this, rightly embarrassed, the officer put the Asp away with a sense of reality and hopelessness, while the taunts grew in volume and aggression.

I decided to pick off the ringleaders and caught hold of the most vocal of the pupils, a fourteen-year-old girl. As I grabbed her, I felt an enormous burst of pain as she clamped her teeth tighter than a pit bull on my forearm.

Now that hurt.

Had she been an adult outside a pub at 1 a.m. I would have hit her. I tried frantically to prise her teeth free as her friends screamed at her to bite harder.

Eventually, after much struggling, with my arm throbbing and bloody, and minus my hat, which had been lost in the struggle, I booked her in at the police station. She screamed and swore relentlessly. I looked at the desk sergeant, who stared open-mouthed, aghast at her language, and shrugged helplessly.

I was used to being sworn at and could normally laugh it off but to hear things like: 'You will never have my pussy, copper!'

repeated over and over made me feel nauseous. Where on earth had that come from? Her mother? Her friends? Did such language have roots in sexual abuse?

Her father came to collect her. He was well spoken, polite and, on the surface at least, seemed to be an upstanding member of the community. He refused to believe me when I explained what had happened and what she had said.

'I'm sorry, you're wrong, my daughter would never say things like that,' he said.

'But I am telling you that she did,' I replied, boiling with fury. 'Why won't you believe me?'

'Because she would never say anything so horrible. You must have her mixed up with another student. They're all wearing the same uniform.'

I angrily rolled up my sleeve and showed him the bloody imprint of his daughter's teeth. I absorbed his look of horror before pointing at the CCTV camera positioned in the ceiling.

'Would you like me to play back the video, so we can both watch and listen to exactly what your daughter said?'

Defeated, he shut up and stared at the floor. Normally, I would have offered him help. But I was too angry. All I could do was let the situation speak for itself.

Not long after he left, the desk sergeant called me. 'I think you need to come down and see this,' he said.

I stormed back to the front desk, thinking that the father had probably made a complaint. My thunderous look of barely suppressed rage transformed into stunned surprise when I found a group of black school kids waiting quietly for me.

One of them, a boy of about sixteen, handed me my hat. It had scorch marks round the edge.

'We rescued it from some boys who were trying to burn it,' he said. 'It's not too bad, it might clean up.'

Hope among the ruins.

'Hello, Harry!' I snapped back to the present and turned to see Ella, a petite woman in her early twenties with untidy shoulder-length black hair and deep green eyes.

In that first instant, I guessed she was a well-spoken, well-read and well-meaning university graduate who was passionate about her work, but also incredibly naïve about her job and Hackney.

'Hi,' I said as we shook hands. 'This is your first lone home visit, isn't it? Sorry, your boss grassed you up, warned me to expect a newbie.'

Ella sighed, smiled and shrugged her shoulders as if owning up to a guilty secret. 'Yes, yes, OK, you've got me, it's my first,' she said. 'I appreciate your coming along.'

'No problem, it's a pleasure,' I said, meaning it.

Ella's client, Mandy, was unusual in that she actually liked both social workers and police, and although visits to her could be challenging, it at least felt as though she was on our side.

Ella sniffed the air. 'Is that petrol? Is there something wrong with your car?'

The can had splashed petrol over my shoes when I removed it from Nadeema's room.

'No, it's me. I've just dealt with a girl who was planning to set herself on fire.'

Ella looked at me in horror, eyes wide. 'You're joking.'

'Welcome to child protection,' I said brightly. 'Come on, let's go.'

Although I'd been to see Mandy before, I'd forgotten which block she was in. New residents sometimes got lost looking for their homes, thanks to the uniform design and countless stairwells. I consulted a map of the estate, placed on a large wooden board at the entrance. I tried to stare through the tags scrawled over it in black markers.

We found the right entrance and, of course, a group of surly teenagers were lurking in the stairwell, hiding from the CCTV cameras installed everywhere but on the stairs.

'Hiya, you all right?' I said, friendly but also making a statement, that although outnumbered, we weren't intimidated. We walked up another two floors and found the brown door to Mandy's flat, also tagged in black marker. It was ajar. I looked at Ella, who shrugged and pushed it open.

'Mandy?' I called out. 'You there?'

Children were running through the flat as we entered. I noted the familiar and distinctive dank odour that anyone who has worked in this field knows only too well: the slightly doggy smell of a household out of control, where everyday concerns do not include housework.

Mandy was a one-off. Although I knew others like her, she was the extreme version. She had had seven children with seven different fathers and the kids all lived with her in a flat with bashed-in doors, coverless and yellowed duvets, walls covered in scribbles, stains and sticky finger marks. Although the home was chaotic and in a constant mess, the kids were happy and there hadn't yet been any cause to remove them from her care.

Mandy was in the kitchen, which looked like it hadn't been decorated since the 60s.

'All right, 'Arry? Long time no see.' She smiled at me and it was impossible not to focus on the black space where her two lower front teeth should have been. Mandy was thin, had wild brown-blonde hair. There was something about her that made her seem a bit fairy-like, as if she were a very down-at-heel Tinkerbell.

Mandy was one of the few people we visited who always had a smile for us. She'd been known to social services for years and her file was about a metre high, caused by the constant visits over concerns for her children's wellbeing. She wasn't an alcoholic, a drug addict or a gambler, she just needed guidance and a dedicated helping hand. Her problem was sex, which she confused with friendship. This meant that she ended up sleeping with any man she took a liking to – and, as word had spread, she ended up 'liking' a *lot* of men.

For most of the men this simply meant free sex, but Mandy was also in danger of attracting a predatory paedophile. These men preyed on women like Mandy, single mothers with lots of kids, poor and overstretched, grateful for the attention and help of a considerate and generous man. These predators were cunning enough to conceal the abuse and also knew how to escape justice by the time we eventually appeared.

Sure enough, while Ella and I were in the kitchen with Mandy, a reedy male voice came from the front door.

'Mand, Mand, you about?'

'Busy, Phil!' she shouted back. Phil sloped off. He knew what 'busy' usually meant. I didn't catch sight of Phil but my stereotypical cop's imagination flashed up an image of a buck-toothed, wonky-eyed hillbilly in denim dungarees.

'Do you wanna sit down?' Mandy asked.

Ella nodded and got as far as 'Thank—' before I quickly and loudly cut her off.

'No, we're fine here, thank you,' I said as a grubby-faced four-year-old marched past the kitchen door, enthusiastically punching a dirty stuffed panda.

I'd sat down in Mandy's flat once before. Her shiny sofa was rich with stains, the armrests sticky with goodness knows what. I'd ended up with a very expensive dry-cleaning bill – and I'm sure the dry cleaners never looked at me the same way again.

Ella had shouldered Mandy's mighty file after the previous social worker had taken maternity leave. Thanks to Mandy's inability to cope and the resulting frequent visits, social services were part of the family, like a collection of well-meaning and strict aunts. If she was left alone for a couple of months then trouble would quickly sprout and sure enough, a paedophile had once shown interest, necessitating my presence. So, while Ella was there to get to know Mandy, I was there to try and put the brakes on her sexual activity, a walking talking dose of bromide.

I liked Mandy very much (although I wouldn't bring her home for dinner). She was a good-hearted lady who loved her kids and played with them constantly. She was barely able to read or write but that didn't make her a bad mother. At that moment, three boys were in the bathroom, playing in a bath full of water, staying cool and having fun, their own private little paddling pool.

Ella was enjoying this visit to a 'nice' client. Mandy wasn't a lying, confrontational, moaning individual who was conning incapacity benefit out of the taxpayer. Although Mandy was a member of the 'underclass', she was a genuine case and pleasant to deal with.

'Mandy,' I said, 'you have to stop shagging every man in the block. And for some reason, all of your internal doors are broken wide open, the kids must see what you're up to. It isn't good for them.'

'All right, 'Arry,' Mandy replied quietly with a soft giggle.

It was like telling off a child who had been caught truanting for the fifth time.

'And you have to be a bit more choosy about who you let in. Some of these characters are dangerous. You have to be more careful. We can't always be here to protect you and your kids.'

'Yes, 'Arry, I'm sorry. It's just so nice to 'ave a bit of adult company. I love the little ones, but I don't get many other visitors apart from the social, you know?'

'I understand, but you have to hold back with the blokes, OK? How about finding some women friends?'

'That's a great idea,' Mandy said with enthusiasm, as if she'd never thought of it before.

While I accepted that she was sincere, I knew that in a couple of weeks' time, her bedsprings would be groaning incessantly once again while the kids ran about the place, doing whatever they liked until Mandy resurfaced. We had to try and stop the cycle, no matter how hopeless it seemed. After all, we couldn't force her to stop having kids, to stop being a burden on the state and to stop letting strange men into her house.

'Just think of your children,' Ella added. 'They love you and learn from you. Imagine if it was them bringing friends back and sleeping with them, you wouldn't like that, would you?'

Mandy shook her head.

'Well, if you carry on like this, then that's what they'll end up doing.'

'I know I should stop but it's so nice to have company, isn't it? I can't afford a TV.'

I'd already noticed she didn't actually own one, an extreme rarity for this Hackney estate, which had more plasmas than a Dixons warehouse. Of course, TV licences were harder to find. It would be a brave but foolish detector van that drove in here.

'One of my neighbours gave me this leaflet,' Mandy said, passing a glossy flier to Ella. 'I've been thinking about it. So I don't have more babies, you know?'

'What is it?' I asked. Ella's jaw had dropped.

'This is for drug addicts!' she exclaimed. 'Not for you!'

Ella handed me the brochure. It was from a charity called Project Prevention.

'This can't be legal, can it?' she demanded.

The leaflet, which was provocatively entitled 'Don't let pregnancy get in the way of your crack habit', said that it would pay £200 to drug addicts to be sterilised.[4]

'Who gave it to you?' I asked.

'One of my friends,' Mandy said.

'It's disgusting,' Ella said indignantly.

'Mandy,' I said. 'It's your choice, you just need to stop letting so many men into your home and sleeping with them, all right?'

'Yeah, OK. I weren't going to do it anyway. Who would look after me kids while I was in the 'ospital?'

A skinny blond boy ran in with his mixed-race brother. They both looked to be about six. 'Mummy,' the blond boy said, 'can we play outside?'

'Not yet, darlin', Gemma's gotta be fed and 'ave her sleep. Then you 'ave to eat your tea. Then maybe, as long as it's still light.'

Her flat really was a madhouse; there was movement and noise everywhere you looked but it was amazing to see Mandy with her kids. I'd seen other mums lose it with one child, let alone seven, but Mandy was able to keep track of all their needs without thinking. It seemed so ridiculous that she could be a good mum, but so hopeless when it came to men.

Eventually, we said our goodbyes. Ella would be back in a week on her own. The afternoon sun shone brightly on the landing as we left.

A thin white man in a dirty white shirt and blue jeans mooched towards us. I quickly took in the food stains on his shirt, his missing tooth, his tobacco-stained fingers and dirty fingernails and put two and two together.

'Hi, Phil, how's it going?'

Phil was immediately flustered. 'Er . . . Um . . . Hi.' He turned around and jogged down the stairwell.

Ella and I crossed the square, teenage eyes following us.

'I couldn't help noticing that you didn't seem shocked by the leaflet, Harry,' Ella said.

'Well, I've never heard of them until now, but I think they might have a good argument.'

'What?!' Ella was incredulous. 'Are you a Nazi or something?'

'No, but I've seen a junkie lying dead on her bed, her unborn baby dead inside her, both victims of drugs. Our unit has taken dozens of babies away from drug-addicted mothers.'

Ella didn't say anything. I suspected she might change her mind after she'd seen her tenth crack baby plucked from a mother who neither knew how to cope nor cared; who thought about nothing except her fix.

'I'm not saying it should happen,' I added, 'I just mean I can see where they're coming from and why they'd win a lot of support. I could also see lots of prostitute drug addicts who've already given birth to two or three babies going for it.

'Give it time. You're new here, your first visit has been unusually pleasant. You're in for a very rough ride, believe me.'

'All right, Harry,' Ella answered with a smile. 'But I'm ready for anything. That's why I joined child protection.'

We'd reached the car. 'Can I give you a lift?'

'No thanks, it's a lovely afternoon, I think I'll walk, take a short cut across the park.'

I climbed into my car and watched as Ella strolled away across the empty park and passed the concrete skate park. The men were still sat there, sharing a joint. One of them said something as Ella passed and they laughed.

'Just be ready,' I said to myself as I started the engine. 'Just be ready, that's all.'

CHAPTER THREE

PINK ELEPHANT

I arrived at the offices of Hackney's Child Protection Unit bright and early the next morning, carrying a large coffee in one hand and a thick manila folder in the other. I dropped the folder on my desk; it landed with a satisfying thud. In the same motion I sat down and swung my feet up onto the desk and took a big slurp of macchiato.

Clara appeared from nowhere, making me jump. Coffee landed on my tie. 'Shi— Bother!' Clara didn't approve of bad language.

'Have you checked the message book?' Clara asked, frowning at my raised feet.

'No, not yet,' I replied, mopping my tie with the serviette that had come with the coffee.

'There's one from Ella in there for you.'

'Ella?'

'Harry,' Clara said, putting on her stern voice, 'there's something wrong with your memory. You met her just yesterday on a home visit.'

'Oh, her, the new social worker, right.'

I took my feet down and reached for the red book. We were supposed to write everything down in this, our weapon against the Post-it culture. After jotting down the date and time, I made a note of the message and number before calling Ella. She answered immediately.

'Thanks for your help yesterday, Harry. My manager said I'd better call you about this one.'

'Fire away,' I said, putting my feet back up on the desk and casually leaning back into the swivel chair, quickly putting them back down again when I spotted Rob frowning at me in disapproval from his desk across the office. As usual, he'd beaten me to work and his mountain of neatly piled files, papers and books stood in stark contrast to my own desk of chaos. Paperwork and I just don't get along.

'We've had a referral about a four-year-old boy called Demaine from his nursery,' Ella said. 'He's been beating up the other boys. He was thrown out of his last nursery for doing the same thing and he's on his last warning with this one.'

'So what's happened to him?'

'His nursery teacher told me he arrived yesterday in a lot of pain. He told her he'd been fighting but didn't say with whom. Can you run some checks, especially on his dad? If there's anything there could you let me know?'

'Sure, I'll call you later.'

In the movies, it usually takes the detective a few quick keystrokes to pull up a suspect's life history from parking tickets to childhood misdemeanours. In the real world it can take hours. You need their full name (no pseudonyms, misspellings, abbreviations or variations) and the right date of birth to check for previous convictions on the Police National Computer.

Then, if you're after intelligence, there are a whole host of systems covering everything from child protection to a general registry, in which you need to specify exactly what kind of intelligence you want, and then there are various sub-categories in each system – suppose you want to check their family history?

Mother and father? Brothers and sisters? If you're looking for someone with a common surname and the date of birth you have for them isn't correct, then it can quickly become a technological nightmare.

This is how people like Ian Huntley, the murderer of ten-year-olds Holly Wells and Jessica Chapman, slip through the net. After Holly and Jessica vanished, it took nearly two weeks for the police to discover that Huntley, a school caretaker, had been the subject of several sexual allegations. One of these had resulted in a charge of rape – later dropped by the CPS. Huntley had also been charged with burglary. Unfortunately, the local police decided that as he had not been convicted, this information should not be released as part of a criminal records check when Huntley submitted his application for the position of school caretaker.

The head teacher later said he would not have hired Huntley had he seen the charge as one of the caretaker's responsibilities was to ensure the security of school buildings.

Tragically, the warning signs were all there, hidden in plain view. Nobody knew where to find them until it was too late.

So it pays to be thorough and the words 'running a check' can translate into half a day's work. As part of every crime investigation I performed a minimum of seven lengthy and detailed searches on each child and recorded every result for the file.

My coffee grew cold and forgotten as I hunted through Merlin and various other fantasy-themed software systems that were surely christened by computer nerds.

Like Ian Huntley, Demaine's dad Jordan had popped up on the system – but only just. He'd been arrested and charged a few times, but each time they'd been dropped for lack of evidence. He'd also attracted the interest of various specialist police units. All the intelligence screamed that this man was a drug-dealing 'gangsta'.

Unfortunately I wasn't able to share most of this information with Ella, as it was sensitive intel, for police eyes only, and did not relate to child abuse. I would, however, be able to give her a hint and I would certainly accompany Ella on what would be a much more testing home visit.

I'd left the station and was walking to my car, deep in thought about Jordan and Demaine, when I heard a woman's pleading cry.

'Please, babe. *Please* sort me out, babe.'

I looked up and saw a skinny white woman with curly black hair standing with her back to me. She was wearing a short black skirt, black hoodie and dirty white trainers. She was all over the man in front of her, a young black guy in shades. She was holding his arms just above the elbow, desperately trying to prevent him from getting away.

'Sort me out' is Hackney-speak for 'Sell me drugs'.

The man's face was blankly indifferent as he shook her off. Her credit was no good. She was simply embarrassing him. Losing patience, he shoved her roughly to one side and strode onwards, shaking his head in disgust at the situation he'd helped engineer.

The woman, who was now sobbing, sat down on a low wall next to a small green on the edge of a council estate and pulled out a mobile phone. I guessed she was in her early twenties; the first signs of crack addiction were plain in the disintegration of her features, the slight sagging of the mouth, along with the drooping and creasing of flesh.

If this had been my Hertfordshire suburbia, I would have stopped to ask: 'I'm a police officer, can I help you?' In inner-city London, however, this was normal. Most people don't see it but it's everywhere. All you have to do is look.

I was once talking to a TV producer who wanted to make a documentary about the rise of crack cocaine. We were in

London's trendy Shoreditch area, home to dozens of TV companies. Jamie Oliver's office was just across the road.

As we walked and talked, a thin bedraggled woman in her slippers emerged from a block of flats, looking the worse for her addiction. A quick trip across the road and she was back with her rock. Then another addict appeared, and another. This was 10 o'clock on a Tuesday morning. The TV producer watched open-mouthed in surprise when I pointed it out to him.

'I'd never even noticed,' he said.

The reality of London's drug problems meant that I could never really help this young woman. I might perhaps have offered an umbrella of safety for a few minutes, but that was all. As I was keen to get to the bottom of Demaine's case, I had no intention of asking if she needed help.

Drawing close, I saw that composing a text message with shaking hands was too much for her. She looked ready to chuck the phone away in despair. I gave her a wide berth, almost walking on the kerb.

Her clothes were stained and dishevelled. I couldn't know for certain that she was a sex worker but the signs were all there. There's a great deal I don't understand about prostitution. I'm not alone. Many people still think it's illegal, for example.

I've seen what crack does and so can totally understand why a woman would hire out her body for five minutes with a stranger for £20. What I struggle with is not what *she* is doing, but the guys that readily pick these women up from the street in these circumstances. Each client is just the latest in a long line and it's not as if the prostitute washes after each session. They smell bad. Often there are sores, or in bad cases, ulcers.

Of course, as long as the condom doesn't burst, they're probably safe, but many punters pay extra to have sex without a condom, which just beggars belief. And there's hepatitis, which can be passed on via kissing. A prostitute once told me that no woman in the sex trade would do this unless they fancied the punter.

In a way this woman typified the difference between police and social services. As cops, we walk in and out of people's lives at great speed. We're there to achieve immediate goals: make someone safe, prevent or solve a crime. If this woman was beaten badly enough to end up in hospital or was killed, or had sold someone drugs or died from an overdose, then we would appear, do what we needed to do and vanish.

Unlike social workers, the detectives of the human psyche, we don't have the skills, training or time to unravel the lives of our most vulnerable citizens. Somewhere out there, a social worker was probably trying to sort out the chaotic mess of this girl's life. Her problems appeared to me to be so deep-rooted and so complex that it seemed an impossibly tall order.

She was fumbling in her pockets. Cigarettes, I guessed, and was proved right when she pulled out a pack of ten Mayfair. As she did so, something fell to the ground.

I quickly decided if it was a lump of cannabis then I'd ignore it. It wasn't; it was just a small and grubby soft toy, a pink elephant. Through the surprise of seeing the elephant, I looked up at her face and studied it more closely, the behaviour of a true cop. Members of the public understandably have no desire to stare directly at a scene like this, or into the eyes of a 'fallen woman', and do their best not to see what's going on around them.

She smiled at me, trembling, pathetic. As she bent down to retrieve the little elephant, a wave of recognition hit me; my mind flipped through the thousands of images held on my internal database, looking for a name.

Got it.

'Lisa?'

She stood up, surprised, on her guard. Then a look of

recognition crossed her face. When she spoke her voice was husky from cigarette and crack smoke.

'Oh, hello. You're the copper who took my baby, aren't you?'

Oh God, I thought. She now appeared calm and so I confessed that I had, readying myself for the 'You fucking bastard'. If I'd been the social worker, the phrase would usually be altered to 'You fucking *interfering* bastard'.

'I am. How are you?'

The moment I said it, I realised how stupid this must sound to a woman I'd just witnessed begging for her next fix and crying by the side of the road.

I couldn't remember her baby's name. In fact I was struggling to remember whether it was a boy or girl. I'd already removed several babies from crack prostitutes by now. My mind drew a blank, so I went for neutral.

Pointing at the little pink elephant, I asked, 'Is that baby's?'

Lisa nodded. She put her phone away and held the pink elephant in both hands, staring at it intently.

I thought about where that little pink elephant had been. Crack houses, the back of countless cars on East London trading estates, alleyways and alcoves; it had been present at meetings with social workers and interviews with police officers; down the benefit office; it had sat in her bag, rolling around next to packets of condoms and rocks of crack.

Somehow, despite everything, she'd held on to it, a small talisman, a reminder that her child was out there somewhere, a child that she and I could only hope had been given a decent shot at life, a child that would never know about that little elephant.

'Take care, Lisa.'

'Yeah, you too.'

I walked on.

CHAPTER FOUR

THE SILENT KILLER

As part of their near constant demonisation, social workers are often pegged with the wearing of bad clothes and sandals. I have never seen a social worker in a pair of sandals, but they do 'dress down'. Ella had done just that. She was wearing trainers (a good idea in case you have to run for your life), a blouse with a floral print and dark jeans. She was also wearing a heavy-looking ruck-sack. She looked as if she was prepared for anything.

Tayshia, Demaine's mother, answered the door. Tayshia was young and attractive and lived in a very well-kept council flat. Even I, with my appalling sense of fashion, could tell she was wearing carefully chosen designer clothes. What my eyes were most drawn to, however, were her extraordinarily long nails painted with bright pink, gold and black bands. She invited us in.

She remained calm as I made the introductions; there was no change in her friendly expression when I uttered the words 'police' and 'social worker'.

'Tayshia,' I said, 'we're worried about Demaine.'

'Aw, Demaine,' she said in a strong Jamaican accent, with a hint of East End. 'He take after his dad, he fearless and like to play rough; he always injuring himself. You know what young boys like.'

That sounded a bit like a 'prepared statement' to me.

'Would you mind if I spoke to Demaine alone?' Ella asked.

'Of course, no problem. Demaine! Come 'ere!'

'It's OK, I'll go and talk to him in his room,' Ella said, getting up.

Another lesson learned. Victoria Climbié was asked about her injuries in front of her abusers. Of course she disclosed nothing and died after suffering unimaginable torture.

'How often does Jordan see Demaine?' I asked.

'Ev'ry coupla weeks,' Tayshia said. Looking down she added, 'He saw Demaine last night.'

'Has he ever been violent?'

'Jus' with me but that was a long time ago, and it was nothing. Look, Jordan is a man, right? He's jealous sometime; he love me and Demaine; he die for us rather than see us come harm.'

Although my twenty years of dealing with domestic abuse told me otherwise, I knew not to challenge her. Tayshia was a victim and like thousands of other women, she was suffering in silence and denial. Inside she was scared of 'making things worse', especially if Jordan found out she'd had a cop and a social worker around for tea and a chat.

Ella came down and stopped at the door to the hallway. 'Excuse me,' I said to Tayshia. 'We need to speak in private.'

'Demaine says he's hurting on his side,' Ella said, 'from playing rough with the other boys.'

'Can you see any injury?' I asked, knowing that bruises are harder to see on black skin.

Ella shook her head. 'I don't think he needs medical attention,' she added.

'And we have nothing to go on,' I said. 'We have a suggestion of past violence and hints of criminality, a slightly bruised child who said he hurt himself playing. The home is clean, Demaine is well fed and, on the surface, seems happy.'

'So what do we do?' Ella asked.

'A wise man once said, treat every kid as if they will die overnight and then ask yourself if you've done everything you should have. As long as you do that there'll never be another Climbié.'

After talking to Tayshia, she agreed to come to the Homerton Hospital the following morning. We couldn't make it any earlier as urgent cases had priority.

As we were about to leave, a little girl, who looked to be about nine years old, came into the room and sat down on the sofa.

I smiled at her. 'Who's this?'

'This is Marisha, Demaine's sister.'

'Hi, Marisha,' Ella said. 'How old are you?'

Marisha looked down at her hands and pressed close to her mum.

There was no eye contact. Tayshia bent forward a touch and whispered, 'Go on, tell them how old you are.'

'Ten,' Marisha said, in a tiny voice. She said little else when Ella asked a few more questions. Experience told me this wasn't a good sign, an indication that a child is frightened or trying not to get tangled up in lies. Of course, some kids are just shy.

Oh well, I thought, we'll learn everything tomorrow.

In the meantime, my phone had been buzzing in my jacket pocket for a while now. I answered as we emerged into the sunlight.

It was Rob. 'Got an address for you to go to ASAP. A tough one for you, I'm afraid.'

Twenty minutes later, I swung into the street and started to count door numbers, but stopped when I spotted the Instant

Response Vehicle (IRV). I squeezed my little Fiesta into a nearby space, grabbed my red incident book and climbed out into the muggy afternoon heat.

There are many beautiful Victorian London streets with original front doors framed by red brick, elegant white pillars that enclose large bay windows with original pine shutters that look out on to immaculate front gardens with neatly arranged recycling bins. This wasn't one of them.

This street paid homage to the worst excesses of 1980s refurbishment; it was yet to attract the bravest of Hackney's *nouveaux riches* looking for an investment. It was rich with PVC porches, stone cladding and pebbledash, burgundy paint splashed over original brick. The odd sofa or mattress sat rotting in unkempt gardens, bins had been left where the rubbish collectors had thrown them after squeezing their truck past the cars that lined both sides of the entire street.

I'd been a cop long enough to know not to allow stereotypical thinking to take over, but the street only added to my expectations of the drama that I was about to join. My role in this tragedy was familiar enough but no case was the same and every child was unique.

As I got out of my car and walked towards the house, the passenger in the IRV climbed out, rubbing the sleep out of his eyes. 'Long shift?' I asked, smiling sympathetically.

My smart suit and large red incident book told him I was a cop. He nodded and straightened, stretching stiff muscles, and handed me the crime scene log so I could sign myself in.

Following imaginary stage directions – *There is a knock on the front door, Detective Sergeant Harry Keeble enters* – I stepped into the crime scene.

A policewoman in her early twenties was sat on the sofa, her arm around the shoulders of a woman her own age. The woman's shoulders shook uncontrollably each time she lifted her head to take a drag of her cigarette. Her blonde, slightly greasy hair was tied back behind her head, her face swollen from a night of tears. She was dressed in a red tracksuit and wore dirty trainers with no socks.

Without asking her permission, the need rendered ridiculous considering the circumstances, I sat down, opened my book and introduced myself.

Just then, a thin white man with brightly coloured tattoos that covered every square inch of his arms emerged from the kitchen. A half-smoked cigarette dangled from his mouth. He squinted through the smoke as he nodded at me and mumbled, 'A'right.' Looking at his partner, he said, 'Babe, I gotta take Tyson for a walk, will only be a couple of minutes, he ain't been out yet.'

The woman didn't look up; the bottom of her wrist remained firmly pushed against her forehead, the cigarette smoke curled up towards the ceiling. I noticed that the original Victorian rose, thick with many coats of white paint, had yellowed, and that the flex of the light was surrounded by wisps of old cobwebs.

To one side of the old gas fire was the gaming chair, well used and worn. This was the seat on which this thin little man had raced Jenson Button, defeated evil sorcerers, fought in the Battle of Arnhem and scored the winning goal in the World Cup Final. The huge screen of the TV looked out of place, a malevolent black hole, irresistibly drawing the attention of anyone in the room, with its promise of a brighter world, where dreams become reality.

The man barked, 'Tyson! Walkies!' A thudding sound came from the kitchen, followed by the heavy breathing of a happy Staffordshire bull terrier that didn't give me a second glance as it ran too quickly up to the front door and crashed into it with a thud. Another stereotype ticked. Man and dog exited stage left, via the front door, which slammed behind them.

What the hell is he going to say, I wondered, when he bumps into the regulars down the park and they ask him how he is?

The sofa had shiny patches, but it wasn't uncomfortable. The coffee table, upon which I'd placed my book, was 'old' new pine. It was full of post, including a letter, I noted, confirming the continuance of the man's incapacity benefit. Sandwiched between various papers was an ashtray, overflowing with cigarette and joint butts. I stared at it for a touch too long before I snapped back into the job and started talking to Mum. I poured out my sympathy. She nodded through the tears, mumbling the occasional thank you.

This young mother, with all the stereotypical attributes of a 'chav', now had to be strong in the face of tragedy. She was doing her best to face up to what had happened. Making eye contact, I ploughed through my list of what would happen next. She nodded, still trembling, and I doubted whether she was taking anything in. Tears spilled over on to her cheeks as she fought to pay attention.

'Right,' I said, making ready to get up. 'I need to have the scene photographed and then remove any exhibits.' I placed my hands on my knees and pushed myself up out of the deep sofa.

The woman was so deeply immersed in grief that she continued to stare blankly into the space where I'd been sitting.

I crossed the lounge and started up the stairs. There was no carpet and my shoes clonked noisily. I put my hand on the stair rail bolted to the wall; evidence an elderly person had once lived in this house. Most of the wallpaper had gone, partly scraped away in a half-hearted attempt at DIY. A child's drawings and scribbles covered the lower part of the wall. I focused on getting up the stairs.

The paramedics had gone beyond the call of duty as usual, slogging their guts out trying to bring back baby long after the point of no return, hoping for a miracle that never came.

'You never forget the young ones,' a paramedic once told me, 'because they lose a whole lifetime, they haven't even lived.'

The thought of the tasks ahead burned in my mind. The lifeless body was in the hospital, waiting for me to perform my examination. For many, overcoming the in-built instinct to resist handling the dead isn't easily overcome. I had been through a few cases by now and knew what to expect. I would prepare myself mentally by imagining the chest, bruised by compressions, and the many marks left by various tubes.

The term 'lifeless' means little to those who have not actually experienced it. Lifeless in this case is to hold a baby without breath, unable to move, with no reflex, no muscle movement – no soul to hold the package of limbs and organs together as a cohesive whole. It's an unforgettable experience, in the worst sense of the phrase.

My job was to look for the obvious, something like a stab wound. It's rare but it does happen, particularly with tragedies like this that can overwhelm the senses and the emotions, where the undertaker calls to ask the police to 'pop back' because he's found a knife in the back of the victim.

As I entered the room, I saw that attempts had been made to make it baby-friendly. A glittering mobile, twisting slightly, lit by the sunlight streaming through the window, above the cot. Among a handful of soft toys on the floor were the baby blankets, thrown aside in desperation after the horrible realisation that something was wrong, followed by panic, before Mum had hit the nines.

This was a crime scene and, although it was the most likely culprit, the last assumption we made at this stage was that this was a cot death. Every other possibility had to be checked. I checked for medication, baby milk and drugs, anything that might help the coroner. There was nothing.

A male PC thudded up the stairs behind me. 'Bag the blankets,' I told him.

I looked underneath the cot and spotted a little soft toy, a Winnie the Pooh bear. I knelt down on the thin, dirty carpet and plucked it out. No buttons or plastic parts were missing.

I glanced out of the bedroom window, which overlooked a nearby park, and froze when I saw the unemployed and supposedly sick father, 'walking' Tyson. While Tyson ran back and forth in the sunshine, full of life, the father was standing still and smoking. He was a miserable, pathetic figure. How could he think of walking his dog? OK, so they didn't have a garden, but he could have asked a neighbour, or could have quickly taken him out in the street. Instead he was leaving the mother of his son to face the responsibility of dealing with the police. How long would it be, I wondered, before he hit the on-switch of his X-Box?

Anger boiled inside me as I watched – they had a history with social services: 'minor' neglect, some domestic violence. I'd seen this sort of life often but because of the dead baby, I found myself thinking that, living like this, so carelessly, so selfishly, so miserably, so hopelessly, filling the house with tobacco and weed smoke while their baby slept in an airless room, then what did they expect?

I stopped myself and took a breath. Had I become that cynical? I'd been working in child protection for a good few years now, and had seen a great many horrors. The parents didn't deserve this.

People handle grief in different ways; the father was no doubt in shock, in denial. No one really knows the causes of cot death and babies die whether the parents are smokers or not. It was hard not to get angry though, to find someone, something to blame. That baby had had a future in a world that I was supposed to be helping make safer.

There was just something in this house, something about the man, that left me with a nagging frustrated feeling, as if I were missing something, one vital piece of the story.

I sensed movement behind me. The mother was in the doorway, looking over my shoulder out the window.

'His life revolves around that bloody dog,' she said.

'You shouldn't—' I started.

'His life also revolves around signing on, smoking weed until God knows when every night, playing on the Xbox with his friends and that –' and here she emphasised the point, 'that *fucking* dog.

'He says he can't work, that the incapacity benefit ain't enough, but he's a liar. The only good thing in our life was Alfie.'

She faltered, her anger evaporating and with it her strength.

I took a step towards her, blocking her view of the cot, and held out the bear.

The woman looked up, tears still streaming, reached out slowly and took it, hugging it to her chest.

When she spoke, it came in a whisper. 'We killed our Alfie, didn't we?'

My answer came quickly, instinctively. 'No, you didn't.'

But I wondered.

CHAPTER FIVE

NEW YEAR'S HONOURS

'You eat far too much, Harry,' Clara said in disbelief.

I was in the police canteen and my mouth was watering at the prospect of taramasalata followed by a huge double portion of lasagne. Canteen cuisine had come on a long way during the last ten years.

Clara was still standing. Her light salad, wholemeal roll and yoghurt glared accusingly at me from her tray.

'That may be so,' I replied, my fork poised over my starter, 'but I'm not fat, am I? I burn it off.'

'It'll catch up with you one day.'

Just at that moment, Rob, who was ten or so years older than me, joined us. I stared at his huge bulk as he set down a tray that was the precise duplicate of mine.

'What?' he asked as he noticed Clara's smug I-told-you-so smile.

My mobile rang. Saved by the bell. It was Ella. Her tone was grim.

'Harry, you'd better get down here now. The doctor isn't happy. She's found lots of bruising and she wants X-rays now, a full skeletal on Demaine.'

'OK, I'm leaving now.'

Much to Clara's distaste I finished my lasagne in sixty seconds flat and left the canteen at a trot.

Ten minutes later I passed through the sliding double doors of Homerton Hospital, jogged straight up to the Starlight Children's Ward and rang the buzzer to be admitted. There was no reply. This was typical for one of the busiest children's wards in the country. It took me a good few minutes to get a nurse's attention by banging on the glass and waving my warrant card.

The doctor, an attractive, fresh-faced woman of about thirty, met me. She had Demaine's skeletal survey with her.

'Did we interrupt your lunch?' she said with a smile.

'Excuse me?'

'You have tomato sauce on your face.'

I did my best to clean up as we stepped into an office where she switched on wall-mounted light boxes before thrusting the X-rays into clips that held them in place. Once they were up, she took me through them.

'Demaine has a classic metaphyseal lesion, also known as the corner or bucket-handle fracture of the distal tibia.'

She pointed at another X-ray. 'There are old breaks too. Posterior rib fractures here, and scapular fractures here. He has yellow bruising on his buttocks, the bruises are at least a week old, caused by being hit with a fixed object. He has newer ones, just a day old, on his upper arms.'

'How were the fractures caused?'

'From the angles and by the fact that there are two old spiral fractures, I'd say they have most likely been caused by an adult beating and throwing him.'

'You seem very certain.'

'That's not all.' She handed me a body map, on which all Demaine's injuries, old and new, bruises and scars, were marked on a child's outline.

It took me a moment to take in the doctor's scribbles and then a few more to regain the power of speech.

'Poor little guy.' I took a deep breath. 'Thank you,' I said. 'Believe it or not, we could have easily missed this one.'

'I'm glad to have helped. We'll keep him here overnight for treatment. Just make sure I don't have to see him again, OK?'

I nodded, my shock and sadness boiling together into determination.

Tayshia was waiting in a small room nearby and stood up when I entered.

'Look,' she began testily, 'we've been here for long enough.'

'Demaine has a broken bone,' I said. 'Can you explain why?'

Her shock and sheer bewilderment appeared genuine enough. 'No, no, I don't understand.'

'OK,' I said evenly. 'The doctor has given me enough cause to take Demaine into police protection.'

I was eternally grateful that we had the power to instantly protect a child. It was the legal equivalent of scooping them up in my arms to keep them safe.

Tayshia offered no opposition, just stunned silence.

'As soon as the doctors have finished treating him and are satisfied he's well enough, we're going to interview Demaine.'

As I left with Ella, I asked how she was. Her normally bright expression had faded and she seemed lost in thought.

'You can stop asking how I am all the time for a start,' she snapped suddenly. 'I get it. I know where it comes from and thank you but I'm fine. I'm ready for this. I know why Demaine got a good beating.'

Ella paused for a second, taking a deep breath before continuing in a rush of emotion.

'After all, a beating never did Demaine's father any harm, did it? Gang violence, glorified in the network of hot dusty streets in the Jamaican ghetto, where the "big man" is the one with the gun. Demaine's dad is showing him he's the rooster and that if the hens step out of the coop, they can be beaten back in. And that nothing matters more than respect, "Cause that's all we got, son", except his kind of respect is the kind you achieve through bludgeoning anyone who dares to say or do anything you don't like into submission, especially as real respect is hard to come by when you're an absent father who pays no maintenance and wears designer clothes, while one of his many baby mothers looks after the big man's gun.'

Ella obviously had a lot more fire in her than I'd imagined. She was walking so fast I had to take bigger strides to catch up as we neared my car.

'And do you know what the worst thing is? He's driving Demaine towards his own twisted values and beliefs. Well, not any more, not if I have anything to do with it.'

Both the doctor and I were keen to move on with the interview. 'The crack is small and already healing,' the doctor said. 'He just needs to rest it, so he can definitely go.'

'I want my mum,' Demaine told me when I next saw him.

Fair enough. I warned Tayshia not to talk to Demaine about his dad, especially about what we suspected, and to try and stay calm, as close to normal as possible.

Our interview suite, which had its own entrance, was around the back of the police station. It was light and airy, with children's posters on the wall, a few simple but popular toys (we don't want to overexcite children with anything too flashy) and comfy furniture in neutral colours. Everything had been done to try and eliminate formality and to reduce anxiety.

As Ella had already established a rapport with Demaine in his bedroom at home, it was decided that she should conduct the interview with Sarah while I watched on the cameras in the observation room.

I'd carried out and sat through many of these types of interviews and although they were always challenging and stressful, I knew what to expect. This, however, was Ella's first. Despite yesterday's speech, I was nervous for her.

You can't really teach someone how to carry out a memorandum interview of an abused child. You can study discourse analysis, child psychology and interviewing techniques but once you're in the interview room, looking into the eyes of an abused child, it's very easy to forget all your preparations and let your emotions take over.[1]

Then there's the pressure. The fact that a child's life may depend on your questions and how you deal with their responses in just a few minutes is a heavy burden. Whatever the outcome, it's on your back – whatever anyone says, you can't help but blame yourself for any slip-ups that help a child abuser stay free or return a child to a life of horror.

Ella looked to me as if she was feeling the pressure. She cared about Demaine so much and knew his immediate future depended on her. She nervously shuffled her notes together. These covered everything from Demaine's date of birth to the list of names of relatives and family friends he regularly came into contact with, to the page that described his long list of injuries in detail.

Ella's hands trembled as we checked and rechecked the equipment. The last thing you wanted was to find that the tape recorder or microphone had conked out, or that you'd forgotten to check that blank tapes were in the machine.

Once everything was set, I asked Ella if she was OK. She looked at me, knowing what was on my mind.

'I'm fine,' she said, her jaw hardening in determination.

'Good,' I replied, and retired to the observation room.

Demaine was barely old enough for a memorandum interview and Ella would have to adapt linguistically. I'd once watched a flustered and tongue-tied social worker ask a sexually abused five-year-old: 'And did your stepfather ever tell you that if anyone ever asks the same questions as me, you better not say what he told you not to say; that what we said wasn't what happened?'

A four-year-old has no experience of formal interviews and therefore has no idea what to expect. They may think they've ended up here because they've done something wrong. They certainly have no idea of the weight their answers will carry in a court of law. A nervously asked, complex question will just draw a blank and will leave a child confused, or even scared.

One of the most important things to remember in these situations is that a child like Demaine is constantly trying to make sense of the situation he is in – however bizarre it may be – and this may influence the answers he provides.

Demaine was quiet and well behaved but he was also frightened.

'You're not in any trouble, Demaine,' Ella began. 'I help kids sort things out. We're just going to talk and it won't be for long, OK?'

Demaine nodded.

'If you don't understand something I say, please tell me and I will try to say it using different words.'

After 'warming up', briefly talking to Demaine about a few of his favourite things, getting him used to telling her stories about his life, Ella asked him about his dad.

'How often does your daddy live with you?'

Unfortunately, Demaine, who until then had been chatting quite happily and proudly, shut down. The transformation was immediate and as absolute as the slam of a prison door.

'It's OK to say I don't know or I don't remember,' Ella said.

Silence. This wasn't looking good.

'Even if you think I already know something, please tell me anyway.'

Silence.

It was remarkable. The phrase 'nobody likes a grass' circled my mind.

Even Sarah's skilfully constructed open-ended questions failed to get through. Ella ended the interview a few minutes later, after steering the conversation back to everyday stories, and soon Demaine was chatting normally again.

I wondered whether this wall of silence had knocked Ella's confidence.

'Everything OK?' I asked.

'Yes,' Ella replied testily, 'I'm fine, Harry, but we're in trouble. Demaine's dad has told him not to say anything to us, I'm sure of it. We need to talk to Marisha.'

I agreed. Technically we needed Tayshia's permission for this, but in child protection we're duty-bound to act in the best interests of the child, so we could, if necessary, bypass any refusal. Fortunately, although Tayshia looked anxious, she didn't object.

Sarah was called away to deal with another case and so this time I joined Ella in the interview suite. We went through the rapport-building stage together, taking longer than we had for Demaine.

Marisha's voice rarely rose above a whisper and she spoke while looking down into her lap, avoiding eye contact. I turned the microphone up to maximum.

We'd barely begun when she began to cry.

'What is it, Marisha?'

Marisha shook her head.

'I didn't see anything.'

Ella leaned forward. 'What didn't you see, Marisha?'

Tears started to roll down Marisha's cheeks.

'Just tell us what you remember,' Ella said. 'You won't be in trouble. You'll be helping.'

'I didn't see.'

'Where were you when you didn't see?' Ella asked.

Good question. Keep her talking. Give her another entry into an impossibly difficult story for a ten-year-old.

'In my bed.'

'In your bed?'

Marisha nodded.

'What did you hear?'

This was a great piece of intuition, I thought.

'The bangs.'

'Who was making the bangs?'

'Daddy.'

'What was he doing?'

'Hitting Demaine.'

Marisha was back there again. Her eyes had focused on the memory; she didn't see us any more. Tears streamed.

'What did you hear?'

'Daddy hitting Demaine.'

'When was this?'

'At night. I was in my bed. I tried to cover my ears with the pillow but I could still hear hitting. I wanted to tell Daddy to stop but I was frightened.'

'Frightened of what?'

'What Daddy was doing to Demaine.'

'Did you hear anything else?'

Silence. Ella waited a moment before continuing.

'Please remember that I was not there when it happened,' Ella said. 'The more you can tell me about what happened, the better. So tell me everything you can remember, even things you don't think are important.'

'Demaine was crying but not noisy, like he was trying not to cry. And sometimes something hit the wall, I think.'

Marisha started to cry again and this time she really broke down.

Ella started to close the interview. This was just as important as any other part of the process. Everything up to this stage had been designed to bring Marisha back to the abuse, to get her to the point where she could speak about painful memories. We'd taken her back to the nightmare, now we had to get her out again.

'OK, thank you, Marisha. You've been really, really helpful, we're very grateful. Do you have any questions for us?'

Once Ella was happy Marisha was as back to normal as she could be, we returned her to her mum. I joined Ella for a quick chat in private. This time I didn't ask her how she was but let her speak.

'That little boy is already more of a man than his father,' she said. 'He bravely tried to stifle his cries so as not to scare his sister, a sister now dealing with the guilt of not having risen to the impossible task of going to her brother's aid. Now she's been the bravest person it's possible to be, telling us the truth that her mother either did not know or would not admit to. They'll never appear in the New Year's Honours list, or be nominated for a Pride of Britain Award, even though their bravery was off the scale.'

Tears of anger and heartbreak welled in Ella's eyes as she finished.

'At least now we can protect them,' I said with determination. I had a new mission. One to take on alone, without social services.

Find Jordan.

CHAPTER SIX

THE GAMES
CHILDREN PLAY

Ella set the phone down and ran her hand through her hair. She yawned. The phone started ringing again. A child had run away from a care home last night. Before that, Ella had spent half an hour trying to calm a furious mother, fresh from a contact meeting with her ten-year-old son.

Ella's morning cup of instant coffee sat cold on the desk beside her. And she hadn't even taken off her coat yet. The incoming cases were arriving so quickly they were starting to blur.

The parenting skills of the foster carers were, according to the mother, 'totally crap' and they were 'totally out of order'. Ella had resisted the urge to reply that she was 'totally' pissed off, before reminding the mother that her parenting skills had endangered the lives of her children. She then explained that she had spent two days searching for foster carers before working late every night to make sure all the arrangements had been taken care of and the paperwork correctly filled out.

Ella couldn't remember the last time she'd had a girls' night out. Most of her friends had nine-to-five jobs as solicitors, media

assistants, project managers and bank clerks. One of them made
£40k a year as a telephone cashier for a private bank.

Ella made just over half as much as her clerk friend and lived
in a small and draughty first-floor flat in a grimy part of
Holloway (described by the estate agent as being on the
'Islington fringes'). While her friends obsessed over promotions,
bonuses, cars, savings, holidays, festivals, gigs and property, Ella
worried about meeting the rent.

Houses and holidays were beyond her. She wasn't even sure
she wanted a promotion. Shortly after she started work for
Hackney Social Services, her boss keeled over from nervous
exhaustion. In the days before he disappeared, never to return,
he had jumped every time his phone rang or someone tapped on
his office door.

Offloading her daily trials on her friends was impossible.
Talking about child abuse in the gastro-pub was a real buzzkill.

The phone's ring persisted. Ella snatched up the receiver.

'Yes!?' she demanded.

'Oh. Er, hi, Ella, Harry here. Bad time?'

'Oh, sorry, yes. I've had better starts to the day. What can I do
for you?'

'I need you on a visit. A very young child-on-child reported
by a teacher this morning. It could go either way but hopefully
this will be one for social services.'

'Righto,' Ella said, pulling herself together. Life goes on.
After all, at least *her* job *meant* something. Children, their
mothers and fathers needed her. Every day she made a difference. 'Can you pick me up?' she said. 'I've still got a couple of
calls to make.'

An hour later we were standing in the warm sunshine in front of
a beautiful Victorian Hackney home. Clipped bay trees in pots
stood either side of a black and white checked front path that led

to a pristine and purple Victorian door with sparkling silver let-terbox and knocker.

'Cool,' I said, admiringly.

As we walked up the path a piece of paper fell out of Ella's bag and I quickly bent down to retrieve it. It was the printout of a webpage. At the top were the words 'Castles in the Sky: Internet Dating for Graduates'.

Ella groaned and smiled awkwardly. 'Dating agencies are against my better judgement,' she said, 'but it worked for a friend of mine and what with the hours I put in, it's my best hope. After all, I don't get to meet many eligible bachelors in this line of work.'

We reached the door. 'Original bell ringer,' I said. 'Very swish.'

Ella shrugged; she was distinctly unimpressed.

I yanked the cord and a series of chimes echoed through the house. Ella looked up and I followed her gaze. A very tiny and modern-looking fish-eye camera stared down at us. We weren't expected and I imagined the occupants looking at a black and white convex image of us looking back at them from a TV mon-itor, wondering whether we were there to sell cheap dusters or to preach from the good book.

I was quietly confident that I'd eventually be able to leave this one to Ella, but I was also on full alert. Judging a book by its cover in child protection only leads to misery for some poor child.

A shadow grew behind the front door's frosted glass. A man in his late forties swung back the door. He had a pleasant and relaxed face. The lack of grey hairs meant he'd either recently discovered *Just For Men* or had a stress-free job. He was wearing black jeans and a white open-necked Ralph Lauren shirt.

'Hi,' he said. He looked a bit puzzled, but not suspicious.

I showed my warrant card and introduced Ella.

'Please, do come in.' His voice was deep, clear, relaxed and confident.

We made our way down the broad hallway (oak floor and white walls skimmed to perfection with brushed steel switches and perfectly positioned down lights).

'The name's Andy,' he said. 'We can talk in the kitchen, lots of room there.'

As we reached the magnificent kitchen I made an impressed face at Ella. She shrugged back. Not having one of her better days, I thought, as I marvelled at the bright orange handle-less units, white Corian work surfaces and beautifully tiled floor. Huge frameless folding glass doors led to a garden that looked like something out of the Chelsea Flower Show.

We pulled out white chairs and sat behind a long glass table. I took out my red book and opened it. Andy's eyes flitted to it, obviously wondering what on earth we could want with him.

'Coffee?' he asked, pointing towards a perfectly engineered, stainless-steel Gaggia machine that outclassed anything in Costa's armoury. My mouth watered but, knowing it would take time and that we had to crack on, I declined.

'I'll have one, thank you,' Ella said brightly.

Bloody hell. Where had that come from?

'Great,' Andy said, and turned back to me. 'Are you sure?'

'Oh, erm,' I said awkwardly, 'OK then.'

As he began emptying beans into grinders and frothing milk, I turned and gave Ella a mock frown of disapproval. We weren't here for a chat about joining the local reading group, after all.

She looked back at me innocently. '*Somebody* interrupted my morning coffee,' she said accusingly.

Finally, after a few noisy, steam-filled minutes of intense activity, our coffee arrived. I took a sip. My God, that was good. Ella gestured with her finger at her top lip. Whoops. Telling this story with a froth moustache would not be good.

*

The teacher, Miss Masters, was sat in her empty preparatory classroom with eight-year-old Henrietta.

One of Hetty's friends, Maya, had left Miss Masters reeling when she asked if it was OK if someone 'pushed their finger inside you'.

'Who told you such a thing?' Miss Masters asked.

'Hetty, Miss, she said someone done it to her.'

'Did, Maya,' Miss Masters said absently. 'You say "did" not "done".'

'Yes, Miss.'

Now Miss Masters was wondering how to broach the subject with Hetty in such a way that would not leave her worried or frightened, while bearing in mind the next call she would make might well be to the police.

To interview well and to understand their answers properly, you have to put yourself in the child's mind. This takes tremendous skill on the part of the teacher and plenty of trust and courage from the child. While the task is daunting, teachers are perhaps best placed to understand every aspect of a particular child's thinking, which is dependent on memory, conceptual and emotional development, as well as linguistic skill and idiosyncrasies. Every child is different but a teacher who knows her class well will have some idea of what their pupil understands about many concepts, such as height, weight, age, time, the truth, secrecy and sex.

The tricky part is that the interview is very different from a lesson. Normally, Miss Masters, in talking about a science project for example, would correct wrong answers or would ask the child to make a guess. This way, she would know whether the child was interested in the project (if they were genuinely trying to get the answer right) or perhaps where they were going wrong with their calculations. There's nothing wrong with an incorrect answer and Miss Masters would always make sure the child eventually got the answer right.

The rules are very different when you're questioning a child about a crime you're uncertain has actually happened, or know little or nothing about. In this case all Miss Masters had to go on was something Hetty's friend had said.

'Hetty, I just wanted to talk to you for a moment, all right?'

'Yes, Miss.'

'You're not in trouble at all and I won't get angry about anything you tell me. If you don't know then just tell me you don't know. Do you understand?'

'Yes, Miss.'

Where to start? Get to the point as clearly and as simply as possible.

'What did you tell Maya this morning, Hetty?'

Silence.

'You know what I mean, don't you?'

Hetty nodded. 'About Anthony.'

'Tell me what happened.'

'We were in the playing field and he ...'

'He ...?'

'He put his finger up my rudey and ...'

'And ...?'

'It hurt lots. I wanted to know if Maya had it done too. It hurt and I ...'

Hetty tailed off into silence.

After a lengthy pause, Miss Masters asked, 'How do you feel now?'

'All right, Miss.'

'No pain?'

'No, Miss.'

'Just one more thing. Do you mean Anthony, who is in Mrs Briggs' class?'

'Yes, Miss.'

'Thank you, Hetty, you've been very good and helpful for answering my questions.'

Miss Masters had played this perfectly. She wrote down everything word for word, made a note of the date and time, called us and described what had happened over the phone.

Andy's relaxed smile vanished when I began repeating Miss Masters' conversation with his daughter Hetty. He paled and squirmed awkwardly as I continued. I really felt for him as images, questions and thoughts sent his mind spiralling.

It's hard to know what thoughts take predominance in a parent's mind in a case like this. Obviously, thoughts about the pain and terrible experience of what the poor child had endured are usually at the top of the list. Then there are worries about whether she'd be left mentally damaged in some way and whether it would affect her adult relationships. Some parents become terribly concerned about the involvement of the school, their knowledge about what has happened and the fact that police and social services are involved.

Then there was the question of why nine-year-old Anthony had done what he'd done.

Andy was clearly reeling. While he was a successful and confident man with an amazing home and a lifestyle beyond most people's dreams, this incident had instantly reduced him to a state of helplessness.

He couldn't even get angry. There was no obvious paedophile to vent fury on; just a nine-year-old boy.

These thoughts would be with him, churning through his mind day and night. Andy needed me and Ella to help him, to put the incident in perspective and to lead him carefully through what would happen next.

'You must be mistaken,' Andy said finally, his voice hoarse. 'This other girl. She might have been wrong. She meant something else.' This was the coping mechanism of denial.

Ella continued. 'Miss Masters, who is very experienced, was very clear and Hetty repeated the same story to me.'

'I see,' Andy said slowly, nodding thoughtfully. 'Sorry,' he said, 'I don't know what to say. It's a real shock.'

He walked over to a two-metre-tall white fridge and filled the glass with water from a tap.

'So,' he said, trying to restore some self-control to his voice. 'What do we do now?'

'We will see you through this,' Ella said. 'Try not to worry too much. Hetty is fine.'

'Where is your wife?' I asked. 'We really need to speak to her as soon as possible.'

I'd once made the mistake in a similar case of only talking to one of the parents. I didn't ever want to repeat it. There was a danger in putting a plan into action here and now with the dad, only to have Mum disagree and ask questions the dad might not have thought of. It's also vital to involve Mum as early as possible if we're to earn and keep her trust.

'She's visiting a friend who lives just down the street. I'll call her.'

Penelope arrived a few minutes later, an attractive brunette, smartly dressed in designer jeans and a very expensive-looking cape. She dropped her large handbag on the floor and hugged Andy in the hallway, before joining us in the kitchen. She was friendly but totally overwhelmed at the same time; her hands shook as she reached for a chair and sat beside her husband, facing me and Ella across the table.

'So,' she said clearly and confidently, 'what happens now?'

'We will need to interview Hetty tomorrow,' I said.

'Oh God—'

'And of course we'll speak to the child that did this, too.'

'I can't believe this is happening,' Andy said.

'It's OK,' Ella said, 'Hetty is our number one priority, no

question. She will be interviewed by an experienced officer. We're not going to push her too hard but it will help to have her story recorded in her own words.'

As Ella talked, I could see waves of realisation hitting Penelope; that this had happened, that it was real, that her daughter had been abused.

'But is this really abuse?' she asked. 'Can a nine-year-old sexually abuse an eight-year-old?'

'A nine-year-old can't commit an offence as such,' I answered, 'but little Anthony has overstepped the line so far that it is clearly "abuse". Try not to worry too much. I know the term "child sex abuse" conjures up terror and fear, much like the word "cancer", which could mean anything from having a tiny mole removed to death in a few weeks. Without the facts, "child sex abuse" is an unhelpful term.'

Penelope nodded. 'I understand. In other words, don't panic.'

'It's a shock,' Ella said. 'So do let it out, tell us and ask us anything you need to, no matter how small or strange it may seem. We're here for you and will be with you every step of the way.'

'It's nearly lunchtime,' Andy said. 'Irena will be bringing Hetty home from school soon.'

'Who's Irena?' I asked.

'The nanny,' Penelope said. 'What do we do? Do we talk to Hetty about it?'

'No,' I said, 'she needs to return to normality, keep your stress from her. We will talk to her tomorrow.'

I stood up. 'Ella and I will make the arrangements and will call you later.'

We shook hands and made our way out, leaving Andy and Penelope to pull themselves together in time for Hetty's arrival.

As soon as the door had closed Ella and I turned on our

phones. They both began to ring simultaneously. We looked at each other and smiled.

'Different job, same stress,' I said.

'Too much work and not enough time,' Ella replied.

'Still,' I added, as I lifted the phone to my ear, 'we should hopefully have this one wrapped up tomorrow.'

Unfortunately, I was totally wrong.

CHAPTER SEVEN

UNTHINKABLE

Anthony smiled at me from the sofa in our interview suite. He was small for his age, a dark-haired, green-eyed, nine-year-old boy with pale skin. He looked happy though, not what I'd expected at all. Still, I should have known by now; there's no right answer to what an abused child should look like.

It was a remarkable development. When Ella and I answered our phones, our respective bosses told us that Hetty's friend, Anthony, had just complained of having a very sore bottom to his teacher, Mrs Briggs. Mrs Briggs knew of the events surrounding Hetty's disclosure and had called the police.

Mrs Briggs, who had been a teacher for thirty years, belonged to another era. She sat straight-backed on her chair, her grey hair secured in a bun with a pin, exuding quiet authority. When she spoke, her voice was like that of a well-trained Shakespearean actor.

'Anthony's a delightful boy,' she said, 'but extremely quiet. He wouldn't say boo to a goose and, in my judgement, he's extremely vulnerable.'

To our relief, Mrs Briggs had written everything down (in

exceptionally neat handwriting that shamed my wild, spidery penmanship) and signed and dated it.

'It's sometimes hard to understand Anthony,' she told me. 'The poor thing barely speaks above a whisper. My hearing isn't what it was, but I'm totally convinced about what he told me. He said that someone had put their fingers inside his . . . his . . .'

Mrs Briggs pushed her large, thick-rimmed glasses back on her nose and cleared her throat. Her composure softened. 'I mean . . . it's terrible,' she said. 'I don't understand it. Who would want to do something like that?'

Sarah and Ella had brought Anthony into the suite that same afternoon, before school finished. A medical examination confirmed the abuse. Unlike Hetty, where we knew exactly what had happened, we needed to interview Anthony straight away to find out who had done this to him.

When Julie, Anthony's mum, arrived, she seemed to be just as worried as any mother should be. Her dark brown hair was tinted red and she looked older than her thirty years. She had watery green eyes and the shiny, slightly swollen face of someone who relied on alcohol to get through each day. Her large sunglasses pushed back on her head and her summer clothes were designer label.

I couldn't explain why, but there was something inherently dislikable about her. She barely let me get a word in edgeways after I'd told her what had happened.

'I want to see Anthony, right now,' she demanded. Her voice was sharp, her tone unpleasant.

'Of course, but we'll have to be there with you.'

'What? I want to see him alone.'

'That's not possible,' I said calmly. 'We have to talk to him to—'

'Well, I want to see him now. No one's keeping Anthony from me.'

'Anthony has made a serious disclosure. We need to urgently investigate what he's told us so we can make sure he's safe.'

'Safe? What the hell are you going on about? I can tell you what happened,' Julie said bitterly. 'Nothing, that's what. That bloody teacher's an interfering busybody, always sticking her beak in where it's not wanted. My poor boy, being put through all this. It's a nonsense, it really is.'

'I'm sorry, there's more to it, I'm afraid. One of Anthony's classmates has told her teacher that Anthony abused her,' I said. 'This is extremely serious and we have to investigate.'

Julie fell silent, stunned. 'I don't believe it for a moment,' she said eventually, as I gently steered her towards the suite's waiting room, where she was given a hot and sweet cup of tea.

You could never tell how a parent would react. Julie's response seemed normal, anger followed by denial, but my cop sense was telling me there was something else. Was it guilt?

Craig entered the room and made a face that said: 'Can-I-have-a-word-in-private?'

'What is it?' I asked once we were in the corridor.

'There's no father,' Craig said quietly. 'He left Julie years ago and hasn't been in touch for over twelve months. But Julie has a boyfriend by the name of Brian Wilkes, a forty-year-old IT consultant. We're trying to get hold of him but he's working out of town, so it might be a while.'

I nodded. 'Thanks,' I said, thinking that the boyfriend would be a prime candidate. 'Can you sit with Mum while we do the interview?'

Leaving Craig, I found Sarah and a nervous-looking Ella. This was her first time dealing with child sexual abuse. Sadly, I knew that in just a few months, thanks to the number of cases we saw, she would become accustomed to them.

Sarah would lead the interview with Ella supporting. Sarah was a rock; she always thoroughly studied every case and never left the office until she was absolutely certain that everything had been done correctly. She was always at the forefront of the many heated discussions and debates we had about the best way to protect children. She was fearless, never afraid to tell anyone when she thought they were wrong about something.

Ella's youth was useful in cases like this. She was closer to Anthony's age than I was to hers. However, Ella radiated pity for Anthony. Young kids, still in the midst of their cognitive development, rely on a heightened emotional sensitivity to help them make sense of the world. I hoped this pity wouldn't come across in the interview and affect Anthony's answers. The important thing was to provide Anthony with stability and that meant taking a calm and friendly approach. Anthony seemed happy and I wanted him kept that way. I was struck by his courage, his ability to smile despite the trauma, trauma that we were about to make him relive.

We began the rapport phase, a pre-interview chat, designed to help Anthony relax and to help instil trust and confidence in us. He was sat on a plastic chair in front of a table where he'd been drawing.

'Hi, Anthony, I'm Harry.'

He looked up, his long dark lashes blinking across his emerald-green eyes.

'Hello,' he answered quietly, with a small smile.

'Are you comfy?'

'Yes.'

'Good. I'm pleased to hear it. We're here to take care of you. If you need anything, anything at all, like a drink, or to go to the toilet or to have a rest, then you tell us, OK?'

He nodded.

'Excellent. Do you know why you're here?'

'Because of what Mrs Briggs said.'

'Yes, that's right. We want to make sure you're safe and I want you to know that you were quite right to talk to Mrs Briggs. That was a good thing. We want to talk to you about that a bit more. Is that OK?'

Anthony nodded again, swinging his legs as he did so.

Sarah and I asked open-ended questions about school, books and TV programmes. By familiarising Anthony with storytelling and encouraging him to talk as much as possible, we would hopefully increase the amount of information he would spontaneously provide when we got to the nasty part of the interview. We had to place Anthony in an emotional bubble, a place where he was able to feel as secure as possible, to lighten the worries that must have been pressing down on him.

Child sexual abuse victims often feel shame, or a terrifying sense of having done something wrong. Once the secret is out, they are often frightened about what will happen to them, as well as how others might react. In this case there was an extra dimension in that Anthony himself had done something terribly wrong. They key thing here, though, was to find out why he had abused Hetty. The obvious answer was that Anthony had been abused, but by whom?

Child abusers often threaten their victims. They tell them that horrible things will happen to them and their family, that they will never see their friends and family again and that we won't believe them and will punish them for telling stories. We have to deal with these fears as quickly as possible and try to give victims a sense that we are there to make sure their future will be a safe and stable one.

While chatting to Anthony, I noticed that Ella looked tense; her expression was urgent. Her emotions were taking over. This was understandable, but she had to find a way to disengage from the horror and the pity, to master her feelings. If she failed, then

Ella would not be a child protection social worker for long.

A memorandum interview is like hypnosis. After we've done our best to put the child at ease, to get them to relax, we ever-so-gradually lead them back into the darkness where emotions, sounds, smells and sensations are revisited and memories are evoked. As the memories resurface, so do the feelings, often reducing the child to tears. The skill is to keep them talking, pressing on for as long as possible before the tears make speech impossible.

Although Ella had read case studies and studied child psychology, she was yet to witness a child endure the interview first-hand. Her expression, part pity, part fear, told me she needed to pull back and regroup because the pre-interview chat – although it was a crucial part of the process – was the easy bit.

In an interview like this, no metaphors or knowing looks can be used. The child has to describe as best they can what happened to them in the most graphic detail. The interviewer has to be able to talk about anything without flinching or shying away when they reach the nasty stuff.

I wondered whether Ella should be there. Although we were supposed to be running more joint police/social worker cases as part of a new initiative, we could interview Anthony without a social worker. I couldn't risk Ella breaking down when we reached the heart of Anthony's nightmare. Doing so would jeopardise our investigation.

We chatted to Anthony about the ground rules of the interview, letting him know the level of detail and what exactly would happen (that we'd be recording everything, that I'd be sitting around a table in another room, that it was OK to tell us if he didn't know the answer to a question, and that we'd never be angry with him).

Finally, we were ready and I departed for the control room, still worrying about Ella. Before the interview had started I'd taken her to one side.

'I know I'm always asking but this time I want you to really think about this. Are you going to be OK in there? It's going to be tough.'

Defiance fired in Ella's eyes.

'Yes, Harry. I'll be fine.'

'OK. I had to check.'

As I walked to the control room, a pang of guilt hit me. By asking Ella if she was OK, I was covering myself, in case she crumbled during the interview. But what did it matter to me? Anthony would be the one worst affected if Ella broke down. That had to be my first concern.

And so the interview began.

Sarah expertly led Anthony through the various stages as I took notes. Every now and again I glanced up at the screen, checking body language. Anthony was holding up well. Ella seemed OK, she was sitting very still, just listening for now.

Sarah asked about Julie's boyfriend.

'What do you call him?'

'Uncle Brian. He's not my daddy, Daddy is. Uncle Brian is my new daddy.'

'Do you see Uncle Brian often?'

'Sometimes. Usually at weekends.'

He looked down at the floor.

'When did he last visit?'

'Last weekend.'

Aha. The soreness had been reported just after Uncle Brian's weekend visit. Sarah was nearing the crucial part. There was no room for ambiguity, confusion or misunderstanding. Uncle Brian's life would never be the same again from the moment we acted on what Anthony told us. We had to get it exactly right.

'What kind of things do you and Uncle Brian do together?'

Anthony shifted. He looked uncomfortable.

'He comes to see Mummy. I don't think he likes me very much. He hurts me.'

'How?'

'He does things.'

'When did you feel sore down below, Anthony?' she asked.

Anthony looked down. 'It was on Saturday, after *Ant and Dec*.'

'Who was there?'

'Uncle Brian.'

'Was that when you got sore?'

'Yes.'

'Who made you sore?'

'Uncle Brian.'

Anthony looked uncomfortable again. Something else had happened here, I was sure of it. I looked at Ella. Still no movement, no sign. And then she spoke.

'Anthony,' Ella said quietly but clearly, 'where did this happen?'

'In the bedroom.'

He then went on to disclose what we thought was the full horror.

'Where was Mummy?' Ella asked, leaning forward over the desk, trying to get Anthony to look up, to regain that all-important eye contact.

'She was there.'

Again the pause. Again, a feeling of tension. Shockwaves.

Good God.

Sarah reacted by lifting her head up in surprise. What? What did he just say?

'What do you mean?' Sarah asked.

Although Ella's insight was an inspiration, we had to be careful with leading questions like 'Did she hurt you?' before establishing what had happened. We could not put words in

Anthony's mouth. If we did and the case went to a trial, the defence would quite rightly demolish us.

'Mummy was there. Mummy was always there. She told me it was OK. She said not to tell.'

I had by this time dealt with countless cases of paedophilia but this was my first encounter with a female paedophile, and my first case of maternal incest.

We were all trying to rebound from the shock. The gentle flow of the interview had been totally knocked off course. We hadn't been ready for this. For Anthony's sake, Sarah and Ella had to maintain the interview's stability. Their expressions, changes in posture and shock had given Anthony's finely tuned child senses a clue that something was wrong, but like an actor who's made a mistake on stage, you have to forget it and move on before the whole performance is ruined.

We were at a new and unexpected crucial stage. We couldn't go back. We'd brought Anthony to this point. We needed to get him through it, so that he wouldn't have to go through it ever again. It's hard enough for children to speak about sexual abuse, let alone when it's the mother that's hurt and upset them.

Sarah asked the next question. 'Is there anything else you do with Mummy that you're not supposed to tell anyone about?'

Anthony nodded. As gently as she could, Sarah helped this brave little nine-year-old boy relive the horror of the abuse.

'Did Mummy say what would happen if you told?'

'She said if I told anyone what we do, that I'll be put in a forest home and never see her or my friends again.'

Of course he meant foster home. His mistake simply reinforced his innocence. This threat was devastating. Anthony never saw his aunts or uncles and was rarely allowed to visit friends at their homes outside of school. He wasn't a member of any after-school groups, such as the Scouts, or any sports clubs.

He had been isolated and dominated to serve his mother's and stepfather's cruel urges.

Once the main part of the recall was over, Sarah went back over the interview, asking yet more questions, drawing out details that would help the forensic side of the investigation, as well as establishing how often the abuse happened and whether anyone else knew about it.

'Anthony, you've been brilliant,' Sarah said when she was at last done. After gently steering the subject back to more mundane matters and chatting for a while longer, the interview was finally over.

'Is there anything we can get you?' Sarah asked.

'I want me mum.'

Mum was all he knew. Mum was the caregiver, the one who took care of him, the anchor that held his life in place. Anthony had unknowingly cut himself adrift.

I rewound and ejected the tapes and went to find Ella. She was in the suite's 'kitchen', a small room with a microwave and kettle.

I looked her straight in the eye and said —

'I'm OK, Harry,' she said, beating me to it.

'Sure?'

'Yeah, I think so.'

She exhaled, as if she was out of breath, a symptom of stress, of 'forgetting' to breathe properly. We were both silent for a few seconds. Neither of us could find the words. We were simply two professionals bonded by the terrible abuse of a small child.

Rob appeared at the door.

'Sarah's just told me,' he said. 'I think you could use some help with this one.'

CHAPTER EIGHT

CRUEL AND UNUSUAL

'The sexual abuse of children by women,' Rob said, 'is still unthinkable in today's society.'

Rob, Sarah and I were sat in the conference room. As was usual in these difficult situations, Rob had taken us out of the office for an urgent briefing. There was no time for interruption; the rule here was to listen, absorb and then crack on with the investigation.

We were still getting over the shock. I'd not come across a female offender before. I realised that, along with so many other 'recently discovered' forms of child abuse, such as ritualised torture, our ignorance had meant the problem had been largely ignored until now, a point that Rob was quick to reinforce.

'Until recently, and despite the existence of a great deal of evidence to the contrary, many academic papers have stated that female paedophiles do not exist. This was even true for the psychiatrists' bible, the *Diagnostic and Statistical Manual of Mental Disorders*, as late as 1994.[1]

'Studies have since shown that the male-to-female ratio of sexual offenders is approximately twenty to one, and that female sexual offenders are responsible for at least 5 per cent of all sexual offences.[2, 3] That means that a great many people who have been sexually abused by women are being ignored by society. All too often, when someone accuses a woman of sexual abuse, let alone their mother, their claims are disbelieved by friends and relatives, or end up being ignored or dismissed by professionals.[4]

'A relative might say: "But she's your mother, of course she wants a cuddle." Even worse, the child may end up being punished for having made such an outrageous accusation. After all, if someone mentions the words "child sex offender", people will instantly picture an innately evil older male stranger with uncontrollable sexual urges who attacks both male and female victims. The stereotypical image of a mother couldn't be more different.

'A mother is more likely to get away with it. She has every opportunity to commit abuse without anyone noticing and without younger children realising that anything is wrong. Besides that, children who do realise that something is wrong are faced with an incredible dilemma. They want the abuse to end but the only way to do this – by telling on their mother – means they will lose the one person they count on for everything in life. This is an incredible conflict.

'I'm telling you this so that you understand the mindset of the person you're about to interview. I know you're used to dealing with twisted people but this is very different; there is something so wrong with the mind of a mother that abuses her own child that the justifications she is likely to come out with will shock and possibly confuse you. It's vital that you take whatever she says in your stride.

'In all the cases I know about and have read about regarding pre-pubescent children, women have always molested children they knew. Many have worked with children as a teacher's assistant, as a nurse in an adolescent psychiatric unit, as a fairground worker and as a nursery worker, so we'll need to know what and where Anthony's mother works or volunteers, just to be sure no other child has been abused by her.

'Women like Anthony's mum are not criminals in the traditional sense, in that they don't have records. There might well be a history of drug abuse and sexual abuse, domestic abuse, teenage alcohol abuse. Encourage her to talk about this. It may lead to a disclosure.

'I also want you to understand that cases like this are much less likely to lead to a conviction. That has got to change and I want us to set an example here. One study of eighty-three women who had sexually abused children found that only *one* made it to court, despite the fact that 56 per cent of these women committed brutal acts like burning, pinching, beating, biting and, in a few cases, had bound the children they were abusing.

'Female offenders may not even be given restrictions with regards to coming into contact with children and many are not required to undertake treatment or evaluation, even though the destructive nature of the offence is just as serious.

'And that's another thing. A belief persists that being abused by a woman is less damaging than being abused by a man. One only has to talk to the victims to realise what utter nonsense this is. More worrying still is that new research – and I'll stress here that more work needs to be done on this, but I think this is something we must bear in mind – suggests that male children abused by women are more likely to offend against women in the future.

'A high number of violent sexual offenders have reported that they had been abused by women when children. They all shared a strong mistrust of women and, in some cases, hatred.[5] It is by no means the case that every child abused by a woman will go on to offend, for the vast majority this is the last thing they would want to do. But all the same, this is another important reason for us to be open to the idea of abuse by women as well as men, and to act decisively in cases like this.

'One of the key things that Anthony has told us is that his mum is not acting alone. This is not so unusual. I need only to mention the names of Rosemary West and Myra Hindley. More than half of female abusers have a male partner; some, like nursery worker Vanessa George, are led and encouraged by a man, while others are forced into abusing children. In these forced cases, the woman is thought to act out of fear of physical punishment or sexual assault at the hands of her partner, or suffers from some kind of extreme emotional dependency. Over time, the woman might participate more actively in the abuse and may start acting independently.

'If Julie has ever abused Anthony on her own then she's very likely to be predisposed towards children. She may have suffered child abuse herself and I suspect that her adult relationships will tend to be unhealthy, in that they are full of violence and sexual abuse. Women abusers often suffer from low self-esteem, extreme anger, anguish or distorted thinking – with regards to things other than their sexual deviance.

'Finally, although this is perhaps hard to imagine, women paedophiles are often very different from men in that their pathway to offending is uniquely female.[6] Unlike male paedophiles, whose attraction to children is irreparably hard-wired, there's good research to suggest that most women are not 'programmed' this way. These tend to be the most disorganised offenders, those who act impulsively with minimal planning. Others might have been coerced by a male partner and did not want to take part in the offences – they only did so out of weakness and fear. This is where sharp-witted and passionate social workers like Ella will prove invaluable. With the right cognitive behavioural therapy and close supervision and support, it seems that some of these women can return to society.

'OK,' Rob said with a sigh, 'that's everything I know on the subject. While Craig hunts for the stepfather, you two can arrest Anthony's mum.

'We know she's a monster but we need to find out what kind of monster she is.'

CHAPTER NINE

A NEW MONSTER

'I was frightened of Brian,' Julie said. 'He was violent to me. I couldn't stop him.'

It would be too easy to accept this excuse because the alternative was too terrible to consider. I saw it for what it was in this instance: a classic distraction technique, a waste of time. 'Remember,' Rob had said as he wished us luck, 'in the interview you might hear some excuses that may make even you think twice.'

'Anthony is only nine,' Sarah said. 'That's a pathetic excuse.'

Julie stared back, but without looking. Her solicitor, a young woman about Ella's age, shifted uncomfortably on the plastic chair. I bet they don't prepare you for this at lawyer school, do they? I thought. I sympathised, because I wasn't ready for this either. Somehow, I was able to handle Brian abusing his stepson, but Julie's presence was something else.

'Let's move on,' I said. 'Anthony has told us that Brian exposed himself and touched him in your presence. That you undressed Anthony, cuddled him while he was naked and while Brian put his fingers inside him.' Of course, that was just Brian warming up.

Julie was perspiring. She looked confused. I knew we weren't wrong about her, but I didn't have a clue what was going on in her mind. What would a mother who stood by while her boyfriend sexually abused her son think? How would she justify it? What could possibly make it acceptable? I needed a lever to prise it out.

And then it hit me.

Love.

'Julie,' I said, 'do you love your son?'

'Of course I do,' she snapped back. 'More than anything.'

'How would you describe your relationship with Anthony?'

'Loving, caring ... erm, like mothers and children everywhere.'

'And you sometimes cuddle your son to show him that you love him, don't you?'

'Of course, I do, that's exactly right, like any mum.'

I glanced at the solicitor. She looked completely out of her depth, as if she'd like nothing better than to get this over with as soon as humanly possible. She wasn't alone.

My next question should wake her up, I thought.

'Do you think you went a bit too far when you showed your son how much you "love" him?'

It was a nasty question. In any other case a solicitor would bang the desk at that one. The solicitor looked at me. I pursed my lips, hoping she'd stay quiet. She did. I let the silence build. From Julie's confused expression, I guessed her mind was in turmoil.

She was thinking: if she said 'Yes' would this stop? Was this the right answer? What we wanted to hear? Would we then go away?

Sarah and I looked straight at Julie, calmly, giving her all the time in the world. There has to be an answer to every question, it just takes time. I let the tension do its work.

The silence was torturous for all of us – my hands were sweating – but none more so than for Julie. I stayed calm, not giving anything away in my body language, expression or tone.

'OK, it's all true, but Brian was going to hurt me ...'

Clang goes the cell door.

Throughout the interview Julie had consistently paralleled her behaviours with expressions of love and devotion. In her own mind she'd neutralised the sexual abuse. She'd lost her maternal nurturing.

The solicitor looked like a small furry animal trapped in the headlights of an Ice Road Trucker. She could have objected to this by now, slowed things down, broken my rhythm, asked for time with her client, but she hadn't, so I pressed on.

'Were you ever drunk when this happened?'

'Yeah,' Julie said, nodding slowly, her tone softening for the first time. 'It happened when I was drunk, most of the time.'

Sarah and I kept digging, exploring the mind of this new, strange and terrible monster.

Once Julie had opened up a small crack, the rest was surprisingly straightforward. Perhaps talking to us wasn't nearly as bad as she'd thought. Perhaps she thought that by being honest she wasn't in as much trouble.

We learned that Julie talked about sex with Anthony way too much, making crude comments and discussing his sexual development on a daily basis. She talked as though they were adults. I made a note to see if we could find any witnesses who would support any of this.

'Where was your partner while this was going on?'

'Brian? Oh, he's not around much. He's always travelling with the job. He's always down the pub or round his mates'.'

'Does he show any normal interest in Anthony?'

'No, as I said, he's not around much. He's not interested in his everyday life.'

To me that just made it worse, if such a thing were possible.

Julie was the dominant partner. It was clear that 'Uncle' Brian, who seemed to be virtually autistic in that his first love was computers, took little part in Julie's childrearing activities and decisions. He contributed to the housekeeping, paid the mortgage. In return Julie provided a home, hot meals, 'normal' sex and Anthony.

Anthony had been isolated. There was no one to protect him, no real father figure. No brothers or sisters. Julie had discouraged Anthony from making friends, stopped him from joining after-school clubs, taking part in school trips and extracurricular activities.

As far as Julie was concerned, Anthony had a dual purpose: he existed to give love, affection and attention to her and sex to her boyfriend. Anthony may even have reached a stage where he thought that abuse meant love. That 'love' had come out in the abuse of his friend Hetty. All he'd wanted to do was to show her love, to make Hetty his friend the only way he knew how, the way his mother had taught him.

No wonder Anthony had found it so hard to tell us what had happened. He did not know that his mother's cruel behaviour was criminally inappropriate. He was a confused and frightened little boy. This was confirmed once the interview with Julie was over. We returned to the suite to see Anthony and a plaintive little voice cut through our conversation.

'I want my mum.'

Tears filled Ella's eyes. She'd held it together when she needed to but now she had to let it out, the anger, the sadness, the tragedy of that small green-eyed boy who did not know any better than the cruelty of his mum and her boyfriend.

In cases of child abuse there are no winners. We had done our jobs. We had got the right result. Hetty was safe; already back at school, the memories fading. Julie and Brian would be punished. Anthony was safe.

But little Anthony would always want his mum.

CHAPTER TEN

YE GODS

'Oh God. Oh, you can't be serious. Oh God. No. '

As I stared at the file in disbelief, Craig crept up and peered over my shoulder.

'Oh hooo!' he hooted, 'you've hit the jackpot, old boy! Good luck with that one. Try not to say "Oh God" when you're down there though, won't you?'

'Thanks, Craig, that's very helpful.'

I read the referral over and over again. There was no escaping it. It wasn't any potential danger that I was scared of: it was politics.

I was tempted to delegate the job to Craig for being so cheeky but I knew Rob would take me to task if I did. I sighed. No, it had landed on my desk, so I would see it through.

The referral was simple enough: children at the Finsbury Park Mosque were being beaten with canes to 'help' them learn the Koran.

I stapled the yellow referral sheets together and wrote: 'Telephone strategy discussion with social services and education', in my red book. Then I picked up the phone and rang Siobhan, a newly promoted social services manager.

'That's one for the Department of Education, Harry,' she said in her cheerful Irish accent. 'I don't mind telling you, I really don't envy you that one.'

She started laughing.

'What's so funny?' I asked.

'Just imagining you walking in there, a Jim Carrey lookalike in your M&S suit, telling them how to run their mosque. Oh, to be a fly on the wall.'

'Well, come with me then.'

'No, thanks!' Siobhan said, as if I'd just suggested she join me for a weekend break in Mogadishu. 'Although,' she added thoughtfully, 'you could take Ella with you.'

'Really?'

'Yeah, she could use the experience. It's good for her.'

'You just want to see her face when you tell her, don't you?'

'Well, yes, I do,' Siobhan admitted with a laugh, 'but this is a good opportunity. She's had it easy so far.'

I wasn't sure that was exactly fair, especially considering our encounter with the female paedophile, but I was grateful for the support, so thanked Siobhan and hung up.

Next, I called the Department of Education. I eventually spoke to a manager who couldn't bat me away fast enough as soon as I mentioned the words 'Finsbury Park Mosque'.

'Y-you need to go on, on, erm, a, erm, to find out the facts,' he stuttered. 'Yes, that's it,' he added, his bureaucratic confidence growing. 'A fact-finding mission. We couldn't possibly get involved until we know all the facts.'

I chuckled. That's exactly what I would have said if I'd had the chance. So, off Ella and I went, armed with a handful of details. Even Ella, who was usually full of optimism and confidence at the start of each case, seemed a little pale at the prospect of having to reprimand a mullah.

Still, as long as we were acting in the children's interest then that was all that mattered. One slip-up, however and we'd be on the *Six O'Clock News* before you could say 'institutionally racist'.

Finsbury Park Mosque (since renamed the North London Central Mosque) sits prominently on the North London skyline. It's clearly visible from the main overground commuter line that runs through North London to King's Cross, along with the roof of a nearby bowling alley that, at the time, featured a billboard poster of a semi-naked young woman attempting to look seductive while lying across a bowling lane.

Abu Hamza al-Masri, the former nightclub bouncer who'd seemingly risen from nowhere to end up as the head of the mosque, was the archetypal cartoon villain. With his one eye and hooked hands, this extremist imam was an easy target for newspaper photographers and he frequently featured on the front page of the *Evening Standard*, where he was described, accurately enough, as a 'Hate Preacher'.

In January 2003, about 150 officers raided the mosque and recovered chemical warfare suits, fake passports, a stun gun, handcuffs and hunting knives. Although Hamza wasn't charged in relation to this raid, he was dismissed from the mosque before eventually being imprisoned for inciting racial hatred.

I felt like a lit match wandering around a fireworks factory as we passed through its doors and were shown around. The mosque had often been in the news. Negative media attention had rumbled on during Hamza's trial and this, combined with general public concern about terrorist activity, meant that the new trustees appointed by the Muslim Association of Britain had an extremely tough job as far as restoring public relations went.

Soon we were introduced to a kind-looking white-bearded imam in his fifties. 'People always ask me,' he said quietly in a

London accent, 'whenever I go and give a talk, they say, "What is it like in that notorious mosque?"'

He chuckled. 'I tell them that it is like any other mosque, very peaceful and friendly, and they look so disappointed. I don't know what they were expecting me to say.'

He waggled his finger at us. 'What do you think they were expecting?'

Ella and I took this question to be rhetorical and stayed silent.

'There are no media stories about us now because only good things are happening. If something went wrong, or some scandal took place here, then they would be all over us, demanding we be sent home.' He paused for a moment before adding with a laugh, 'I live in Wilberforce Road, so that wouldn't take long!'

I did my best to join in but only managed a half-hearted chuckle. All I could think about was the fact that I was about to ruin this man's day.

'Seriously, though,' he continued, 'those who strongarmed the mosque into their control for the purposes of hatred and violence instead of helping the community and teaching Islam are long gone; they are not welcome here. This is a place of peace and harmony.'

Oh boy.

'Now, what can I do for you, Detective Sergeant Keeble?'

'Well,' I said hesitantly, 'talking about teaching Islam . . .'

'Yes?'

Ella leaned forward and spoke quickly and directly. 'We've received a report that one of your teachers has been hitting children, to reinforce the learning of the Koran.'

The imam's mouth fell open. I held my breath. Ella had been clear and unequivocal, just as we should have been. Personally, I would have dressed it up a bit more, but it was too late now.

After a few seconds, the imam started to smile, then let out a loud guffaw. Ella and I looked at one another as he continued to laugh until he struggled for breath. What had we said that was so funny?

'I'm sorry,' the imam said, wiping a tear from his eye, 'I think someone has been pulling your leg. This would never happen here, it is ridiculous. Forgive me, I don't mean to make fun of a serious accusation but it is simply ludicrous. Did your report include a name?'

I passed him the report. He put on a pair of glasses with round lenses and squinted at the paper.

'We have no one here by that name. You do know that there are more mosques in Finsbury Park?'

'Er ...' I said, 'there are?'

'Yes, of course! Although we are the focus for the local Muslim communities, there are many imams who preach in their homes. Perhaps this is what your tip-off refers to. If you like, I will make some enquiries for you.'

'That would be very kind.'

As we left we passed a group of teenagers carrying bin liners, wearing reflective tops and rubber gloves.

'A street litter collection,' the imam said. 'Just a small way we can make a big difference to our community.'

'I'm impressed,' I said, thinking of a certain Christian phrase.

'This is what our role in community should be about,' he said as we shook hands at the gate. 'If all Muslims simply banded together to make the world a better place to live in, we'd be universally admired.'

As Ella and I left, my phone rang. It was Rob.

'Some new info on an old case has come in,' he said.

'Which one?'

'Cyril. His wife's just called.'

'Christ, what else is there to say about him?'

'No idea, but I want you to go and talk to her. I know this wasn't one of yours originally but everyone else is busy at the moment. I've ordered his file from the general registry, it should be here shortly.'

'I'll be right there.' I hung up.

'Something important?' Ella asked.

I looked at the young litter collectors hard at work.

'What was it the Bible says about cleanliness?' I asked.

CHAPTER ELEVEN

NEXT TO GODLINESS

Four doors to a floor. I found the one I wanted and walked forward, pausing at the fish sign above. A Christian home. 'Follow me and I will make you fishers of men,' Jesus had once said. Well, I didn't follow Jesus as such, but I'd certainly fished for a fair few lost souls in my time.

I pressed the button and a loud half-buzz, half-ring rattled through the flat. Unlike the other flats, a security grille didn't cover the white door. The paint was worn thin but its surface was graffiti free, spotless in fact. The landing smelled slightly of bleach; almost clinically clean.

I heard scuffling then a soft elderly female Jamaican voice said, 'Who is it?'

'Harry Keeble.'

I didn't say 'Detective Sergeant' because Florence was expecting me. The lads loitering on the stairs at the taxpayers' expense didn't need to know the 'Feds' had come calling.

'Just a minute.'

The door opened on the chain. Florence peered over her glasses and through the gap at my ID and shook her head; she couldn't see. I passed my warrant card through to her. She shut the door and I had a minor panic attack. Had I just lost my warrant card? If I didn't get it back I would be in for a severe telling-off from Rob.

Thankfully, the door opened and I heard the sound of the chain dropping. 'Can't be too careful, dear,' Florence said. 'Especially living 'ere, you know?' She returned my precious card and welcomed me in.

Light filled the hallway of the small flat. Florence beamed at me. She was in her seventies and was slightly overweight. Her thick greying hair clashed with a brown and orange floral print dress that might have been fashionable in the 1970s, maybe even the 60s.

I followed Florence down the hallway that darkened as the door closed behind me. Most hallways in council flats don't have much natural light.

'How are you, Florence?'

'Oh fine, fine. Call me Flo, dear, everyone does round 'ere.'

The flat was dated but extremely clean. Florence had lived here for decades and it was a real home. Often, council estates provide shelter to young families and people on the move, yet to establish a base, and so don't usually have a homely feel. Unfortunately, many of the estate's less salubrious residents end up trashing them.

Florence was surrounded by her treasured memories. Framed photographs filled every space. Children and grandchildren held teddy bears, footballs and diplomas. There were wedding pictures, including Florence's own.

'Me and Cyril were married in 1965,' she said. 'Still got the dress, you know. Wanted me daughter to wear it at 'ers.' She sighed. 'But fashions have changed, haven't they?'

I looked at Cyril. A young man, smiling broadly from almost half a century away, proud of his stunning new wife.

Florence had pride; she treasured her family and her life,

which she lived in the best Christian traditions. It was a pity to think that once she was gone her possessions would be swept up; her ornaments dropped straight into the bin or off to the charity shop. That flat would be stripped, cleaned, maybe even modernised and handed over to the next family. Florence, like so many, would not leave much of a legacy.

I sat on the sofa, which was, like everything else, spotless.

'I wish I could keep my home this clean,' I said, genuinely impressed.

'Well, I bet you have kids, don't you?'

I nodded.

'See, you wait until they leave home, then you can clean all you want. Then you'll miss all the sticky handprints and mess.'

There were china dolls on the shelves and clean white linen squares on the back of the sofa, one for each cushion. On the small coffee table in front of me, a teapot sat waiting. This was quite lovely and relatively rare in my line of work. There was another silver-framed picture on the coffee table.

'That were me in the fifties,' Florence said. 'Just arrived in London, green as you like.'

'It must have been an amazing experience.'

'Oh, we had some adventures, I can tell you. There was good and bad. The housing was terrible and there was lots of racism, lots of ignorance. Cyril couldn't stand it. He spoke up and never backed down when he encountered racists. He got a few black eyes.'

She paused and leaned forward, touching my forearm, and in a whisper said, 'One or two of those black eyes came from policemen.'

I wasn't sure whether to apologise on behalf of the Met or simply sympathise. As I searched for the right expression, Florence sat back and laughed. 'It's OK!' she said, waving a hand at me, 'I know you're not like that, 'Arry.'

'That's terrible. It must have been very tough.'

'Yes, it was,' Florence said. 'I was a singer, you know? I sung in a few clubs and even went on tour as a backing singer with some top bands towards the end of the sixties.'

I was impressed. 'I had no idea.'

'Well, I was getting pretty good pay and wanted to get me some new clothes. I went along to some fancy shoe shop and when I wanted to try on the shoes, they said I had to wear special socks and gloves if I was going to touch anything. White people didn't have to.'

'So what did you do?'

'Said I didn't need to try them on, that I'd buy them right then and wear them immediately. You should have seen the look on 'er face!' Florence giggled.

I thought of how little this woman asked from life, from the rest of society, and how much she clearly gave. She was so different from anyone else I usually encountered in these blocks. Florence was a mile apart from her neighbours. She didn't fit in any more and although I felt like 'rescuing' her from these sometimes 'troubled' flats, I knew she wouldn't budge. This was her home. She couldn't imagine living anywhere else, just like the old folks who, true to the Blitz spirit, refused to budge from one of the blocks on the Hollywell Estate when the bulldozers rolled in.

Florence took a sip of her tea, placed the cup back on the saucer and looked at me with a serious expression. 'I have something else to tell you about Cyril.'

Cyril, Florence's husband, was two years into a thirteen-year prison sentence for raping their two granddaughters.

Although his case had been closed, we never threw the files away. All the papers were tied up together, placed in a box and sent off to a huge warehouse in West London where they were filed in the Met's ambiguously titled 'General Registry'. The papers would stay there for at least thirty years, just in case. Paedophiles can't be 'cured' and these files sometimes come in very useful.

'Do go on, Flo,' I said.

Cyril's file had landed on my desk that morning. The interviews detailed the many, many times the two girls had stayed in the flat. Mum and Dad worked long hours and odd shifts, so Florence and Cyril stepped in, like many other grandparents across the UK, as free babysitters delighted to spend time with their children's children.

Cyril, however, was delighted for all the wrong reasons. He was in his mid-sixties and complained of his 'bad back', brought about by many years of work as a postman. The marital bed was too soft, he said. He needed to sleep on the sofa, in the lounge, he said.

Florence had not suspected a thing. How could she?

'He was guilty, so I said, "Let him go to jail, where he belong." But he was still my husband. I could not divorce him; it would not be Christian.' Her voice trembled slightly as she continued. 'If I did not stand by him, I thought, then how could he be saved in, in . . . there?'

To Florence, Cyril had been split in two. He was the young and courageous man she'd fallen in love with as a teenager. He was the man who'd betrayed her in the foulest manner imaginable. He was the man who had raised their children, who'd laughed as they learned to ride their bikes and hugged them when they passed their driving tests. He was the man who had raped their grandchildren.

Their photographs sat side-by-side, abuser and abused, separated by silver frames. I noted there were none of Cyril from the last decade and, as far as I could tell, they weren't pictured together anywhere.

'I asked God why, in his wisdom, had he allowed this to

happen? That was the hardest thing. I did not know why. But there was no answer. Sometimes there isn't, is there?'

I could certainly agree with that. I nodded.

'All I could do was speak the truth and support my children and our grandchildren, so that is what I did. Those poor little girls.' She smiled. 'You wouldn't think it to look at them now. They don't come 'ere any more, of course, but I visit sometimes, when I can.'

I had looked long and hard into that file. And something had jumped out at me. They always made disturbing reading but this one contained something I'd never read before.

The granddaughters had been asked to tell the interviewer what the abuse had been like. One of them had said something truly extraordinary. She described the pain to start with, but then later how the sensation was 'warm', almost as if the experience had been pleasant. Of course, it wasn't, not by any stretch of any perverted imagination. The child had described her experience like this simply because she had no real concept of what sex was.

I'd felt nauseous with anger.

Cyril pleaded guilty, a tactic employed in cases like this, where the interview evidence is utterly convincing because the abused child simply could not know how to make this stuff up.

By pleading guilty, Cyril had hoped he would get a 'light' sentence.

He got it wrong. He got a 'lighter' sentence.

And even though Cyril wasn't due for parole until his late seventies, it was still far too soon.

'Fifty years,' Florence said, shaking her head. Her tone was almost incredulous as she continued. 'I mean, fifty years I'd known that man and look at what he did. Look at what he did. How could I not know?'

Florence was clearly serving her own sentence. I'm sure her

decision to stay in contact with Cyril would seem alien to most mothers fortunate enough not to be faced with such a nightmarish duality. While many would no doubt argue she was being weak, taking the easy line, I could see Florence was battling demons that had pushed her faith right to the edge. Whether she was right or wrong, her strength of conviction had been tremendous.

'I had forgiven him, you know,' Florence said, 'and I prayed for his soul every day. I really did.'

I looked up from stirring my tea. What was that? My spoon froze. Florence was speaking in the past tense. Something else had happened. Something had broken her conviction.

Florence took another sip of tea. Her hand shook as she placed the cup back on the saucer. She nervously picked up a teaspoon before putting it down again.

'Cyril always assured me it was just our granddaughters, you know?'

I stayed silent, giving Florence all the time she needed.

'I visited my sister yesterday. She has a granddaughter, Rita. She told me ... that ... that Cyril ...'

I nodded, encouraging Florence to find whatever words she needed to tell me what I now already knew. I hoped, after what would amount to a huge amount of time and effort, we'd get another conviction that would see Cyril die in prison.

Florence's prayers had been answered, but not in the way she'd hoped. But her dignity, honesty and the way she had dealt with Cyril and her granddaughters had inspired fifteen-year-old Rita to come forward. Now I would do all I could to make sure both she and Cyril received the justice they deserved and life would go on.

Once I was outside, back on the spotless landing, I heard a vacuum cleaner start up behind me. When the stain of bad memories came, Flo reached for the mop, vacuum and duster.

CHAPTER TWELVE

HOME SCHOOLED

'You're not like the *kaffir* [non-Muslims],' the teacher said as he marched up and down in front of a row of ten small boys who were sat cross-legged on the classroom floor.

'Those people who don't believe, who don't wear the hijab, who smoke and drink, are responsible for all the evil in the city. You should hate them! They are evil. Even worse are the Muslims who live like Westerners, who shave, dance, listen to Western music. Women who don't wear their headscarves properly must be punished and will be tortured with a forked metal rod in the afterlife!'

I was with the imam, looking at his computer screen.

'This is what we want to stamp out,' he said. 'This horrible man is infecting the minds of young children, teaching them to hate their neighbours.'

The man in the footage, which had been taken secretly, went on to verbally attack Hindus, Jews, Christians and atheists.

The imam had found my suspect, who taught in a private madrasa. Madrasas in the UK are part-time, after-school or weekend classes, often held in mosques, where children are taught to read the Koran.

'Before you go and see him,' the imam said when he called me with his tip, 'I want to show you something. Could you come and see me?'

I'd driven straight over and he'd shown me this shocking video.

'This school was praised by government-approved inspection teams for its interfaith teachings,' he said. 'Apparently, according to the report, pupils learn about the beliefs and practices of other faiths and are taught to show respect to other world religions.

'They obviously weren't scrupulous enough,' the imam said, 'perhaps out of fear of crossing some line or other. I'm furious about this. I want us to be as crystal clear and as open as possible, so that people know we only preach peace and love. This sort of thing must be stamped out.'

The man in the video got up and walked behind the boys. The children flinched as he passed. He suddenly leaped forward and slapped a young boy hard on the head before kicking the child next to him on the shoulder. It was clear that these boys were well used to the beatings.

'Where is this place?' I asked.

'It's not in London,' the imam said. 'It's already the subject of a police investigation. I wanted to show you that I know that this does go on.'[1] He leaned closer. 'More importantly, I want you to know that if you find anything like this here, in North London, I want you –' He paused for a moment and emphasised the point by thumping his fist on the desk. 'No, I *need* you to investigate it fully. If we don't protect our young now, then the consequences will be disastrous in years to come.'

I could tell we were at the right address thanks to the large sticker in Arabic above the door.

An imam in traditional tunic and trousers answered the ring. He was about forty, well built, with a good-sized potbelly.

'Yes, what can I do for you?' he said, looking from me to Ella with curiosity.

I made the introductions, and asked if we could talk inside. He smiled and beckoned us in.

'Should we remove our shoes?' I asked.

'No, no, not at all, it's not necessary,' he said.

Interesting, I thought. I'd once turned up at a suspected crack dealer's address with my squad to search for drugs. He was Muslim, he said, and he asked us to remove our shoes, a request we politely declined. At the time, I wasn't sure if I'd made the right choice, even though he did turn out to be a drug dealer.

The imam, who introduced himself as Mushtaq, led us down the hall into a large lounge. The house was austere; there were no ornaments and the furniture was cheap and basic but spotlessly clean. I could tell that Mushtaq was wary of us but I felt that the fact we'd made it through the front door was already a good sign.

'We're here to gather information about an allegation,' I said.

Ella stayed quiet this time, letting me do the work. I had to admit I danced around the topic a bit, trying to be delicate, to let potential tensions settle. Mushtaq seemed to sense this and relaxed. It was now obvious to him that I was not a member of the heavy-handed brigade.

'As you know, we work in child protection and we're interested to know more about what goes on in this madrasa.'

The man nodded as I spilled one sentence out after the other. I couldn't tell if he thought I was weak, scared and vulnerable or if I was displaying sensitivity and professionalism.

'Yes, well my mosque is what you would call a fringe mosque,' Mushtaq said flatly. 'There are many others in London based in people's homes.'

Any man can come along to a public mosque, but these private mosques sometimes forbid strangers. A minority of these host extremism. Mushtaq began to explain about teaching the Koran. We went through how long the lessons were, what they had to do and how the lesson was structured.

'These are young kids, eight, nine years old,' he said with a strained look. 'It's easy to lose discipline.'

The lessons sounded like they were too much for an eight-year-old. Hours of learning by rote – and after school to boot. While I wouldn't have let my kids take part even if they wanted to, I had to put my own feelings about these lessons to one side. I wasn't in a position to judge. After all, I wasn't an Ofsted inspector.

'I'm not surprised,' Ella said. 'I don't think I could learn the Koran off by heart. It must be hard to keep eight-year-olds focused.'

Mushtaq frowned at Ella. We were nearing the important part of the interview.

'We have to ask you,' I said, 'because we have received information that to reinforce learning and to keep discipline, it has been alleged that—'

Ella broke in. 'You hit the kids with a wooden stick.'

I glared at her. I'd spent ages leading up to that point and there she went again, jumping in from nowhere.

Still, this was forgotten when the imam replied, 'But of course.'

He got up off the sofa, went over to a cupboard and produced a small piece of rectangular wood, about the same length as a ruler, but a bit thicker.

'I use this,' he said with a shrug, 'but gently on the palm, like so,' and he lightly tapped his hand.

If this had been any other police enquiry I would have stopped the conversation, seized the bit of wood and arrested him. But this was child protection, a branch of policing that stands apart from any other. I had to find a genuine solution to this problem that was in the best interests of the children.

Mushtaq sighed. He wasn't stupid; he knew my cogs were

whirring as I decided on a course of action – no doubt he was wondering whether I was going to arrest him.

There had been no reported injuries, so arresting the imam, followed by a major inquiry that would involve interviewing dozens of children, was clearly not the best way forward. I just needed to put matters right.

'Mushtaq,' I said in a serious tone, 'I know you see your methods of discipline as a moderate correction and this is not an unusual view. Private schools across the UK were still using the cane up until the late nineties. But they have stopped now. The reason is that any type of corporal punishment is against the law, and has been since 1999.'

'I am sorry,' Mushtaq said, 'I'll stop using the stick.'

'If you have a problem with discipline,' Ella said, 'then tell the parents. It's usually very effective.'

Mushtaq continued to make all the right noises and, relieved and satisfied, we left.

'Hopefully we've made those kids' Koran lessons more enjoyable,' I said.

'Yes, that went well,' Ella said. 'Much better than I thought it would.'

'We may never know,' I replied. 'This is the eternal problem. Mushtaq seemed genuine. He made all the promises we needed to hear and we'll check with the parents that they're OK with the situation. All we can do then is write it up, make sure it's in the system, so if another report surfaces our reaction will be severe. It may be that we end up back there.

'While my heart says we should treat this as a success story, we've only walked away with a promise. I have no idea if he is going to give those kids hell the next time or not. I know that all sounds very cynical, but if you write up things in full detail, then if you got it all wrong, you can always rely on what you genuinely thought at the time.

'Oh, and if you do get it wrong, expect to be on your own. I bet they didn't tell you *that* at social work school, or whatever it is.'

Ella laughed. 'No, no they didn't, they just said if you get it wrong you will be supported.'

'I take it you didn't believe them.'

'Of course not. I know what's in store for me if things go awry.'

'And in Hackney, they will, Ella, believe me. Just be prepared for it, that's all.'

CHAPTER THIRTEEN

A DETECTIVE CALLS

The large black door swung back. I introduced myself.

The man's face fell. No one wants to see a police officer at the front door. We rarely appear unannounced to deliver good news.

I could hear music in the background, accompanied by laughter. I'd interrupted a small party. I quickly double-checked that I had the right name and address. Yes, I did.

'May I?' I said, stepping forward across the threshold. It wasn't a question.

'Can't this wait?' said the man, who was black, greying and in his fifties.

'I'm afraid not,' I said, struggling to keep my voice even. 'Are you celebrating something?'

A successful businessman, he had just secured a new contract. This, along with his daughter's engagement, was cause for celebration.

The large house was immaculate. It should be, I thought.

In the lounge, among the plants and ornaments, a large pair of golden crucifixes had been fixed to the wall. The man's wife, their daughter and her husband-to-be were drinking champagne.

'I'm here about Jemi,' I said, unfolding a crumpled scan of a visa application photograph of a fourteen-year-old girl that had been handed to me earlier that evening. I passed it to the man. He knew the face only too well, but I wanted him to look at it when I told him.

The girl in the picture had such a huge smile it was infectious; like when somebody else yawns you yawn, when you looked at Jemi's picture you couldn't help but smile. She radiated happiness.

'What is it?' the man asked with a tired, impatient sigh. 'What's she done now?'

Jemi had arrived in the UK from Sierra Leone under a false name with, as Customs and Immigration were led to believe, her 'mother'. In reality she was a family friend, known to Jemi as 'Auntie'.

Jemi had been given a new name, a new name for her new life, she thought. Her excitement, she told us later, was extremely hard to contain. Jemi didn't know she was an illegal immigrant; she wanted to study and to work, to be a part of our world. Jemi's family had worked hard to raise the money for the flight. She would work just as hard to make sure it was paid back as soon as possible.

She'd marvelled at the tube, the people in their strange clothes, smells, the newspapers they read, the brightly coloured adverts, the metallic sound of the tube driver's announcements, the incredible amount of people, their mobile phones. She was in commuter hell but thought it heavenly.

Jemi didn't have her own suitcase. All she'd had were a few clothes stuffed into Auntie Femi's bulging suitcase. These had been abandoned after Auntie had a long and hopeless argument at the check-in desk about charges for excess baggage.

Where they were going, Auntie said, there were three

children, two boys younger than her and their older sister, who was in her late teens. Jemi smiled in delight as they boarded a bus. She spent the trip across East London with her nose to the window, looking back at her auntie every now and again, to point out something of particular interest. They passed a park with an adventure playground before arriving at the house. It was the size of a palace. Jemi really was in heaven.

She had so many questions but Auntie said she was tired from the trip, so Jemi tried to keep as quiet as possible. She was the only passenger who was disappointed when it was time to leave the bus.

Auntie rang the doorbell. It was answered by another auntie. This one was bigger and looked angry. Jemi became worried when her old auntie left her there but when the new auntie said Jemi would sleep on the sofa, Jemi was delighted. To sleep in this large room, with the TV and the soft sofa, was to be a princess.

The other children were at school. Jemi asked if she could go too. 'Not yet,' her new auntie said, 'we need to sort out some papers first. But in the meantime you're going to help, aren't you?'

The new auntie then explained. Jemi was here to do the washing, dusting, ironing, vacuuming and cooking. She would take out the rubbish, prepare packed lunches, walk the children to school and back again, take them to the doctor when it was needed, to the park to play and would look after them when auntie had to go away. She would live off scraps and she wouldn't be going to school. This was her life.

Jemi was a slave.

Eric, the manager of the children's home, knocked on the door. Jemi had been found in the small hours, sitting in a high street shop doorway by a police officer. The officer thought she was mute, as she didn't seem able to speak. He checked to see if a missing girl had been reported. Nothing came back, so a bed was found for Jemi in a children's home.

Jemi had finally spoken, asking for something to eat. Eric held a plate of food in his hand.

Eric tried to open the door. It was blocked. Knocking and banging brought no answer and, after placing the plate on the ground, he forced the door open, just wide enough for him to enter.

What he saw next would stay with him for the rest of his life.

I looked the father in the eye. I wanted to see his reaction.

'I'm sorry to have to tell you that Jemi has tried to commit suicide.'

His wife, Jemi's new auntie, gave a little scream. 'My God!' she said, and crossed herself. The young couple looked on in open-mouthed shock. The man sat staring at the picture, saying nothing. He covered his mouth with his free hand.

'What happened?' the daughter asked.

'She was found wandering the streets,' I said. 'The day after she was brought to a children's home, she tried to hang herself. Luckily someone found her just in time.'

More gasps of shock from the two women.

I remembered Eric's shaking hands, the sweet tea; Jemi in the hospital bed, the sympathetic nurses.

Jemi looked at me nervously with big wide eyes. The welts on her neck were already fading but she had been marked by far deeper wounds. She wanted to trust somebody but she was a very different girl from the one who'd travelled on the Piccadilly Line all those months ago.

After telling us how she arrived in London and what her new

'family' had expected of her, Jemi refused point-blank to say any-thing more about them. She was scared. Until she ran away, she had only ever left the house with the children, on some errand, to take them to school or to the adventure playground or to carry Auntie's shopping.

She wouldn't tell us if there was some specific incident that had motivated her to run away and although there were some faint scars on her young body, it wasn't enough to say for certain that she'd suffered physical abuse.

Jemi said over and over that she wanted her mum. This was something we could help with but, with her mum being in Sierra Leone, it would take a while.

The case was a difficult one, in that without Jemi's help, pros-ecuting the family – who denied everything – was going to be impossible. She had no understanding of how the British justice system worked. Although we tried to explain, she still wasn't confident enough to tell us what we needed to know to see jus-tice done.

Even if she did talk, it would simply be a case of her word against the family. If the CPS let us take it to court, I doubted whether she would survive a relentless cross-examination.

Of course, there was the crime of 'failing to send a child to school'. The child benefits angle was another; Auntie had lied on the forms, but it would take a long time to prosecute and even then it was hardly enough. I had compiled a file to try and squeeze a false imprisonment charge or something, anything out of our system – and to keep the pressure on the family – but I wasn't hopeful.

Of course I wanted the family punished, but sometimes it just doesn't happen. This leaves one with a feeling of uselessness. We are the police; we take down bad guys. But sometimes we're forced to watch criminals slip away.

Although Jemi was safe and her new life could now begin, her future remained uncertain. Her name had been added to the long, sad list of thousands of 'unaccompanied' minors that place incredible demands on the social care system. Ultimately, I resigned myself to the likelihood that I would never know. I hoped that with the right foster carer, Jemi would eventually recover and that smile in the photo would one day return.

Modern slavery is developing into a huge problem. It takes many forms, from children like Jemi, packed off to the UK from a deprived country, to young gypsy brides wedded into a life of drudgery.

The program *Big Fat Gypsy Wedding* attracted enormous audiences. It cleverly exposed the life of slavery some teen brides can expect after a few short hours spent dressed as candyfloss princesses. Leaving school early and without qualifications to become lifelong caravan cleaners is hardly the end of a happy fairytale. I saw at least one child protection referral on the programme.

Child slaves are sometimes found when social services notice that the family is claiming benefits for a child that is not registered at any school. For the most part, they go undetected, until perhaps they run away – and even then people simply don't believe their fantastic tales: 'Come on, slavery in modern London? I've seen the *Cinderella* movie too, you know!' Most of the time, they're accused of being here illegally and are treated as such.

The Met Police set up Operation Paladin in 2004 to deal with the incredible numbers of children brought into the UK to work as domestic slaves. The few studies that have been carried out suggest the number of child slaves easily runs into the thousands (and these figures do not include those trafficked for prostitution).[1]

Prosecuting guilty families is nigh-on impossible; the

evidence is often historic and the people who bring them into the country are transient and possess multiple identities. There's little incentive for victims to cooperate, especially if they fear deportation, a fear often instilled by their abusers, who nearly always tell them the lie that they will be free one day – they just have to repay the money it cost to get them into the UK first.

Even when they are rescued, many slave children have no permanent UK status. Some are given temporary visas, while others are kept waiting for years without visas, trapped in limbo, unable to work or move on. The holy grail of indefinite leave to remain in the UK remains a rare thing for these young victims.

Public vigilance is our best weapon against child slavery. If we can collect evidence and witness statements, and arrest the people concerned, then we have a far better chance of prosecution. At the time of writing only one person, Lucy Adeniji, a Nigerian pastor, has ever been convicted of bringing a child into the UK for the purposes of domestic servitude. One person. This beggars belief.[2]

One of Adeniji's victims, who can't be named for legal reasons, was only eleven when she first arrived in the UK. She spent eight years being beaten and tortured by Adeniji; pepper was rubbed in her eyes and between her legs and she was cut with knives. She was expected to care for Adeniji's five children and clean her five-bedroom home.

Unbelievably, Adeniji worked part-time for Newham Council in East London as a youth worker. She'd also written two self-published books on childcare called *Parenting God's Way* and *Carry a Seed* in which she described her joy at becoming pregnant after fearing she was infertile.

Parenting God's Way was still on sale at the time of writing. Her author biography included the sentence: 'She is now a proud and fruitful mother of five children of her own and few others adopted [sic].'

At the trial in March 2011, it was Adeniji's word against her victims. Proceedings had to be stopped when one of the children broke down screaming. The jury were utterly convinced and found Adeniji guilty. She was sentenced to eleven years in prison and will be deported to Nigeria once she's served her time.

Adeniji had robbed these children of their childhoods and there are many, many more still out there and getting away with it. All too often in child protection we have to think the unthinkable. The public also needs to believe the unbelievable.

Signs that a child is a domestic slave include a young person regularly bringing children to and from school but not attending herself, or a child that looks thinner, scruffier and doesn't smile with other children in the same 'family', or a child on their own loaded with shopping bags, or a young child that visits a local GP without their parents.

Between the police and the public, it must be possible to free more of these invisible children from their never-ending nightmare.

After interviewing Jemi, I showed her around the police station and took her to the police canteen for a fizzy drink. She watched the cops laughing and talking.

I spotted an old mate, Liam, I hadn't seen for years. We shook hands warmly; we had loads to catch up on.

'I'm a bit busy right now,' I said, 'but if you're about in ten minutes I've got time for a chat.'

'Great, see you then.'

Jemi watched Liam return to his table. 'That's what I want,' she said.

'Which one?' I asked, thinking she was talking about the drinks.

'I want to be like you. I want to be a policeman like you.'

Fifteen minutes later, I was cradling a latte and catching up with my old friend Liam. He was on an exciting, well-funded and high-profile street crime unit.

'So, what are you up to these days?' he asked. 'Last time I saw you, you were charging into crack houses and had made the front page of *The Job* (the police magazine). Did you go on to a sexy drugs unit or what?'

I always dreaded this question. I took a breath and said, 'Nah, I went for Child Protection.'

He froze and stared at me intently. I knew what was coming. It usually went something like: 'You, Mr Proactive Policing, in the Cardigan Squad? Are you winding me up?'

The Cardigan Squad was the unfair nickname some cops gave to Child Protection. They assumed that all we did was give upset kids a bit of a cuddle before we passed them on to social services. Attitudes were starting to change, but it was slow.

Liam leaned forward. When he spoke, it was with real intensity.

'Don't fuck it up, Harry. Between you and me, I was in foster care and beaten up loads when I was nine. Fucking nine years old, and got the shit kicked out of me for months. I was rescued by a social worker; she saw the look in my eyes and did whatever it took to get me the fuck out. I don't know how she did it but she got me into an amazing foster family. She saved my life.

'I can't tell you what it means to live in total fear. Leaving that home was the best day in my life. I know why you do that job. It's the reason I became a cop: I'm not going to let any victim down.'

He paused for a moment. I looked away awkwardly as I saw he

was fighting to control old emotions and memories, things he hadn't thought about for years.

'It's only when you've been through it that you really understand,' he said. 'Just don't fuck it up. It's too important. Good luck, mate.'

He drained the last of his coffee, shook my hand, stood up and walked back over to a table with his friends and joined straight back in the banter, as if our conversation had never happened.

CHAPTER FOURTEEN

HERE'S TO YOU, MRS ROBINSON

'What if I could prove it?' Donna asked, pushing her long, dark hair back, which caused her large, looped earrings to swing back and forth.

'How would you do that?' I asked.

We were sitting in a police interview room. So far, I'd been getting nowhere. A few minutes ago, Donna's husband had arrived and had passed something on to their solicitor, who'd then called me back in.

Donna, an attractive lady in her mid-thirties, wearing a long, figure-hugging black cardigan and designer jeans, looked me in the eye. 'I'll admit what happened but you have to believe me, I didn't know he was underage.'

She nodded to her solicitor, who pushed a black moleskin notebook, about the size of a paperback, across the table.

I picked it up and started reading.

January 15
Well, my jottings are about to take a most unusual and unexpected turn. I am bursting to share these thoughts but can confide in no one, only my diary.

I came across Hadis running in Victoria Park last week. He literally bumped into me at the gate, sending my handbag flying.

He's beautiful, black-haired, brown-eyed, strong-jawed and with a fine physique. He's building up his stamina to give him the edge, he said, in football. He's determined to be a professional. His voice is a clear, freshly broken tenor. It's a delight to listen to.

I want to sleep with him.

Now, hold your indignation for a moment, put down the stakes and flaming torches. I may be 35 and nearly 20 years older but I am not a monster and really, what is so strange about the idea? Shakespeare married an older woman and he did pretty well. I may be a drama teacher, but I'm not a teacher in his school, so there can be no betrayal of trust.

Many people accept that a young boy looking for his first sexual experience will be naturally drawn to an older woman, and that we women are instinctively driven to look for young, strong and healthy mates.

Everyone knows that some fathers take their sons to a brothel; maybe some sleep with the au pair hired to look after their little brothers and sisters, while others, after a few ciders, slither up to a well-known slut-about-town who throws her legs apart for the sheer hell of it. Well diary, that's not me.

These are hardly ideal ways for a boy to lose his virginity. While I don't think prostitution should be encouraged, in many ways these options are no worse than sleeping with an inexperienced female peer. I – the older woman, that is – am wise, kind, soothing. A girl of his age will be nervous, uncertain and ignorant. She will be a disappointment and may even be cruel.

Hadis and I met independently of anyone. The attraction

is mutual. I am married, with a good job. Surely no safer pair of hands exists. I will be kind to him, calm his nerves and show him what a woman wants. In return he will be able to dazzle inexperienced young ladies with his lovemaking skills in the future.

I will make him a kind lover, rather than those awful rugby boys who I know make bets with one another to see who can sleep with the ugliest and most unpopular girl in the school.

I hear and see the frantic race for sexual maturity every year. I've had boys who've shouted 'Show us your tits!' at me in the street. I *know* what teenage boys talk about – the sex lives of celebrities, who they'd like to 'do' and so on.

I don't even need to seduce him, not in the sense people are familiar with, making lewd suggestions, dressing provocatively, looking a certain way. He already has a crush on me. All I need to do is not discourage him and he will get there all on his own.

Hadis is young but his body is mature and his eyes are full of sexual longing. When he looks at me that way, he seems much older. He has been spared the curse of acne. His hormones have travelled at such a rate that he's shot through adolescence, straight over the border into manhood.

He's just not certain enough to act. I will help him overcome this, gradually, carefully.

February 3

Hadis told me he liked me. Then that it was more than 'liking'. I kissed him on the cheek. Then he told me I was beautiful. Do you know how long it has been since I was told that? I laughed and he thought I was laughing at him, the poor boy. He was shaking, trembling. He's always so

freshly shampooed and brushed and smells of fabric
softener, the scent of which now reminds me only of him.

And then – well, to lie beneath his slender, light body,
feel his unfamiliar hands on me, exploring me, cautiously,
timidly even ... at first. I'd forgotten how exhilarating this
is, the excitement of danger, the fear of revealing yourself
to a stranger, of kissing a stranger after a decade of the same
man every night.

I'm alive again, I've awoken, as if the clock has been
reset at 18 and I get to do everything over – but differently
this time and with all that I now know.

God, I want to preserve what has happened because I
know my extraordinary happiness is finite. A clock is
always ticking, speeding up as it counts down to the end.

I have set up a hotmail account (in a different name, of
course), so Hadis and I can communicate freely, arrange
our liaisons and send each other comments, little
reminders throughout the day that make life oh-so-
exciting.

My descent was gradual at first but within a week I was
addicted, checking my messages on my secret Blackberry
has become a compulsion. The rush I feel when I see a message from Hadis, just the simple question, 'Lunchtime?'
sends me into orbit.

And although no one could possibly believe him if he
told anyway, I've made him promise. I told him we would
both be in a lot of trouble if he ever dared to boast and I
would deny everything. He looked hurt, silly boy.

March 12
We meet whenever we can. We only live a few short streets
apart. Perhaps it increases the danger but the convenience
and the excitement are too much.

We have to be quick in the week. Afterwards he showers and runs out the door, to be home at more or less the usual time.

Thursdays are different, he told his mother he'd joined an after-school club to prepare for his GCSEs, which I suppose he has in a way, although the extra lessons he's getting are different from the norm.

Hadis is gentle, careful and considerate – and a very fast learner who needs little encouragement. I can tell him to do anything and he does it obediently, without question or hesitation.

For the first time I have thrown away my mask, have abandoned my dissatisfaction with life for a pure rush of pleasure. And talking of dissatisfaction, that brings me to my husband, poor middle-aged Gary, with his expanding stomach, thinning hair, worn-out pants and holed, mismatching socks he sometimes deigns to throw in the general direction of the washing machine. Gary is simply too focused on his work to notice.

I'm nicer to him now, sympathetic. After all, he doesn't have what I have and, let's be frank, has no chance of getting it. I almost burst out laughing when he said I was looking particularly 'fresh' this morning. I almost told him then and there. I want to throw my old life away. It is a mask.

April 26

Tonight my precious boy picked a quote from *Hamlet*. 'This is the very ecstasy of love,' he told me.

I was so surprised I was speechless. It was like scratching a little puppy behind the ear and instead of wagging its tail, it opens its mouth and says 'A bit lower, please'.

'No,' I told him, and paraphrased from *Henry VI*:

'Heaven may be made in a woman's lap but what you feel is not love.'

He insisted he was falling for me. I told him not to be so silly, that this was just an attachment to the intimate pleasure we shared. We're just having fun, well I'm having the time of my life in fact, *and* I'm giving Hadis guidance that will stand him in good stead in later life.

It just seems absurd to me, when the world is full of so much truly terrible evil, that people would feel morally outraged when something of this sort happens.

After all, I'm not evil. I'm no do-gooder, either. I'm not naïve enough to think that a few poems and an understanding of Shakespeare is genuinely going to enrich the lives of the people who come to see our school production.

'It's the *Lolita* versus *The Reader* argument, isn't it?' Ella shouted over the rain.

'What do you mean?' I asked.

We were hurrying through a summer thunderstorm to the car under my large but wobbly £3 umbrella. The next strong gust of wind would blow it inside out.

'Well, in *Lolita*, Humbert Humbert, a middle-aged writer, seduces Lolita, whom he describes as a "nymphet", in between girlhood and adolescence, not quite thirteen.'

We reached the car and leaped in just as the umbrella exploded. The car windows immediately fogged up, forcing me to wind down my window a touch.

'In *The Reader* Michael is fifteen and is seduced by Hanna, a 36-year-old tram conductor, who dominates their relationship. In *Lolita*, Humbert murders a man, while Hanna was a former Nazi involved in the gassing of Jews.

'People still get more irate over *Lolita*, over this despicable man who seduces a child, who is – according to Humbert anyway – willing. In *The Reader* the underage element is not considered a problem and although the psychological conse- quences of the affair are mentioned in the book – in that Michael is unable to form lasting relationships with women – this is just put down to Hanna's sudden arrest. Critics always pass over this, and the issue is barely covered in the film.

'The question is: if Hanna had been a man, would anyone feel sympathy for her?'

'What you're trying to say,' I said, with a slight tone of con- descension, 'in an extraordinarily long-winded way, is that if we swapped the sexes in this case, so that it was a 35-year-old man and a fifteen-year-old girl, then we'd react differently?'

Ella ignored my jibe. 'Yes, that's it. That's the only reason why we feel a little bit of sympathy for Hanna. Readers can live with the fact that Hanna was a sex abuser but not Humbert. The revulsion stays with you throughout, even though Humbert pro- fesses to truly love Lolita and she's a willing sexual partner. It stays even though he commits no other crime, until the end of the book, when he kills in Lolita's name. It's certainly nothing like playing a role in the gassing and incineration of millions of Jews.

'All the arguments and excuses for female seducers of teenage boys fall down when you swap the sexes. Mrs Robinson might try and win sympathy by saying, "My judgement was clouded by desire," but put the same argument in a man's mouth and it's instantly dismissible.'

Ella waved the photocopies of what we referred to as 'Mrs Robinson's diary' at me.

'Imagine if this was written by a man,' she said. 'Would you feel the same?'

The ink was barely dry on Ella's degree and so everything was new to her and, so it seemed, also black and white. I knew from my own experience that the first few child protection cases

definitely have the greatest impact and create the deepest
memories. You're suddenly dealing with the most extreme people
in society, extreme in the sense of their depravity or suffering.

Ella certainly had the passion for the job. She reminded me of
me when I first joined child protection and I would have debates
with Rob. Now, it felt like I was taking Rob's role with Ella,
which often involved playing devil's advocate.

'Well, I'm not sure it's so clear cut,' I said, navigating the
chaos of Homerton high street. 'The thing is, the diary *wasn't*
written by a man and the boy is a mature fifteen-year-old. OK, so
he was possibly fourteen when the affair began.

'It's a tricky one. Their affair lasted many months; he went to
see her. He wasn't being forced. There are different levels of
abuse and when you deal with it, you have to keep in mind the
interests of the victim and his family. This isn't paedophilia, *per
se*. "Mrs Robinson" is attracted to a young man, not a pre-
pubescent child. There are about 200,000 teachers in 3,500
secondary schools in charge of millions of teenage pupils. It's
going to happen. The stars will cross every now and again and a
passion will be born that goes beyond the desire to learn ...
erm ...'

'Whether Catherine loves Heathcliff,' Ella said.[1]

'What?'

'*Wuthering Heights*. I did English Lit for A level.'

'Yes, well,' I said, 'I don't go as far as ex-chief inspector of
schools Chris Woodhead. He had a relationship with a former
pupil eleven years his junior back in the 1970s. When he went
public about this in 1999, he said that affairs between teachers
and sixth-formers could be "educative on both sides".'[2]

'That's an insane thing to say!' Ella exclaimed.

'Yes, it puts a whole new spin on "extracurricular activities".'
I smirked. Ella wasn't amused.

'Anyway,' I said, 'although Hadis may be embarrassed and not want to take Mrs Robinson to court, the consequences may come later, like in the book you were talking about.

'In cases like this, it takes a lot of guts to speak out. If a boy discloses abuse, he may not be believed. If he enjoyed himself, he does not think of himself as a victim, despite the fact that he may be suffering. Then there is the inevitable breakup, heartbreak, emotional turmoil, perhaps feelings of betrayal, which will fuel distrust of women in later life. His friends will be jealous or will see him as a hero and will expect him to live up to his reputation. He's going to need an eye kept on him.'

Ella, who would be that eye, thought for a moment. 'OK, I see what you're saying. But it seems as though a crime has been committed and damage has been done to the boy.'

'Well, that's what we're here for. Although I've got a feeling this is going to be anything but straightforward.'

We reached the address and ran through the rain that was still hammering down, up the tiled entranceway to the original Victorian door of the nicely restored semi.

The chimes of the doorbell had barely stopped echoing when the door was flung open. There was an awkward pause as Saliha, Hadis's mother, examined my warrant card and absorbed my introduction.

Ella shouted over the noise of the rain, 'Can we come in, please? Out of the rain.'

'Oh yes, yes, of course!' the woman said with a forced smile, waving us inside.

We hurried into the hall, wiped our feet, and followed her to the kitchen where we placed our coats over the backs of chairs surrounding a large antique farmer's table.

'Hello, nice to meet you,' she said confidently, thrusting her hand out to me, then Ella.

A small pool of rainwater had appeared on the tiles under our coats.

'Sorry,' I said. 'Is there somewhere else—'

'Don't worry, forget about it,' she said, running her fingers through her hair.

Like most Turkish women she was naturally dark, but Saliha had dyed her hair blonde. She was wearing Calvin Klein jeans and a Karen Millen baggy T-shirt with a wide neck. She looked smart. I wanted to take her seriously but struggled thanks to the enormous pair of Goofy the Dog slippers on her feet. It was like she'd stepped into a pair of cuddly toys.

The house was immaculate, obviously recently renovated with clean white walls, wooden floors, and fitted bookshelves. She introduced us to Hadis, her fifteen-year-old son. He was a tall and good-looking lad. It was easy to see how his dark hair, slight stubble and strong physique made him look older than he was. He didn't get up from the sofa, just nodded an almost inaudible 'Hullo'.

Normally I'd bowl straight over and throw out my hand for a warm, firm handshake, but this time I chose to stay put. Hadis was withdrawn; he'd thrown up a barrier and crashing through it now wouldn't help him in the slightest.

We sat down.

'It's so shocking,' Saliha said. 'My poor Hadis. I am so very angry. I hate that bitch.'

When rumours reached Saliha about Hadis and Donna, she confronted her son. He didn't deny it. Saliha's reaction had been simple and instinctive. She tracked Donna down and attacked her in the street. Screaming insults, she grabbed a fistful of hair and they fought until the police arrived.

It was the kind of case every police officer dreads, where everyone is a suspect and everyone is a victim.

With regards to the catfight, I really didn't want to know; enough police time had already been wasted in arresting, cautioning and interviewing them.

Saliha's blood was still up, however. 'That bitch has been abusing my son,' she said. 'She's a child molester, an abuser. She should die for what she has done!'

As Saliha spoke, I glanced at Hadis. He looked like he wished the sofa he was sitting on would swallow him whole. I sympathised. Firstly, he'd been off school and everyone already knew why. When Hadis returned, he'd have to face his peers. A lot of the guys would be jealous – and very interested to know more.

I knew Hadis would be worrying about the girls at school; would they think he was a pervert? Did this mean his chances of having a girlfriend had been reduced to zero?

Adults often look down upon these sorts of teenage worries with a patronising lack of concern. But sometimes, kids who are teased or have their affections rejected end up killing themselves. What may seem like harmless banter to an adult, or a simple romantic hiccup, can be utterly soul-destroying to a teenager.

I needed to make Saliha shut up. She thought she was protecting her son's innocence, but labelling him as a victim of sexual abuse would only make Hadis feel worse and increase his fear of how his peers might react. Her violence towards Donna could also be a sign of guilt. She had missed the signs and she had failed to protect her son.

I needed to be very firm, to take control quickly so that Hadis would speak. As long as his mum was screaming child abuse, I knew he'd say nothing. I certainly wouldn't, if I was in his place.

'Saliha, listen to me. You need to calm down and put this into perspective. Forget for a moment about what the law says and let's just calmly talk about what has happened and how Hadis feels, before we go any further.'

Ella shot me a sideways glance. I could tell she was surprised at my approach but I ignored her and kept my eyes fixed on Saliha. After what seemed like an age, but was probably only a few seconds, Saliha exhaled and relaxed her posture. She felt like she was carrying a burden and she didn't know what to do with it. The sooner she understood that Ella and I wanted to take it from her the better.

'We need to discuss this calmly,' I repeated, 'and make decisions in terms of what's best for Hadis. We need his view, it's as important as yours.'

I wasn't really being honest here. Hadis's view was paramount. We would do what he wanted – within reason. Saliha nodded.

I turned to look at Hadis, who was staring into the screen of a portable PlayStation.

'OK, Hadis,' I said, 'do you want to tell us your story on video and possibly give evidence?'

'No, definitely not.' He put the device down and looked across at his mum. 'Mum, please, this is so embarrassing, I just want to forget about it.'

Saliha stared back at him and stayed silent. Good. I had taken the burden.

'Fine,' I said. 'What we can do is this. If you do not want to go to court, we can record your account of what's happened. We are going to arrest Donna anyway, but if you don't want to give evidence, no one is going to make you. If you change your mind later, that's fine, but this conversation could be made use of in court.'

Hadis turned his gaze on me and repeated what he'd told his mother. 'I don't want to give evidence, I just want to forget about this.'

'OK, I will make a record of this conversation anyway,' I said, taking out my notebook, 'in case you change your mind. Please tell me everything you can.'

'Look,' Hadis said, gesturing with his hands palm up in a plea. 'I don't see what the fuss is about. I know this isn't exactly normal but Donna is an attractive woman. I'd jokingly tried it on a few times, like my friends. If she'd knocked me back just once, that would have been it, but she didn't, she played along.'

He paused. 'I liked her, I mean really liked her.'

Saliha started to interrupt. 'You can't possibly mean—'

A quick look from me was enough to stop her.

'Mum, since Dad left you've been really busy. I haven't seen Dad for ages. Things have been tough at school. I've been struggling to make the football team. Donna was kind to me. I miss that part of her. I used to do anything to see her. I'd even sneak out at night.

'I know it's wrong. We used to argue about it. Donna was much better at arguing than me, knew more things than me. I'd then shout something like, "Of course you know all that because you're so much older." And she'd cry.

'And now I just want it to go away. I know I have to talk to you about this, Mum, but you have no idea how hard it is. I don't want it to ruin our relationship. We need to let it go, put it down to experience. If we drag this through the courts it will be a nightmare. I won't be able to go to that school any more. I won't be able to look you in the eye.'

Now that was one mature young man.

Hadis may have been a victim, but he was a victim who had consented and had enjoyed everything that had happened, except for the fallout, caused by the age of consent. He had just reasoned the best way out. I could tell that Ella was impressed with him.

A trial might well attract national media coverage. Donna, whom Hadis still had strong feelings for, would be labelled a 'predator'. Hadis would find himself featured in assumptive and salacious stories, where he would be described as the 'handsome young schoolboy'. Journalists would chase them and their families for quotes. They would dig into the family's past and would label Hadis's mother a divorcee, hinting at a difficult home life.

At the moment, Hadis at least had the protection of the male stereotype. He'd 'done it' with an older woman and would be admired by his peers, most of whom would have seized the chance to sleep with Donna. I know that as a fifteen-year-old boy I would probably have done the same, given the opportunity. Things would eventually settle down and Hadis would finish his GCSEs.

Life would go on.

I sat across from Donna in the interview room.

'Well?' she demanded nervously. 'You see how I thought he was sixteen.'

Although I was grateful for this written confession, ignorance was no excuse. 'Should Donna really go to prison for several months?' I wondered. 'Should she be placed on the sex offenders register for committing an act that, a few months later, would not have been a crime?'

Like so many things in child protection, I wasn't sure. While I was certain that what I'd done was in Hadis's best interests, I wasn't sure that Donna deserved her fate. I'd read about a woman teacher called Nicola Prentice, who'd avoided a prison sentence after seducing a boy of sixteen, because the judge felt media coverage of the case, based in part on her victim talking to a newspaper, equated to a 'Biblical stoning'. The judge's decision was also influenced by the fact that the boy did not want her to go to jail. This was despite the fact that she had targeted the boy before losing interest after her conquest was complete.[3]

Donna and Hadis had had fun. It had got out of hand and was never going to work but there was no malicious intent from either party and now both of them simply wanted to put the experience behind them and get on with their lives.

I mentally swapped their sexes. Would I really go for a jail sentence in those circumstances? I would. Then why did it not feel right in this case?

'You've admitted the affair and dropped the assault charges against Mrs Saliha Takis,' I said.

'Yes, and?'

'I've spoken to Hadis and he doesn't want to take this any further—'

'Oh, thank God,' Donna said, relief flowing prematurely through her.

'But,' I added, 'you are still getting a caution. This will mean that you will have a criminal record and you will be placed on the sex offenders register—'

'With paedophiles and rapists? You can't be serious!'

'And your school must be told. It may be that you won't be able to teach any more.'

'But that's what I live for!' Donna said, shocked tears already flowing.

I left the room and passed the husband who was sat in the reception. He was lost in a thousand-yard stare. I wondered whether he'd stand by her, whether she'd show him the diary or whether he'd already read it.

Whatever the case, Donna's life was in tatters. I still had a niggling feeling that this wasn't the right outcome, but couldn't explain why.

Ella, as ever, had a more direct opinion. 'Donna deserved what she got. She knew what she was doing. She was using a young boy's love for her own end. I've been doing some research.'

She took out a collection of research papers and leafed through them, looking for a reference.

'Here we are,' she said, and started to read. 'The damage done by older female abusers on teenage boys can be severe. One woman who sexually abused an adolescent boy told him he'd be charged with rape, as he was the male.'

Ella paused. 'Can you imagine what that would do to you? Research also says that boys like Hadis often suffer from self-blame, low self-esteem, sexual problems and substance abuse. I'm going to have to keep a close eye on him and his mother.'

We were silent for a moment as we walked down the corridor. Ella would write up her report while I briefed Rob on this unusual case. As it turned out Hadis did go on to finish his GCSEs, and his escapades with Donna faded into urban legend over the summer holidays.

'It's amazing, really,' Ella said, shaking her head. 'All the signs were there, but no one spotted them.'

'That's often the way in child protection,' I replied. 'The unthinkable often bears thinking about.'

CHAPTER FIFTEEN

ONE DAY, AT THE AIRPORT

I passed the crime scene tape, just beyond which a CID detective was interviewing a witness, an elderly black lady. I overheard her say, 'The screams seemed to go on for hours before they stopped.'

'Why didn't you call the police?' the detective asked.

'I did. It took ages for someone to come. It sounded just like a dying animal.'

I passed the detective, showing him my badge.

'Don't worry, I'm not here to tread on your toes,' I said. 'I'm here for the flat upstairs.'

'Oh, that one. Right then. Good luck.'

'You too. Looks like you've got your work cut out.'

One crime above the other. Just another day in Hackney.

I entered the stairwell, jogged up to the floor above and pushed open the door to the flat.

'Hello?' I said.

A young uniformed constable appeared in the hallway.

'DS Keeble from Child Protection.'

'They're in here.'

I stepped into one of the bedrooms to see two girls, aged ten and six. They looked at me with wide, fearful eyes. I beamed at them cheerfully.

'Hello, my name's Harry. What's yours?'

Heathrow is a fascinating place. Just about every law enforcement agency in the UK is up to something in Europe's largest and busiest airport, either looking for or following suspects. Thousands of holidaymakers and businesspeople go about their travels, unaware of the countless crime dramas unfolding around them every single day of the year.

The man in the suit, a detective from Heathrow's very own police station, scanned the sunburned arrivals from Izmir on the Turkish coast. He saw several refreshed-looking couples, their hand luggage stuffed with souvenirs; a group of six lads all hungover from an extended stag do, comparing conquests; the elderly couple who'd run out of things to say to one another and couldn't wait to get home for a decent bit of toast and cheddar; and a pair of skinny, hungry-looking backpackers seeing Europe on a shoe string.

None of these interested him, though.

Samantha produced her passport and beamed at the immigration officer. Her head was pounding. The flight had been awful, four hours with a slowly worsening hangover.

She'd not gone to bed but had instead stayed out all night in Club Triple-X, then straight to the airport, swaying from the cocktails, ears ringing from the pounding bass of house music.

She'd felt eighteen again. The guys in Turkey had adored her; she only had to roll up to a bar or step into a club and she was bought a drink. Not to mention the waiters, barmen and the guys working in the hotel. Money was tight, so the financial support was greatly appreciated.

It really was as if she were a new woman, no one knew her

from Eve. Everyone was a blank slate, no baggage, just searching for a good time. Sun, sea and sex. For a precious few days, Hackney, land of rain, dirt and – for Samantha – boredom, had seemed a million miles away.

The man in the suit stepped forward. 'Samantha Brice?'

'Yeah, who's asking?' she answered, looking him up and down.

'Would you come with me, please?'

'What's this all about?'

'Just follow me if you would, so we can talk privately.'

They walked side by side. She could feel him watching her out of the corner of his eye. He stopped at a security door, typed in a pin number and took her along a corridor with rooms with glass doors on both sides, some of which were already in use, civilians on one side of the table, customs and police officers on the other.

They reached an empty room, entered, and the man offered Samantha a seat.

'A Detective Sergeant Harry Keeble from Hackney's Police Child Protection Team has asked me to speak to you.'

Samantha leaped to her feet in shock, hangover gone; her face white, panic in her eyes.

'Are my babies OK?'

'What did Mummy tell you, Nadia?'

I looked across the table at ten-year-old Nadia. She was tall for her age, mature too, a lovely girl. She spoke clearly and answered our questions without hesitation.

'Mummy had to go away for a few days. Granny was sick. Mummy had to look after her.'

'I see. And who was going to look after you while Mummy was gone?'

'I'm old enough to look after myself and my sister. I took her to school. Mummy left us enough food and showed me where

Aisha's spare inhaler was. I marked off each day on the calendar until she was back.'

'So what did you do while Mummy was away?' Ella asked.

Nadia looked at her nervously.

'You've done nothing wrong,' Ella said. 'And you aren't in any trouble.'

Nadia smiled. 'It was fun. We played games, had picnics and I read Aisha bedtime stories. When can we see our mum?'

The man in the suit broke the silence.

'Well?'

'You don't know how hard it is. Struggling for years on your own with two kids. I have brought my kids up all on my own. I've never had a break. I should have gone to social services, I know. I needed help, but the social don't give you any, I just needed a break, that's all. Nadia is a good girl and her Auntie Janie was there.'

'There?'

'Yes, looking after her.'

'What do you mean?'

'On the estate, in case anything happened, she lives across the block. Janie was there looking out for them. They were never in any danger.'

The man in the suit absorbed this for a moment.

'Samantha Brice, I am arresting you . . .'

'Can you tell me what happened last night?' I asked.

'We played a board game,' Nadia said, 'and I read Aisha a bedtime story.'

'And what happened after you had fallen asleep?'

Nadia's voice trembled. 'There ... there was a man. Screaming.'

*

At the crime scene, the murder squad detective told reporters it was the worst case he'd seen in thirty years as a detective. Other detectives would roll their eyes at this stereotypical comment but this time, he assured his colleagues later, it really was.

'The occupant of this flat was subjected to a brutal and horrifying attack,' he said. 'His killers tortured him, demanding he give them his pin number. It appears that after he resisted their sustained efforts for a number of hours, his murderers strangled him with an electrical cord.'

'At least we got to them before the tabloids,' I said once we were outside the interview suite.

'I can't imagine how terrifying that must have been for them,' Ella said, 'listening to the torture going on below.' She wiped away tears. 'How are they ever going to sleep through the night again? Christ, I'm so angry with their mother. What's going to happen to her?'

'We'll prosecute her,' I said firmly. 'Child abandonment is very serious. Samantha will be going to prison. All for a drunken five-day break in Turkey.'

'Is that the best outcome for her kids, though?' Ella asked. 'They're so good, she's done a good job raising them.'

'Well, you're right, it may or may not be the best outcome. But Samantha's broken a very serious law; she has to face the consequences. There will be media coverage, so we need a strong message. The best thing you can do is search for a decent home for Nadia and Aisha in the meantime. Perhaps a family member.'

'God, I wish I could take them,' Ella said quietly, staring back through the door. 'They're such lovely kids.'

We were silent for a moment.

'I'm going to look long and hard for a good home,' Ella said with determination. 'Whatever it takes.'

I held the door open as Ella returned to the suite. She sat down with Nadia and Aisha who were now playing together in the lounge.

It had been a tough day, with no good outcome, except for one thing; a realisation that hit me at that moment. So much had happened recently, that I hadn't even noticed.

Ella was on her way to becoming a remarkable social worker.

CHAPTER SIXTEEN

THE SOCIAL NETWORK

In some ways, the bedroom looked like any other. It was in a first-floor flat inside a large terraced house. There was a double bed, exposed floorboards and a large white wardrobe. What distinguished it from most other bedrooms was the enormous wall-to-wall desk. Several computer drives, leads and screens were all connected by a complex spaghetti of cables. Two modems blinked busily. On the right, next to the largest screen, sat four A4 ring binders, packed to bursting.

The man, sitting on a lightweight designer ergonomic chair, typed something and hit 'enter'. The noise of the sent message pinged softly. A response came a few seconds later, a cheerful, innocent-sounding 'beep'. The man pushed his chair across the wooden floor with his foot. He automatically reached out and grabbed one of the ring binders, which was labelled 'Buddy List', and opened it.

He flicked through it. Inside were photographs of children's schools, football teams, rugby teams and lots and lots of pictures of children, all carefully catalogued: name, age, date of birth, favourite sports, celebrities, food, chat rooms and what time they usually logged on.

The man, who called himself 'Joe', pushed the chair back across to the screen, and then searched in the folder until he found the picture he wanted: Rachel Forbes, thirteen years old. He ran his finger down a list of likes and dislikes before checking the location of her school.

He smiled.

Gotcha.

The constable, pen poised, thought for a moment before asking, 'So what music is Rachel into?'

Melanie shifted uncomfortably, knees together, her hands resting on them, nervously twisting a tissue. She was all cried out. She had been overtaken by a hopeless, despairing fatigue.

Rachel, her thirteen-year-old daughter, had not come home the previous night.

'I don't know what she's into. Why would that help?' she asked.

'If it comes to it, we can ask her favourite singer to personal message Rachel.'

'How would they do that?'

'She might still be checking her email, using Facebook, MySpace, Bebo and so on. It can be quite effective.'

'What?'

'You know, Facebook, the social network, you must have heard of it?'

'Personal message?'

'Yes. Rachel has a Facebook account.'

Melanie shook her head. 'I didn't know.'

'Her computer was on in her room,' the cop said, a new concern crossing his face. 'Facebook was Rachel's homepage.'

had a sh_it day
what happened?
Got picked on by the cool girls.

Can't believe it u are the cool girl did you tell mum and dad?

Mum drunk. Dad watching TV. Tried to talk to him but grunts like caveman.

Sounds like my parents. Skool is tough ✷ but u get thru it

U cant spell

IK! U don't need 2 in the real world

I wish I didn't have 2 go 2 skool tmrw. Wish I was 20 like u

wish I could see u

me 2 your the only 1 who gets me

& u get me ✪

really?

(An emoticon showing a bunch of flowers appears)

Ah yr sweet! Lonely here

Where are your brothers?

They are out always in trouble

Wish I could keep u company c u at last

Me 2

Talk tmrw x

Tmrw x

How we take statements varies slightly from officer to officer. Ideally, it's best if you can get the person to open up while you stay as silent as possible, taking notes while they talk. This gives you an opportunity to get matters clear and in order.

Melanie was sobbing in front of me. She'd already sat through too many of these interviews with cops over the last twenty-four hours. The detectives trying to find her missing daughter had asked her for more and more information about Rachel as time went on, looking for any clue that could lead them to her, until they found Rachel's computer.

Now it was my turn. I needed to know to what extent Rachel had been a victim of her parents' neglect. Rachel had already been missing for twelve hours before her mother and father had noticed.

If I was a nurse at a hospital, Melanie would have probably got a hug, but all I could do was adopt what I hoped was a sympathetic look. Male cops don't hug, we all know why. I waited for a few moments before breaking the silence.

'It's OK, take your time.'

Melanie nodded. 'I'm all right,' she said.

She was an attractive, large lady in her late thirties with medium-length, light brown hair and red painted nails. She was dressed in worn light blue Levis, open-toed, high-heeled sandals and a loose white blouse. She made little eye contact at first and she spoke very quietly, as if she was simply speaking her thoughts aloud. I had to ask her to speak up a couple of times.

'Rachel, "Shel", we call her, for short,' Melanie said quietly. 'She hated Rache, after *Friends*. She doesn't like being compared to Jennifer Aniston. She's the youngest, my baby girl, my princess. I don't know what it was, but the more I tried to make her into a princess, the more she rebelled and tried to be like her two older brothers. They were more of an influence than I ever was.

'By the time she was ten, she wanted to wear denim, not silk, and on Saturdays she wanted to play football, not visit Brent Cross shopping centre. I still loved her, of course. As far as taste and interests went, we were as different as anyone could be, but we got along; I let her be who she wanted to be. Pete, my husband, on the other hand, *was* a problem.

'Our problems started after Shel was born. He showed less and less interest in the kids and me. I was sure he was having an affair, so, when the opportunity presented itself to me, I did little to resist.'

She stopped and looked up at me, as if suddenly realising someone was taking note of everything she was saying.

'Did Rachel know about this?'

'I really don't know. It's taken this to make me realise I don't know my own daughter any more. I was too wrapped up in my own life. I could tell you more about Steve than my own daughter.'

Melanie shook her head in self-disgust at this insight.

'Steve was a security guard who worked nights. We'd meet in secret, all sorts of places, it was very exciting. He really loved me. At least I thought he did. Then things between Pete and me started to get really bad. There was a lot of repressed anger between us. It started to come out; we had terrible rows and the boys got into trouble at school.

'To be honest, I became a bit of a basket case. I spent all my time moaning about my husband and how I wanted to leave him. Steve was married too, but still loved his wife and didn't want to risk losing his kids, so eventually he dumped me.

'My life was over. Raised three kids with a man I never really loved. About to cross over to the wrong side of forty, living in a small terraced house in Hackney, on the edge of a council estate with railway lines at the bottom of the garden.'

Melanie released a short bitter laugh. 'Hardly living the dream, is it?

'I became depressed, so I drank. It used to be half a bottle of Shiraz in the evening, but I started popping the cork at lunchtime. God knows what my kids got away with. The boys were always in trouble at school, but I ignored them. It wasn't that I didn't love them; I just didn't have the energy to play such a big part of their lives any more. Booze clouded my mind. I spent three years like this, three years of barely saying a word to my husband.

'And so here we are. I don't know what else to say except this is enough to drive me sober. I'm not touching that stuff again. Especially when the cop asked me all those questions I didn't know the answer to. I want to know what music my daughter likes, the gossip she's into, her little idiosyncrasies. I've become a stranger to her, someone she's forced to share the same house with, that's all.'

> **mum is having an affair she thinks I don't no but its obvious I hate my parents**
> my parents split up 2
> **really? Im sorry** ☆
> It was bad for a while but theyre happyer now it helps if you have friends to c u thru cos it gets messy
> **I'm scared. I don't have any friends**
> Yes u do!
> **✪ I no but here with me**
> Wish I could b there with u
> **Me 2. Talk tmrw**
> Tmrw x
> **x**

I looked at the image on the screen. A pretty thirteen-year-old girl, who was trying too hard to look like she was eighteen, stared back at me, smiling shyly. She had straight, long, dark hair and wore a tight bright pink vest. Like many her age she'd also gone a bit crazy with her makeup.

Other pictures in Rachel's personal gallery showed her in shorts and with an exposed stomach, the sort of pictures most parents – had they seen them – would have removed in a flash.

At thirteen, Rachel was, according to Facebook's regulations, just old enough to have an account. She hadn't bothered with any privacy settings. What for? Surely that was the whole point of social networking?

Joining Facebook is like joining a party in an infinitely sized room, where the entire world's population can come and go as they please, and where it's possible to talk to any one of them in private about any subject in the known universe.

There was a lot of competition for attention and time was short, so the sooner people knew all about Rachel the better. Then she could get down to the interesting stuff. Rachel used her full name and quickly began 'Friending' people she didn't know. She listed her favourite music, movies, subjects and celebrities and joined a dozen groups.

Rachel then created a photo gallery, starting with the classic Facebook portrait, shots taken with a phone held at arm's length. She quickly grew more confident and tried her best to look older, exposing more and more skin.

After school, she'd dive in through the door and run up to her room, logging on to AOL, Facebook and MySpace at the same time. Messages were answered, friends were poked; in no time she was fielding several conversations at once in chat rooms packed with thousands of other children her age.

Melanie may not have hit Rachel, she may not have been nasty or cruel, but she had become so wrapped up in her own problems that she had become guilty of neglect. Unintentional, perhaps, but neglect nevertheless. Neither Melanie nor her husband had paid any attention to Rachel's online activities. This was like letting her roam alone through Soho late at night.

Joe had two goals.

The first was to have sex with Rachel.

The second was to record it on film.

I wish I could b there with u

touch u

kiss u

do you want that?

Yes

'Right then, Rachel,' I said, with a gentle smile. 'Is it OK if I begin?'

Rachel shifted awkwardly on the chair and shrugged as if she couldn't care less what I did. She took a sip from the can of Fanta I'd brought back from the police canteen.

'My mum's an idiot,' she volunteered suddenly. 'And Dad's a moron. What else do you need to know?'

'Why is that?'

'Dad keeps saying he wants to kill the bastard because that's what dads are supposed to say and what everyone expects him to say. He'll never understand. Neither will Mum.'

'Understand what?'

'We're here to talk about Joe, right?'

'Well, I'd like to talk about your relationship with your parents,' I said.

Rachel released a small snort of disgust. 'They're useless. For years they're not interested in me and then I meet this amazing man and they freak out. I'll never forgive them for this, never.'

'Forgive them for what? For not protecting you?'

'No!' Rachel sat up, angry now. 'Why doesn't anyone understand? Joe was nice to me. He looked out for me. I looked out for him. I was nice to him. I fell in love with him.'

'But he was—'

'Thirty-four, yes, I did notice that,' Rachel said, as if I was a little bit thick, 'but he's still so young inside, you know. I slept with him because I wanted to. He *gets* me. Why is it so hard for anyone to understand this?'

And suddenly I did.

Rachel had turned up eighteen hours after her parents had last seen her. At first she denied going to see Joe but, confronted with the evidence, she had to admit the truth.

Rachel was then forced to endure the nightmare of vaginal, anal and oral swabs as well as a detailed examination of her insides, which involved taking several photographs, a record of the damage done. This was followed by a series of forensic interviews. Again, she was reluctant to divulge any information about Joe, where she met him, what he looked like and so on.

And now here she was, defending him still. This man had raped her. And I would have bet my mortgage that he'd filmed the experience as well. And yet, she still talked about him as if they were friends.

Why?

It used to be that the activities of most paedophiles were limited, in that they had to hide in bushes near to playgrounds to get close to children. These days they hide in plain view on social networking sites, thanks to the ease with which one can create a false identity.

As a software engineer, he was well attuned to the online world. For most parents, the language of Facebook, with all of its abbreviations and codes – for example, POS = Parent Over Shoulder, or Legal = Over 16 – is largely a mystery. But not to Internet predators like Joe.

Finding likely candidates was straightforward. Joe began by studying usernames. These are usually an abbreviation of first names combined with something to do with age, a characteristic and/or a hobby. Screen names are supposed to define the user's personality. A lot of teen girls' names are designed to show others that they're physically attractive, and can be quite racy.

It may be as basic as gender: GIRL or GRL, BABE or BBE. Or it could involve a sexual term like FOXY or FXY, SEXY or SXY. A typical username might be SALLY16SK8, which translates into Sally, a sixteen-year-old girl who's into skating.

On top of this, the apparent anonymity of the Internet allows teenagers to use phrases and descriptions that would normally be seen as inappropriate in front of adult strangers.

Joe searched for girls who were discussing sex. He checked their username for suitability (for example, LEAGLEAGLE19 suggests a with-it law student while QT_KIM14, where QT =

cutie, suggests a vulnerable younger target) and then studied all the information they'd revealed about themselves on Facebook, MySpace and so on, looking for their history on chat rooms (remember, once something has been uploaded to the Internet, it's very hard to get rid of, almost impossible in fact).

Joe contacted PRINCESS_SHEL_00 through her personal profile. His profile revealed Joe to be an attractive twenty-year-old (his picture was actually of Joe, but taken when he was a young man). The Facebook newbie immediately agreed to 'talk' privately via Instant Messenger. In no time at all, flattered by the attention, SPORTYJOE98 and PRINCESS_SHEL_00 became inseparable online buddies.

When Shel had a problem at school, from homework to bullying, it was Joe she turned to, not her parents. He knew her better than anyone and he was *always* there for her and always responded immediately no matter what time it was. If she was having trouble with a teacher then Joe said the teacher was stupid; if she'd been insulted by a bully, then he'd say something like 'I'd never say that to you, that's impossible'.

They exchanged messages late into the night. Joe carefully tested the boundaries, easing Rachel into mild sexual fantasies, talking about everything from fashion to underwear and swimwear, as well as telling all sorts of 'true-life' tales, from skinny-dipping to his first sexual experience.

Sometimes he pushed a touch too hard and stepped back, quickly changing the subject, making Rachel laugh or giving her yet another reason to see how lucky she was to have someone like Joe on her side. He took cover behind fake honesty and self-deprecation while satisfying Rachel's idea of the perfect boyfriend.

This was the worst kind of betrayal. To abuse a vulnerable teenager's innocence, to spend months feeding her every desire, becoming closer to her than her best friend, than her parents. To create an unbreakable trust that would be most cruelly betrayed.

'There were loads of weirdos online,' Rachel told me. 'I mean, I'm not stupid, I'm really not. I had strangers contacting me all the time, and some of them tried it on. As soon as they did, I blocked them. Some of my friends told their parents but, well, you know, there was no point telling mine. They were clueless. Joe is different. He isn't obsessed with sex. He wanted *me*. He said I was mature enough to handle it and I am. And then everyone freaked out and ruined it, took away the only good thing in my life.'

Craig appeared in the office doorway. 'They got Joe!'

I leaped to my feet, causing the huge pile of files to slide off my desk in a great paper wave.

'How? Where?'

Even though Joe had used a mirror site to hide from the police, detectives from CEOP, the Child Exploitation and Online Protection unit, hunted him down. The evidence, which included a film of Rachel, was overwhelming.

The film was appalling. To see the bulky, lecherous man and the slender, clearly terrified teenager together was too much for most detectives to stomach. Despite what she'd said, there was no way Rachel had gone to bed willingly with this man.

'He's lucky he made it to the cells in one piece,' Craig said with disgust.

'But whether he survives unscathed in prison is another story,' I said.

Although – in my opinion – sentences for child abusers are too light, an extra punishment comes in the form of other prisoners who like nothing better than to terrorise paedophiles and, if they ever get the chance, to visit what they see as righteous physical retribution upon them. Joe ended up facing twelve years of this.

Unfortunately, although the detectives who tracked Joe down did an amazing job, he was by no means an exception. Perhaps the worst online predator was Peter Chapman, who had 6,000 friends on ten social networks.[1] All of them were women. He posted fake pictures of himself claiming to be a slim and toned teen, when he was anything but. The 33-year-old lured seventeen-year-old Ashleigh Hall to a late-night rendezvous, tied her up, raped and strangled her in October 2009. He was quickly captured and sentenced to 35 years.

In 2007, the American Cyber Crimes Section (ACCS) opened 20,200 cases and arrested almost 10,000 subjects for sexually exploiting children online (we don't have any data for this in the UK at present). The ACCS also reported that about 80 per cent of child victims aged between thirteen and sixteen go willingly to meet their predator.[2]

Social networks are, by definition, difficult to police. Microsoft shut down its MSN Chat service in 2003 in many countries.[3] A spokesperson said: 'As a responsible leader we feel it necessary to make these changes because online chat services are increasingly being misused.' MySpace.com attracts huge numbers of Internet predators and has – as of 2009 – banished no fewer than 90,000 registered sex offenders from across the globe.[4]

The online world is just as dangerous as the 'real' one.

We decided that it wasn't in Rachel's best interest to remove her from her family.

What she needed was her mum and dad.

It was as if a switch had been flipped in Melanie and she had finally emerged from her stupor to become a mum again. Of course, social services would keep a close eye on the family to make sure this was the case.

'The Internet is far more important to teenagers than the

school playground,' I told her. 'Real life is restrictive, parents and society dictate what teenagers can and can't do. Online, however, these kids can do whatever they want, be whomever they want. They can look for love and attention and seek out thrills; the virtual world is now part of their growing up.

'You may find it hard to accept the emergence of Rachel's sexuality but it's coming out, encouraged by TV and, yes, by the Internet, by advertising. You can't say "Don't go on Facebook", because she'll only resent you for it.'

'So what should we do, then?'

'Manage her time online. Take an interest. Get involved. Set up your own Facebook page. She won't let this happen again, as long as you're there for her.'

As Rachel and Melanie left, I thought about how this man had done more than rape a young girl. Melanie and Pete had got their daughter back, but she wasn't the same little girl any more. The emotional barriers she had been forced to raise by her ordeal were already visible in her hardened face. The experience had changed her for ever.

She hadn't been able to trust her own parents to look out for her, show an interest in her, or love her, so Joe was all she had. Rachel had invested too much of herself in Joe. If she faced up to the fact she'd suffered the worst kind of betrayal, then how would she ever be able to give herself to anyone as fully as she had to Joe?

Rachel had been blinded by her innocent love for what she thought was her online dream.

She wasn't ready to let go of that dream just yet.

CHAPTER SEVENTEEN

LOVE, BUT NOT AS WE KNOW IT

The slap landed like a thunderclap.

Sean stood in front of Cheryl, who had dropped to her knees. He swayed slightly, one hand open, the other holding a crushed can of Stella Artois. Through her tears, Cheryl could see more cans on the floor by the sofa.

It was Billy's birthday. Six years old, he was a big boy now. There was going to be a party and Sean had volunteered to get the cake, crisps and sausage rolls. Cheryl had handed him a tenner, enough for eight cans of Special Brew, five of Stella. Five empty cans lay on the floor and it wasn't even lunchtime.

'I'm entitled to a drink on my boy's birthday, aren't I?' Sean said.

What had she expected? It was all part of the game they played. He asked, she gave, not because she believed him but because she was afraid of what he might do if she didn't.

Ella was standing in the main storage room of the child protection department. 'The Library of Doom' was how one older male colleague described it. Countless files stretched back over generations, records of tragedy and abuse.

She extracted a file marked Cheryl Walters and Sean Davis.

The debris of a child's birthday party is usually a record of a happy day. While an exhausted mum and dad may groan at sticky fingerprints on silk-white walls, fairy cakes trampled into their loose-weave rug and the new scratch on the polished hall-way floorboards, they smile at the memories. There's the look of joy on the child's face, the thought of the pictures and the blowing-out-the-candles movie to be uploaded to the computer, preserved for eternity, to be watched over and over. They've filled their child with a sense of wellbeing and showed themselves to be 'cool' parents; after all, every child wants to be able to boast about Mum and Dad in the playground.

As I stepped inside the flat it looked as though a very successful birthday party had just taken place.

So why was I there?

Cheryl knew that this mentality was unbeatable, her argument unwinnable. But she was at the end. She had not only struggled on a low income, she had sacrificed it to alcohol. She had spent years dressing the kids in second-hand, ill-fitting school uniforms and relied on free school meals so that Billy would at least get one decent meal a day.

Jamie Oliver was quite right to fight to make our school dinners more nutritious, but what he may not have realised is that for many poor families, this is the ONLY good meal some kids get.

Billy wasn't poorly fed thanks to a lack of funds; he was poorly fed because his dad spent the family money on alcohol and cigarettes. Billy and Cheryl got whatever was left over, the scraps.

Cheryl tried anyway. She looked up. 'I told you, I need the money for Billy's birthday party.'

'And *I* told *you*, I ain't got it.'

Cheryl stood up. She knew he'd spent it; that it was hopeless, but she was so angry she couldn't stop herself. 'You fucking 'ave, now give it.'

'Cheryl? Yeah, she were here, poor luv.'

Ella was standing in the doorway, talking to Cheryl's neighbour on the third floor of the estate block. The neighbour spoke quickly, hardly pausing for breath, as if she'd been rehearsing the story in her mind and now, finally presented with the chance, it poured out of her in a stream.

'She came 'ere begging for scraps for Billy's party, bless her. She was so thin, you know? Not eaten properly herself, not enough cash for a loaf of bread, that fucking Sean, can't see why she didn't leave him. We ain't rich ourselves, you know? But at least we could spare some jelly as well as a few sausage sandwiches. I told her she needed to get away from that useless bastard, that Billy was suffering and they'd be better off without him. She was angry but scared, too scared to leave him. Nowhere to go, perhaps, no one to ask.'

The doorbell rang. The party was about to start. Billy was overjoyed at the thought. All his friends around for his birthday party. He even had a few presents this year. Mum had saved a pound here and a pound there, doing without makeup, new underwear, relying on bags of broken biscuits to stave off hunger. Not far from the local supermarket she'd passed a dropped cake, crushed but still in its wrapping, and fought the urge to snatch it up, run around the corner and consume every last crumb. But she could never do such a thing. Pride was her last luxury.

'I told him,' the sales manager told Ella. 'I'm sorry, I said, but it's too obvious. You can't hide it any more.'

'Right.'

Sean had tried to work. He was smart, a quick learner and seemed to slot neatly into the high-pressure world of sales for a large minicab company. He won several accounts, but his drive for commission was fuelled only by his lust for alcohol, not to better the life of his family.

'I mean, he was drunk when I sacked him. "Just a beer at lunchtime," he said. It was more like five or six. Did he think we wouldn't notice?'

'What did you tell him?'

'I told him to get some help, dry out and then I'd talk about taking him back on. He's a natural salesman. He'd be brilliant at this job sober.'

'Thanks,' Ella said, 'you've been very helpful.'

I've seen many drunks in the police. For some reason, probably because of misplaced loyalty and the fact that booze still plays a major role in police life, they were rarely sacked – even though everyone knew.

In police days long since gone, alcoholic officers weren't taken seriously and ended up becoming standing, or swaying, jokes. Bosses shifted them from one department to another, making them someone else's problem. Some drunks survived like this for years; a few even made it to retirement.

The start of night duty in one London station involved some of the constables playing 'hunt the stash'. They'd comb the building until one of them cried out in triumph at finding the drunk's secret supply of cans hidden behind the cistern, in a cupboard or buried deep in a waste-paper basket. They then hid it somewhere entirely different, forcing the confused drunk – who now thought the alcohol was affecting his memory – to surreptitiously hunt for his 'misplaced' stash.

I found out about one drunk when, as a young PC, I

accompanied him on patrol. He was much more experienced and very friendly. He even shared his mints with me. After we stopped a member of the public for speeding, I thought I could smell alcohol and asked him to take a breath test. This was met with outraged denial; having heard this a hundred times before, I shut my ears and handed him the Breathalyser. As I did so, I realised it was my colleague I could smell. Now I knew why he rarely drove.

My story was simply added to a series of others that did the rounds of the station, that his room in the section house looked like a bottle bank, and the time he arrived for work in his car and drove straight into the police station's wall. Despite getting progressively worse with age, he survived for a surprisingly long time, until the push finally came.

The day Sean lost his job he went on a bender, no doubt blowing his last paypacket. Cheryl said she could smell the other woman on him when he dragged himself through the door. She didn't like to have sex with him when he was drunk, she told us, but sometimes she was too scared not to. Even when Cheryl had successfully spurned him, Sean went to the estate 'game-girl' who could turn no man away.

Sean had no shame and returned to demand money from Cheryl. The needs of his girlfriend and son were second to his need to stop the shaking that gripped him every morning.

'I was there, you know, at the party,' Cheryl's neighbour told Ella. 'Billy was so 'appy. I was ragin' when I saw her face. Bloody great bruise it was. I knew straight away, she didn't 'ave to tell me.'

The boys were running around the flat; it was Billy's turf and what he said was the law. He was delighted with the attention, proud to be hosting his own party. Of course, this meant making a lot of noise.

Cheryl's anxiety increased as they played. The room started to spin as Sean shouted at her, as the kids screamed, one with tears in his eyes, boo-hooing that something-or-other wasn't fair.

'Welcome to the real world,' Sean yelled. 'Now shut the fuck up!'

Just then, a friend tackled Billy who'd been bouncing on the sofa and they went flying, crashing into the coffee table. An open can toppled over, splashing the carpet with its precious golden liquid.

The reaction was instantaneous. Sean jumped up, raised his hand and hit Billy with his open palm hard across the head.

'What did I fucking tell ya? What did I *fucking* tell ya?' he yelled.

Cheryl's reaction was just as instinctive. She'd been about to cut the cake, a past-its-sell-by-date Madeira. Two strides and she leaped, flying with the knife pointing down. It just missed Sean's arm. She tore at his hair, raked nails across his face before he finally pushed her off and backhanded her. She flew back and landed on one of the other boys, her nose broken and bloody.

'What can I say?' the neighbour said. ''E was out of control, screaming abuse at Cheryl, at me, at Billy and at the kids. Cheryl was lying crying on the floor, Billy 'ugging her, the other kids ran for it. What else could I do? I called the Old Bill. I nearly fainted, I did, when 'e marched up to me but 'e walked past, slammed the front door so hard it bounced back open, so it did.'

Billy and his mum sat side by side on the sofa.

What the hell am I supposed to do with this, I thought. I'd catch up with Sean eventually. But in the meantime Billy had no recordable injury; at worst it was common assault and in prosecution terms this was almost hopeless.

Cheryl was angry and agreed to press charges but I had a feeling she would drop them soon enough. She didn't want to go to court and although she was frightened of Sean, she still loved him. In my experience, this sort of relationship was surprisingly common and the kids always paid the price. All I could do for now was make sure Billy was safe and that Cheryl could protect him. Doing this without long-term foster care, however, would not be easy.

'I'm sorry, Harry,' Ella said.

This was a change, Ella comforting me, and over the phone too. My job usually stopped once the child was safe. That's when Ella's began.

She'd just been round to see Cheryl. Sean had moved back in.

'I managed to have a quick chat with her before Sean turned up. Cheryl says she loves him. It seems genuine, despite everything. I just can't understand it. Why do you think she's stuck with him for so long?'

I knew this and wanted to say I knew, that I'd seen it all before, but I kept silent. This wasn't love as I knew it. It was indescribable, unbelievable.

How could Cheryl take this man back? A man who made her life impossibly difficult, who had struck her and her child, who would let her go hungry and who squandered everything they had on alcohol?

I'd seen this repeated many times; we simply couldn't take every child in Billy's position into care. There just aren't enough foster parents and children's homes – or enough cash in the budget. While our department had no worries when it came to cash, social services was another matter. Billy wasn't in imminent danger, so the argument went, so the money or foster place would be saved for a child who was deemed to be even worse off.

'I'll keep a close eye on them, Harry.'

'Thanks, Ella.'

I knew she would but I wondered how long it would be before I was called back. Would Billy make it to his seventh birthday, I wondered? One thing was certain, as long as Sean was on the scene there'd be no parties.

'Sorry, Harry,' Ella said sympathetically. 'I'd love to talk more but I've got to go. I've got a whole host of home visits today.'

No matter how long you do this job, there are days when it really hurts.

CHAPTER EIGHTEEN

THE ESTATE WE'RE IN

Ella stuffed her phone into a pocket deep within her handbag, walked a few paces along the tower block balcony, saw she was at the right door and rang the bell.

She tried to look relaxed and reassuring.

A few seconds later, the door opened a crack. Half a face peered at Ella curiously, looking her up and down before frowning in disgust.

'Why don't you just fuck off and leave us the fuck alone?'

The door slammed.

Ella sighed demonstratively, even though there was no one there to see it. She looked out over the estate. It was dusk. She rummaged in her bag and took out a squashed cigarette packet. She'd almost given up, but not quite.

'Smoking a cigarette is my only chance to stick two fingers to the world,' Ella had told me when I expressed surprise at her habit.

'I may be wrong, but sometimes being a little bit self-destructive after a door slams in your face, or after you're called an interfering cow for the third time that week, is good for you.'

Besides, Ella still had no one with whom she could unburden

her stress, or at least who would distract her from her job. She'd so far been out on two dates and was seriously starting to doubt the worth of trying a third.

When she was filling out the online form for the dating agency that listed her details, her fingers had hovered for a while over the keyboard when she reached the 'Profession' box. In the end she'd gone for 'Child Services'.

'Nobody wants to date a social worker, do they?' she thought. At least Child Services made her sound like a teacher. She was certain teachers were more popular with men.

The first date, with Julian, a banker in his early twenties with a degree in history, had not gone well.

'So,' he'd said confidently, in an Oxbridge accent, 'I don't usually do these things, but lunchtime speed dating was a washout, so here we are.' Then he'd asked her what she did for a living.

'Are you one of those interfering baby snatchers or a busybody do-gooder?' he asked teasingly. Seeing Ella's face cloud with anger, he'd added, 'I'm joking, of course, I mean it's important work, I know. God, it must be depressing, though.'

Small talk had quickly stalled after this little exchange.

Ella had drunk too much Chenin Blanc too quickly through the first course, trying to work up the courage to tell Julian that she was sorry, she'd received an urgent text and had to go. He beat her to it not long after their main course arrived. She couldn't blame him. It was a tried and tested practice and at least he'd had the guts to be a sneak. She'd finished the bottle and swayed her way unsteadily home to Holloway Road.

In future, Ella decided, she'd get a friend to call her five minutes after the date had started. Then she could decide whether there'd been an 'emergency' that necessitated her leaving the restaurant or not.

She'd known the second hopeful wasn't for her the moment

she saw him. A photographer, he'd obviously Photoshopped his face, which was flabbier, sallower and spottier in real life.

She dragged deeply on her cigarette at the memory. He'd really overdone it with the airbrush tool. Thank God she'd seen him through the restaurant window and had just kept walking.

A couple of lights came on in the block opposite. Behind every window was a story. As she scanned the buildings, it hit her just how many of them she already knew. Unlike me, Ella would stay with families for the long haul, for months and sometimes years, calling on me for the odd emergency, or responding to my call for her to pick up the pieces after I'd dealt with a fast-moving case. She might then spend years with the family, long after I'd forgotten all about them.

Ella knew the deeper stories, the thoughts and everyday feelings of those battling poverty. The woman who'd just slammed the door on Ella was a single mum, typical of a small number of ruthless and selfish women who put themselves before their children.

She had moaned bitterly about 'the social' and how the state failed to provide for her (I'd be interested to know where she would draw the line, the point at which she thought the state's help would no longer be needed), while wasting the resources provided for her children on booze, cigarettes and going out.

Fortunately, these women are in the minority. It's understandable, from reading my books, that you might feel as though our council estates are full of problem families that, when not taking drugs or drinking themselves to death, are abusing one another. Well, you'd be right. There are many people out there with deeply problematic lives, including people who inflict the most terrible abuse on children. Although they're only a small proportion of society as a whole, and are far from representative, they cost us a fortune.

Some people on the estates Ella and I went to were honest,

hard-working and cared deeply about their families. Many also worked hard to improve their homes and their community.

About 20 per cent of the flats in an average council block are home to a single-parent family, the poorest kind of family in Britain. These flats are a vital safety net for our nation's single mothers. They're supposed to be affordable, secure and stable bases that help single mums raise their kids to give them the best possible shot in life. Without this it's very, very difficult for them.

The problem is there aren't enough flats and houses to go round (in my experience a startling number seem to be occupied by single men; I've no idea how this is possible) and cutbacks mean that many of the homes are coming apart at the seams.

In the 1970s about 75,000 new council homes were built every year. By the start of the new millennium it was eighty – not eighty thousand, just eighty. Meanwhile, as we enter the second decade of the twenty-first century, 4.5 million people remain on waiting lists. This means an incredible £21 billion leaves the government vaults every year in housing benefit, much of which ends up in the pockets of private landlords.[1]

This truly is one of the two great scandals of our age.

The other is that more than 3.5 million children live below the poverty line in the UK, which has one of the worst child poverty rates in the industrialised world.[2]

Kirstie, a single mum in her late twenties, lived in a flat the floor below where Ella was standing.

'The council came and did all the repainting on the outside of the estate,' Kirstie had told Ella, 'but I've got mould growing in every room.'

Her walls were damp and being eaten by an indestructible and smelly black fungus. Damien, her ten-year-old son, had a cough that just wouldn't go away.

'I keep writing to the council but they say there's only so

much money in the pot. Sounds like they're just keeping up appearances to me.'

The council had enough money to make the estate look nice on the outside but not enough to treat the social or physical rot on the inside.

Bill, a single-parent father, lived in the opposite block. Carlie, his partner, had walked out the door a few years ago and vanished. Looking after their two children and holding down a job proved impossible. Bill's boss was sympathetic but, after one too many short-notice midday dashes to some family emergency, when the next round of redundancies came around, Bill was top of the list. Unable to find work, he'd lost his home and now struggled to clothe and feed his children. Social services stepped in after Bill had a breakdown and helped with rehousing and support.

His kids, used to living in a small but expensive Hackney terrace, two holidays a year and the odd item of designer clothing, now found themselves being bullied at school. Bill had to leave it as long as possible before buying the next school uniform. Trousers became too short, shoes too scuffed, heels too worn and jumpers too holed. They were picked on for their poverty but especially for coming from the estate.

Their main problem with the flat was the damp.

'It's appalling,' Bill told Ella, after asking her to help with a rehousing application. 'We get ill all the time. I'm telling you, if Hogarth were here today, he'd sketch this estate.'

Recent figures show 47 per cent of children with asthma are from the poorest 10 per cent of families in the UK, and 85 per cent of children living in damp houses suffer from breathing problems.[3]

Damp is easily treated, and is not necessarily that expensive. One wonders, as the Olympic Stadium rises into the Hackney skyline, whether the local children from East London's council estates will be well enough to use it.

'I don't know where the idea comes from that us poor families are stuffing our faces with turkey twizzlers, sweets, crisps and fizzy drinks,' Bill had told Ella, after struggling to come to terms with single-parent-family economics.

While many families on council estates do manage to stuff their kids full of junk food, one in five low-income families reports skipping meals, and children living with single-parent families are twice as likely to go without.[4] Come the school holidays, the precious free lunch vanishes with nothing to replace it, so belts are tightened again.

Hunger and damp make it hard to be happy. Bligh and her eleven-year-old daughter Mel lived two doors away from Bill. Mel, a tomboy, longed for adventure, but had to rely on her imagination. Turning the estate into an adventure playground would have challenged Mervyn Peake – although estates like this were the birthplace of the extreme gymnastic sport of free-running. Many kids are driven stir crazy by their poverty, reinforced when they see the bright perfect alternate reality on the TV every night, commercials featuring happy families enjoying expensive products in perfect homes,

It's not only the adults that carry the stressful burden of poverty. 'We're stuck here,' Mel had told Ella. 'It's boring for us. The grown-ups are losing jobs, we're going to have less and less money.'

Most people would be surprised to learn that, in inner-city areas, over 43 per cent of children have considered suicide and one in six children under the age of eleven has attempted suicide.[5] The reasons include bullying, abuse, poverty, homelessness, and alcohol abuse.

Twelve-year-old Jamie, who lived in the east corner flat on the ground floor, was one such child. 'I thought nobody wants me here and decided I was better off dead. You see it on TV all the time, people hate us, we're dragging the country down and all that.'

Many single mothers manage because they work hard at it.

This is despite the terrible images of single mothers portrayed by the media, from the tabloids to *Little Britain*'s portrayal of comedy single mum Vicky Pollard. The BBC website describes her character thus:

> Vicky Pollard is your common-or-garden teenage delinquent, the sort you can see hanging around any number of off licences in Britain, trying to persuade people going inside to buy them ten fags and a bottle of White Lightening [sic].
>
> Whether nicking stuff from the supermarket or swapping her baby for a Westlife CD, Vicky reacts to any accusation with indignant outrage, while filling you in on 'this fing wot you know nuffin about'.

While I understand that *Little Britain* is playing to extremes, and there are Vicky Pollards in Hackney, it also feeds ignorance, reaffirming a rare and unpleasant truth that has grown into a common stereotype. Bad single mothers are in the minority. The bad ones tend to be women with psychological or drug problems who lose their children to social services. Even the youngest teen mothers don't suffer from ignorance about their situation. Nearly all of them want to work or study (84 per cent according to the 2010 British Social Attitudes survey).

Two floors up and one flat across from Jamie was Sandra. Sandra used to be a cocaine runner who made good money slipping through the warren of estates from dealer to dealer, hiding and collecting gear from bushes, toilets and lampposts. Then a dealer got her pregnant, didn't want to know and, ten years later, Sandra watched the youngsters from her window doing what was once her job.

Sandra did her best to talk the girls on the estate out of sleeping with boys.

'I made my bed and I accept that,' she told Ella, 'but my daughter Sandrine doesn't deserve to live like this. I'm doing my bit to raise her well, but just to have somewhere dry and warm would make it bearable for her, that's all.'

That previous winter, Sandra's early morning routine had started with her scraping away a thick layer of ice from the *inside* of her windows.

There are 1.9 million single-parent families in the UK. Slightly less than half of these are unemployed, claim income support and live below the poverty line.[6] Ella saw just a handful of this vast and silent majority, the very poor, decent women struggling to bring up their kids. They manage it because they work hard at it. Many have part-time jobs, as they can't make the leap into full-time employment, due to the difference between childcare cost and income earned.

Newspapers don't write about these women because they're brilliant at what they do while remaining stoically silent. Somehow they manage the miracle of raising happy, polite and ambitious children with very little money, without savings or credit cards to rely on in emergencies. To do this they often go hungry and do without simple pleasures, and yet they wouldn't dream of trying to cheat the system.

The fact that they're too often forced to live in unhealthy conditions while councils give away billions each year to private landlords is scandalous. The problem is that the system isn't able to distinguish between the Vicky Pollards and the hard-working mums.

'I mean,' Sandra told Ella, 'I don't like asking the council for help. They've given me a home and a chance to raise my girl. I should feel privileged but I don't; I feel like I've been swept under the carpet. And this,' she said, gesturing at the estate, 'is the carpet.

'I want to work. I've heard people say all us single mums are

"happy on benefits", well I ain't. I want to do something, I want
to be useful, but it's just not worth it.'

Right now, single parents are suffering the most from the
latest round of cuts. Depending on which reports you read, the
income of single parents will be cut by between 5 and 8.5 per
cent, roughly the equivalent of a month's current payment. They
will also have to pay for the services of the Child Support
Agency, which struggles to compel absent fathers to contribute
to the cost of raising their children.

Are these really the people we should be asking to shoulder
the cost of the financial crisis? It's not as if they caused it.

'I'm damned if I do, damned if I don't,' Sandra had said. 'If
you're on benefits you're a scrounger. If you're working then
you're neglecting your kids.'

Cuts also mean reducing support and training that helps lone
parents back into work. Even in the recession, 57 per cent of
single parents already have a job.[7] For single parents, it's not just
finding a job; it's finding a job that fits in with single-handedly
raising children *and* with affordable childcare.

Ella told me many times that stigmatising single parents as
ignorant teenage scroungers and financial burdens only serves to
undermine their self-confidence.

'It does nothing to help them get a job,' she said. 'As soon as
an employer hears the words "single mum", they think that way
trouble lies and they're dumped on the rejection pile. This is
stupid. In my experience single parents are mature and responsible people. They're also excellent managers with a better moral
code than most politicians.'

For example, you might be surprised to learn, as I was, that
only one in fifty single mums are under eighteen. The average
age of a single parent is thirty-six, and over half of them had
their children while married.[8]

Some argue that family structure is a key factor in how well a child does in school and later life. Studies have shown time and again that this isn't true. It's the stress of dealing with poverty that affects kids' lives the most. The children of wealthier single mums and dads do just as well as kids with mums and dads who're still married.

At the root of poverty is the estate. So many of these visions of utopia have sunk into crime-ridden depression that it's hard to imagine a way back. But it is possible. It takes something exceptional to transform an estate – unfortunately that something special is usually an especially bad, headline-grabbing murder. Take Broadwater Farm, known to all as 'The Farm', in the neighbouring North London borough of Haringey.

After the murder of PC Keith Blakelock during the 1985 riots, the estate underwent a revolution. Concrete tunnels were demolished and the entrances were all brought down to ground level. Workshops were built so that tenants could learn new skills and how to start their own business. Estate managers were given new powers to help them maintain harmony. Permanent on-site housing officers were on hand to get to know the tenants and respond to their needs.

It didn't happen overnight but today there is a sense of community. Today, almost four thousand people from fifty countries live on the Farm and have helped produce twenty-five professional football players for teams such as Arsenal and West Ham.

The Farm is the estate dream come true, albeit the hard way. All the factors necessary to make it happen came together: political desire, consistent on-site management and plenty of determined tenants.

And money. It cost £33 million.

Twenty years after the riots, the Farm suffered one burglary in the first three months of the year. The culprit was caught and the goods returned. In 1985 there had been 875 burglaries and attempted burglaries.[9]

It's not completely clean, of course, problems with gangs and drugs remain, especially in surrounding areas, but at least the Farm feels more like a haven than hell on earth.

The message is clear. If you build an estate like the Farm and fail to maintain it, while leaving its inhabitants unable to support themselves let alone the community, then it will steadily crumble apart. The fact that so many young people from the UK's poorest inner-city areas exploded on to the streets in August 2011 is proof enough of this. We now have the chance to evict looters and rioters from their council homes. While this sounds like a suitable punishment, where will they go? Is it better for the underclass to all live together on one estate, or in expensive private accommodation paid for by the taxpayer?

The riots showed the country that our estates are in crisis. As the Farm has shown, effective long-term solutions are expensive. The UK's finances are also in crisis. So, I suspect the government will, much like the councils ignoring illness-inducing mould, go for cheap and short-term solutions.

Ella's phone rang.

'Ella, it's Harry.'

'Hi, Harry, I was just thinking about you.'

'Really?' I said, slightly taken aback. 'Well, I was thinking about you too. You're today's on-call, aren't you?'

'For my sins, yes.'

'I need your help. I'm in a flat with a seven-year-old boy who needs an emergency carer. No family beyond the mother and father, who have been treating him like an animal.'

'Where are you?' she asked.

I told her the name of the estate. 'Do you know it?' I asked.

'Yeah, Harry,' Ella said ruefully. 'I'm already there.'

CHAPTER NINETEEN

A DIFFERENT ME

Three sixteen-year-old girls: three different outcomes

Salima

'DS Keeble? It's Nikki from the front office, can you come down, please?'

If I'd been on the burglary squad I would have demanded to know why. If, for example, someone wanted to report that their shed had been burgled, then I would have bounced them across to another department because (apparently) you can't burgle a shed, only steal from it.

Fortunately, such nonsensical divisions don't exist in child protection. We take everything that comes our way and although feisty 'discussions' about certain 'remits' sometimes occur between ourselves and other departments, the victims never have to know.

'I'm not sure if this was covered by child protection or not,' Nikki, a young uniformed officer, said when I arrived a few minutes later. 'I rang CID first and they told me to call you.' She paused a moment, before adding, 'Well, actually what they said was, "Call that Harry bloke from the Cardigan Squad." When I asked him what he meant, he said everyone called Child Protection that. First I've heard of it.'

I sighed and explained. Although it was annoying to hear that the phrase 'Cardigan Squad' was still in use, I sympathised with the CID, who were always overwhelmed with a whole smorgasbord of cases, everything from pickpockets to rape. They needed to know when they could pass a case on.

'Well, that's just rubbish,' Nikki said when I'd finished. 'This case sounds like it's above and beyond the abilities and sensitivities of our CID chap and that's why he's batted it over to you.'

She escorted me to an interview room and opened the door.

Heshu

The sixteen-year-old girl in the video wept as she pleaded to the camera: 'I'm trapped,' she said in a London accent. 'My family hates me. I'm a disappointment to them.'

Heshu Yones had been taken from her home in West London to Sulaymaniyah, in the Kurdish region of Iraq, to be forced into marriage. But things hadn't gone to plan. The day before, her father, 48-year-old Abdullah, had held a gun to her head, telling her she was worthless. She had failed a virginity test.

'I can't give her away now!' he shouted, before his wife and Heshu's older brother persuaded him to lower the gun.

Heshu had fallen in love with eighteen-year-old Nizam back in London. They'd quickly become inseparable. Nizam had never known anyone like Heshu and knew he could never feel that way about anyone else. Heshu felt the same way, so it seemed inevitable that they would sleep together.

Afterwards, Nizam pleaded with Heshu to let him speak to her father about marriage, but she resisted, knowing the consequences would be fatal. To say her father had strict ideas about whom Heshu could marry would be a huge understatement.

Abdullah Yones claimed that he was once a *peshmerga*, a mountain fighter who had battled the forces of Saddam Hussein throughout the 1980s before fleeing Iraq in 1991. He settled with his family in West London, and worked as a volunteer for the Patriotic Union of Kurdistan. While his daughter embraced the West as she grew up, Abdullah retreated more and more to the old ways, and struggled to fit into life in the UK. Forcing Heshu into a marriage she didn't want was just another way to maintain control over her. His plans thwarted, he returned to London with his family.[1]

Sayrah

Sixteen-year-old Sayrah wanted to be a fashion designer, something her mum, Caneze, had begun to encourage, even though she knew Mohammed, her husband, would disapprove when they told him.

Mohammed Riaz was an immigrant from Pakistan's highly conservative Northwest Frontier. He had arrived in the UK aged thirty-two after Caneze was sent from the UK to Pakistan to marry him. They had five children together, four girls and a boy, and lived in Accrington in Lancashire.

His wife, who already had one foot firmly planted in the Western world, encouraged her children to adapt. Mohammed, who had not learned English after seventeen years of living in the UK, became more closed in and tried to isolate his family. He was illiterate, so worked in a number of low-paid jobs and spent most of his spare time in the local mosque. When he came home he criticised his wife and children's Western dress, and demanded that their daughters finish their schooling as soon as possible so they could be married off in Pakistan.

Caneze refused, and also refused to give up work. A bright and bubbly woman, she worked as a campaigner for women's rights, helping women who felt suppressed by their husbands' attempted enforcement of traditional values. Caneze saw herself as a role model, a strong woman who refused to bend to the will of her husband. She was highly sociable; she organised women-only swimming groups and had a wide circle of friends.

Mohammed was incensed by her disobedience but was unable to sway Caneze. Then in 2006, Adam, their seventeen-year-old son, developed leukemia. This 'failure', as he saw it, to produce a healthy son only added to Mohammed's rage. Then Sayrah, with Caneze by her side, backing her up, told him that after she'd finished school she was going to college to become a fashion designer.[2]

Salima

I stepped into the room. Two Asian women in their late teens were waiting inside. One was sat behind the interview table. She had long, thick black hair and looked extremely distressed.

The other was standing behind her, hands on her seated friend's shoulders, doing her best to radiate assurance. They were athletic-looking with sharply defined features and could easily have featured on the cover of a magazine.

'Right,' Nikki said, 'I'll leave you to it, then,' and she closed the door, casting me adrift.

I introduced myself and, sensing their nervousness, quickly added, 'Are you OK talking to me? Would you like to speak to another officer?'

It was quite possible they wouldn't want to open up to a six-foot-four, forty-year-old white male police officer who bore more than a passing resemblance to Jim Carrey. If they wanted an Asian child protection officer, however, then I'd have to search outside of Hackney.

The girl who was standing nodded firmly and said to her friend, 'It's OK, Salima, go ahead. My name is Miah,' she added, 'her best friend.'

She had just paid the police a huge compliment. Although it's been justified on very rare occasions in the past, we're still labelled 'institutionally racist' and 'bullies' far too often by a loud minority. Such accusations don't help the victims of crime and only reinforce the belief that we can't be trusted with sensitive issues.

Until recently, there'd been no standard police policy for dealing with crimes relating to forced marriage and so-called 'family honour'. In the past, police officers had misunderstood the situation, or had sent people away because they did not know what to do, or, worst of all, were afraid to intervene in what they considered to be a 'cultural matter'.

I was delighted to see that these two young women were prepared to trust the police. The key thing now, of course, was not to let either of them down.

Heshu

After the attempt to marry off Heshu failed, her family returned to their home in London where 'normal' life resumed. For Heshu this meant adhering to strict rules enforced by her father – or at least making sure he didn't find out that she'd broken them.

Abdullah had previously beaten Heshu for wearing makeup, so she left the house dressed plainly with her face bare. By the time she arrived at William Morris Academy in Fulham, however, she was fully made up, just like her friends.

Boyfriends were absolutely against the rules. Heshu knew the consequences of seeing a boy without her father's permission (which he would never give anyway), so she went to great lengths to ensure her relationship with Nizam remained secret. This meant playing truant from school, as it was the only way she could see him without her family knowing.

Heshu knew she would never be free and would always be in danger as long as she lived at home. So she planned to run away.

She'd even written the goodbye letter to her family. She was just waiting for the right moment to flee.

'Bye Dad,' the letter said. 'Sorry I was so much trouble. Me and you will probably never understand each other, but I'm sorry I wasn't what you wanted, but there's some things you can't change.' She ended the letter by saying, 'Hey, for an older man you have a good strong punch and kick. I hope you enjoyed testing your strength on me, it was fun being on the receiving end. Well done.'

An inevitable consequence of Heshu skipping school was that her grades, which were normally the highest in the class, started to slip and this fact was difficult to hide from her father. Then Abdullah received an anonymous note, handwritten and in Kurdish, which described his daughter as a slut who spent every day having sex with her boyfriend.

Sayrah

Late on the night of 31 October 2006, Mohammed was very drunk. He locked the doors and windows of the family home. He then took a canister of petrol and poured it all over the kitchen and living room, leaving enough to cover himself. He struck a match.

Salima

Salima and Miah were best friends and both sixteen, which meant they were under our remit (our definition of a child is anyone who has not yet reached their eighteenth birthday).

They were both born here, although their parents had arrived in the UK from Mirpur in Pakistan in the 1980s.

'I suppose you've heard of arranged marriages,' Salima said.

I nodded. This was the tradition where families match-made sons and daughters, but the sons and daughters still had the ultimate say.

'How about forced marriages?'

Again I nodded, although I was on shaky ground here. This would be my first case.

'I was sold for a dowry to a family back in Mirpur when I was ten years old. I've been planning to run away since then but I still love my family, you know? My little bro', he's only ten now, he wouldn't understand. I was still around for the engagement ceremony when I was fourteen.

'When I told my mum I didn't want to marry him she told me not to be such a "silly girl". "You've been engaged to Jamal since you were nine," she said. "You cannot pull out now, it will bring shame upon the family." I didn't know what to do.'

'Listen,' Miah said, breaking in. 'Salima's the dream daughter. A-stars all the way, best at athletics, you know?'

'All right, Miah, that's enough of that,' Salima said, with an embarrassed smile.

'The man's got to understand, hasn't he?' Miah said. 'You're special, girl, you need to know that and I wish your parents did instead of selling you to some stupid peasant halfway up a mountain. What good are your GCSEs up there? Answer me that!'

Miah obviously cared deeply about her friend.

'Anyway,' Salima continued, 'I told Dad I didn't want to marry Jamal and he freaked out. He yelled about shame and family honour and that if I didn't do what he said then "bad things" would happen. Since then they've been not telling me stuff. I keep walking into conversations that end suddenly. We're supposed to be going to Pakistan once I've done my GCSEs, to see my gran. She's dying and I love her so much and want to see her but I'm scared if I go I'll end up in this marriage.'

'This goes on all the time,' Miah said urgently. 'Other girls in our class have gone this way already! She's going to be sold and raped by some mountain mullah! You have to help her! Can't you arrest them or something? Warn them to back off?'

My heart went out to them. I offered to support her and to speak to her parents so that they knew the trip would be monitored.

'No way!' Salima exclaimed. 'If you tell them I've come to you, and you end up sending me home, my dad will kill me – and I mean really kill me.'

'Can't you arrest them or something?' Miah pleaded.

'No. Not without evidence of any crime. But I know someone who can help.'

Heshu

When the police arrived outside the Yones' home they found Abdullah lying in the street.

The officers thought he'd fallen from the balcony. He was still alive, barely. Closer examination revealed that his throat had been cut.

Then they saw the screwed-up bits of paper with Heshu's handwritten cries for help on them.

Running up to the flat, they found Heshu wedged between the bath and the toilet. She had been stabbed more than a dozen times in her chest, arms and legs. Cuts to the palms of her hands revealed she had fought desperately, until her attackers finally stabbed her in the throat, severing her jugular vein.

A kitchen knife, its blade bent, had been left protruding from her body.

Later that evening, Nizam saw the crime scene tape in the street.

Heshu's mother and older brother first insisted to police that the killers must have been intruders of some kind, drug-crazed burglars, perhaps. Heshu's mother, Tanya Yones, was very precise, according to the police report, about the time she left with her son. She also emphasised the fact that she'd left the door unlocked and was also certain about Heshu's state of mind.

'Heshu was laughing,' Tanya told police.

Incredibly, Abdullah survived his terrible injuries. From his hospital bed, he said Al-Qaeda agents had attacked him in revenge for his acts during the war. Detectives were at first prepared to investigate Abdullah's claims but, as news spread of the crime, several women called Scotland Yard, urging the police to dig deeper. Officers then found the video footage of Heshu in Iraq, pleading from beyond the grave for help.

When detectives presented Abdullah with evidence of his violence towards his daughter, he changed his story. He claimed that someone had written an anonymous note to him, detailing Heshu's increasingly Westernised behaviour, saying she was behaving like a prostitute.

When the older man broke and finally admitted his crime in court, no one in the family disputed the reasons he provided to explain why he had murdered his own daughter: Heshu's death, he said, was Heshu's fault.

Sayrah

Firefighters, hardened men all too used to seeing tragedy, were weeping.

Once in a while these terrible fires come along and wipe a family off the face of the earth, but this had been no accident. Caneze and their four daughters aged sixteen, fifteen, ten and three all died.

Incredibly, when firefighters pulled Mohammed out of the building, they were amazed to find he was still alive. He hung on to life for another two days.

One family member hadn't been at home: Adam was in hospital having treatment for his leukemia.

He died six weeks after being told the news.

Salima

Admiralty Arch is one of London's most striking buildings, situated in one of the city's grandest locations. It sits on the southwest corner of Trafalgar Square, where its mighty arches act as the gateway to the Mall, at the end of which sits Buckingham Palace.

In a small office inside this building is the Forced Marriage Unit (FMU), set up by the Home Office in 2005. With the help of the courts, the FMU can stop forced marriages and can order the arrest of anyone involved. The FMU also enforces the new Forced Marriage Act of 2007, which puts into law the fact that choosing the person you want to marry and when you get married is a basic right. Men and women who have been forced into marriage, or who fear they are about to be forced, can apply for a Forced Marriage Protection Order. Since coming into force in 2008, more than 150 orders, which can also be applied for by others acting on their behalf, have been taken out.

I was met at the reception by Martina, a solicitor turned forced marriage investigator.

'Thanks for seeing me at such short notice,' I said.

'No problem,' Martina said. 'Most people don't realise how busy we are.'

'Really?' I said, sounding surprised. 'Well, I suppose even I thought forced marriage was quite rare until recently.'

'We receive between fifteen hundred and two thousand calls from members of the public who want to report a suspected case every year,' she told me as we walked to her small office, which was so crowded with stacked ring binders and manila files that it looked like a scale model of Manhattan. 'We handle about two hundred and fifty to three hundred cases per year, and it's not all women. About 15 per cent of our cases involve men. We've just dealt with one teenager who jumped out of the window and ran away after he overheard his family downstairs debating whether to kill him. He's homosexual.'

Most victims are aged from fifteen to twenty-four, but the FMU recently received a call to its helpline from a 62-year-old widower whose family was trying to force him to marry a 35-year-old woman because they no longer wanted to care for him. Cases also included an underage boy taken to Pakistan where he was forcibly engaged to his five-year-old cousin.

'The message we want to pass on is that victims shouldn't give up hope even if they've been taken out of the country.' Martina pointed to a young man sweeping a load of papers into a brief-case while talking into a phone receiver squashed between shoulder and jaw. 'Sanjay's heading to Pakistan to track down a young girl we think has been abducted. That's where most cases seem to come from, about 65 per cent, although we see cases from all over, from Europe to Africa and East Asia to the Middle East.'

'How many are children?' I asked.

'About a third.'

Martina continued. 'The youngest we've had so far this year is a thirteen-year-old girl.[3] The reasons forced marriages are taking place are changing as well. They used to be status, business and money-related. Now we're seeing a rise in cases with people forced into marriage who are then made to sponsor visa applications.'

Once we were alone in a tiny meeting room I told Martina Salima's story.

'No problem, Harry,' Martina said once I was done. 'We'll make sure Salima's safe. If she feels she's in real danger, we'll help her to get into secure accommodation and will deal with the family.'

*

Three different cases with three different outcomes. Two were utterly catastrophic, while I was fortunate in that the case I dealt with provided the best possible solution in the shortest time. A protective barrier was erected between Salima and her family. She was able to communicate with them and over time their relationship, although always strained, was at least partially restored.

The difference?

Knowledge.

'Had we known what we know now, we would have done a lot of things differently,' said Brent Hyatt, the lead detective who investigated Heshu's murder. 'We just didn't know what we were looking at in those first days.'

The phrase 'lessons have been learned' is used too often by public and private bodies to try and explain why a lack of knowledge led to some kind of disaster. In Heshu and Sayrah's case, however, thanks to detectives like Brent, we really did learn. Many people had already been trying to tell the police about so-called honour killings; Brent was one of the first to listen.

Diana Nammi, the founder of the International Campaign Against Honour Killings, a non-profit group based in London, said, 'No one could believe that it could happen, but we kept giving evidence that honour killings are here.'[4]

We now know there are about twelve honour killings every year in the UK[5] and 5,000 worldwide, a truly appalling statistic.[6]

After Heshu's father had been handed a life sentence, the Met launched a review of murder cases to see if any were linked to so-called honour crimes. A shocking 109 cases were reopened. Of 22 cases that have since been fully examined, 18 were reclassified or remain suspected as cases of 'murder in the name of so-called honour'.[7]

People who still worry about interfering in 'cultural rights' need to put these fears to one side in the interests of the child. If that child is insisting they are in danger, then steps need to be taken to ensure their safety. It's that simple.

Most mistakes are made in the early stages of an investigation. Previously, some child protection officers have got it badly wrong. One officer shockingly argued that it was worse to separate young girls from their family than allow them to be forced into marrying, 'because they can always divorce later'.

In one instance where this logic was applied, a sixteen-year-old Pakistani girl returned to the child protection officer after being badly beaten when he'd sent her home.

While Heshu and Sayrah's family have paid an impossibly high price for our poor awareness, we are now doing all we can to prevent any more of these terrible crimes. A large part of this is education, which can be difficult. Young men growing up in the West can find themselves in a confusing tug of war between two worlds. They want to be a part of life in the West and enjoy all it has to offer but sometimes they find themselves compelled by their elders to work with them in maintaining control over the women in their community. The concept of family honour plays a vital part in persuading them to act as their elders wish.

Family liaison officer PC Steve Cox, talking about the murder of Caneze and her children, summed it up perfectly in an impassioned statement to the press:

Honour is completely the wrong word. It is a control murder. That's what these are. It is not honour crime; it is 'control crime' and fear of losing that control.

It really is beyond belief that he [Mohammed Riaz] felt this – the five graves – was the answer to losing control of his family. What is honourable about this? Caneze had done nothing wrong. On the contrary, she was doing so much that was good. Every one of those children there are testament to that, and they have all suffered because of one man and his completely twisted view on life . . .

Women are dying and being brutalised in this situation many times throughout Britain at the moment. Cultural sensitivity is absolutely no excuse for moral blindness, and there's too much fannying about going on both sides, from both communities, and as long as that remains the situation, then young women are going to keep dying. It's as simple as that.[8]

Public awareness is still poor and those who decide to do nothing and keep silent only help the perpetrators and keep their twisted version of so-called honour alive. A demonstration of this came when a reporter interviewed a man called Mohammed Ahmed, who said he'd fought alongside Abdullah Yones before they immigrated.

'The idea of honour is in our cultural backyard,' he said. 'Ethnically and culturally, we believe it . . . Even in court, the father insisted that he was right and that he did the right thing – and that he'd do it again. I mean, I know it's a crime. We all know he's a killer. But he was very proud, and what he did . . . well, how could he accept his daughter's behaviour?'[9]

The sooner these outdated ideas about 'honour' are erased the better. Public awareness has grown in recent years thanks mainly to media coverage of high-profile cases like Heshu's, but these warped concepts of honour are still a long way from being eradicated. Public and government initiatives are lacking. Although government ministers have said that forced marriage should be part of the sex and relationships curriculum in all schools, many schools refuse to discuss the issue for fear of offending ethnic minorities.[10]

Nizam had honoured Heshu with his love. 'I knew straight away I wanted to be with her for ever,' he said. 'I have never been so nervous in my life than when I asked her out, I just knew I wanted to be with her because she was so special. She was so loving and caring.'

Of this I have no doubt. I defy anyone who reads Heshu's letter to her parents, written when she was planning to run away, to feel any different.

The time has come for us to part. I'm sorry that I have caused so much pain, but after sixteen years of living with you it is evident that I shouldn't be a part of you. I take all the blame openly – I'm not the child you wanted or expected me to be. DISAPPOINTMENTS ARE BORN OF EXPECTATIONS. Maybe you expected a different me and I expected a different you.

One day when I have a proper job every penny I owe you will be repaid in full. I will find a way to look after myself. I will go to social security to get myself a flat or hostel. I will be OK. Don't look for me, because I don't know where I'm going yet. I just want to be alone. But I will be safe. So have a nice day, have a nice week, have a nice life, because the biggest problem in this house has now left.

Bro, I'm not leaving you forever, just for a little while. I'm sorry to do this to you. I LOVE YOU MORE THAN I KNOW WHAT THE WORD LOVE MEANS. PLEASE FORGIVE ME!!! My problem has always been too much talk, too little action. So goodbye. One day you will see that I will make something good of myself. This isn't an end, it's just a new beginning, so enjoy. I'll come and visit you at

school, as often as I can. So you'll be seeing a lot of me,
OK?

LIFE, BEING HOW IT IS, ISN'T NECESSARILY
HOW IT IS. IT IS JUST SIMPLY HOW YOU
CHOOSE TO SEE IT.

CHAPTER TWENTY

THREE AND OUT

Another day, another door.

Ella rang the bell, pressing her finger on the button for a little longer than was polite. We needed to access eight-year-old Jade's medical records, so Mum's signature was required.

I was under time pressure to get to a meeting I simply couldn't miss, so when Ella said, 'I'll go. My 11 a.m. visit's been cancelled, so I can do it no problem,' I accepted after just a moment's thought. Apart from saving me valuable time, an 'unannounced visit' would be great practice for Ella. It would also provide us with a useful first glimpse into Jade's home life.

Jade's mother threw open the door.

'Hello, Louise,' Ella said. 'I need to talk to you about Jade, may I come in?'

The expression on Louise's face was one of shock; she was clearly expecting someone else and struggled to compose herself. When she spoke, she spoke too loudly. 'Oh, you're FROM THE SOCIAL are you?'

'May I come in?' Ella repeated, already lifting her right foot.

'Yeah, well, I suppose.'

Even though she was a newbie, this overanimated

announcement had put Ella on alert. While on the landing she'd seen a figure through the kitchen window. Then the kitchen door slammed.

'Was that Alec?' Ella asked as she stepped inside. Alec was Louise's boyfriend, the man whom Jade claimed had abused her.

Louise, who was taller than tiny Ella by about a foot and in her late twenties with dark brown hair and green eyes, was trembling slightly, as if she were afraid. Her eyes flitted as she searched for an explanation, any lie would do.

'Nah, must've been Jade running about. It's just us here.'

Louise showed Ella through to the lounge where Jade was sitting on a large red sofa, watching lunchtime TV on a large wall-mounted screen. The room was untidy but not dirty, a collection of empty mugs placed around the room, a ring-marked coffee table, slightly soiled rugs and a handful of brightly coloured toys scattered across the floor.

'Jade,' Louise said quietly but firmly, 'go to your room.'

Ella didn't know why, but a sixth sense she didn't know she had was screaming at her to get out, get out of there now.

The huge plasma in the foyer of 50 Ludgate Hill was playing BBC News 24. I half-watched it, just something to stare at while I waited. I briefly wondered how Ella was getting on before more urgent thoughts overtook me. I'd been waiting for this meeting for a long time.

I was at the headquarters of the Crown Prosecution Service, a large glass and concrete block in the City, just across the road from the Old Bailey. I was hoping to persuade the CPS to take on a case of the sexual abuse of three sisters that had taken place a decade ago.

'When I wake up from the nightmare, it's as if I'm ten years old again and as if Uncle Richard is in the room with me,'

Amelia, who was now twenty-one, had told me when I visited her at home.

She looked down and folded her arms, holding herself as she continued. 'My skin is cold and clammy, the fear, the fear is total; like I have no idea what he's going to do to me next. It's hard to explain but when you're young, when you don't know about sex, everything is new and you've never heard of certain things or what's supposed to happen next or what the right thing to do is. When he stopped doing one thing and then touched me somewhere else, a bolt of fear would charge through me.'

Amelia paused for a moment and shivered. Her pupils were dilated with fear. She was back there now.

'I can still smell his breath and hear his panting.'

Her uncle's cruelty had been scored deep into her brain. After her family had moved away, leaving Uncle Richard and the abuse behind, Amelia did everything she could to forget it, drink being her principal aid. But the memories, although submerged in alcohol, were still there. Like so many victims, Amelia's unconscious brain fought to push them to the surface, forcing her to confront and hopefully deal with them.

'And how often do you drea— ... have these nightmares about your uncle?'

'It's every other night. I was terrified of getting pregnant and I even still feel that fear. I mean, at the time I thought I might get pregnant from oral sex.'

'Have you told anyone else about these dreams?'

Amelia nodded.

'Hi, Harry! Haven't seen you in a while.'

It was Katherine, one of the CPS's finest prosecuting solicitors. Tall, confident and fiercely intelligent, she had worked with me twice in the past. Two cases, two victories, and although I knew this would be the toughest one so far, I hoped it would be the third.

Katherine, who was in her thirties and unmarried, drew male eyes wherever her long legs marched her, something I noticed as she escorted me through security and into a crowded lift. As is the tradition, an awkward silence ruled as we climbed to the seventh floor. It was lunchtime, so the journey was slow as the lift collected people heading to the building's restaurant.

I carried with me a most unusual piece of evidence: an A4 notebook, Amelia's dream journal. I'd asked her to keep a record of all her dreams since our first interview. I'd called her the previous night, asking for the latest copy, explaining I wanted to take it with me to present to the CPS, a powerful visual aid, a long and detailed document.

'Same old, same old,' Amelia said with a smile as she handed it over, before wishing me good luck.

Amelia's sister, nineteen-year-old redhead Lucy, had also come forward. Uncle Richard had been prolific, visiting the house regularly when Lucy was between the ages of five and ten.

'He'd touch me all the time,' Lucy told me. 'Whether we were watching TV, "playing" in the garden or in my bedroom. Mum couldn't understand why I didn't want to go and play with him. I wanted to tell her but couldn't. Uncle Richard knew how to put the fear into me.'

Lucy, who had a series of elaborate tattoos on her bared midriff, forearms and shoulders, changed her voice into a quiet, vicious tone: 'If you tell, the police will take you away, you'll live in a horrible orphan's home and never see Mummy again.'

As a result, Lucy developed panic attacks and wet the bed. If a man or boy touched her, she shook with fear.

'I'd try and hide when he came round but this backfired 'cause he'd find me and I was already in a quiet, secret place so he could have his way the moment he found me. It was the sickest, scariest game of hide and seek ever.'

She tried sticking to her other sisters like glue, but he easily managed to separate them.

'He'd say things like: "Why don't you two go to the chippie and get something for all of us for tea?"

'"What a lovely idea," Mum would say. "Thank your Uncle Richard for being so kind, girls." I'd look at Mum; inside I'd be screaming for help. I couldn't understand why Mum couldn't see it. I mean, it seemed so obvious.'

Like Amelia before her, Lucy buried the past once they moved away and did her best to forget about it.

'I used to cut myself when I remembered,' she said, showing me a series of narrow scars on her upper arm. 'That one was with nail scissors. That one I did with a scalpel. It's why I got so many tattoos. The pain blanks everything out, the more and longer it lasts the better.'

Then there was the youngest sister, seventeen-year-old Emma, who was the first to shatter the repressed silence. Emma had just split from yet another boyfriend. She was slim and attractive and never without admirers, but they left her life almost as fast as she dared to let them in.

'I wanted so much to be normal with them, you know? I talked with my friends about what they let boys do when they dated. When I try to do those things, all I see in my mind's eye is Uncle Richard. I go tense, feel sick and the last thing I want to do is kiss some boy. One of them called me frigid at school. My mates defended me, saying it was down to me what I did with my body and who with. They thought I was choosing to wait. But I wasn't. I wanted those boys but couldn't have them. He was right to call me frigid, I am.

'It made me very angry. I tried to bottle it up but I exploded after I split up with John and we were out, celebrating

Amelia's twenty-first. I had too much Smirnoff and broke down.

'My sisters comforted me, thinking I was crying over John, plenty of other fish in the sea and all that. But I wasn't, I was crying about Uncle Richard. I couldn't stop. The sobs got louder and then I screamed, I don't know where it came from but it silenced the bar. And then I said it. I said what had happened. I thought Lucy and Amelia would say I'd made it up, or dreamed it or something. But they had tears in their eyes.

'I'll never forget what Amelia said. It chilled me to the bone.

'"Oh my God," she said. "Not you as well. I thought it was just me."'

Ping.

'Harry?' Katherine asked with a curious smile. She was already in the hallway. 'We're here.'

'Sorry, right.'

We walked to a small meeting room with smoked pale-green glass walls and sat down. The door clicked shut and we were airtight. Safe to talk.

Katherine placed the case file on the table, crossed her legs and looked me straight in the eye. 'So, how did Uncle Richard come across in the interview?'

I wanted to sound as confident and as optimistic as possible, like this was a cut-and-dried case, and launched into the speech I'd spent the last day rehearsing in my mind.

'I know this is not evidential but he looked the part. Long fingernails, yellow tobacco fingers, teeth to match, stained shirt and trousers.'

I wanted to paint the right image; even though this wasn't evidence, a paedophile's appearance could add weight to a victim's testimony as far as the jury were concerned. Despite what they're told, appearances do make a difference to most juries. I've seen silver-tongued sweet old men who looked like everybody's favourite granddad manipulating the court as if it were one of their victims. These monsters can seem very convincing to a jury who have a very different mental image of what a paedophile should look like.

'He has, as you know, a previous conviction for indecent assault on a seven-year-old girl. In the interviews with me about Amelia, Lucy and Emma he simply denied it.'

I paused for a moment. 'He showed zero compassion towards the girls.' Again, this lack of emotion would reinforce the negative image.

'No emotions at all, in fact,' I continued. 'No disgust at the details of the allegations, nothing. He flatly denied the allegations and stated that all three girls were lying.'

Katherine nodded.

'We eventually reached a stage where he started to come up with theories as to why they would accuse him of such terrible crimes. He said that they had "issues".'

Again, this would be fuel for the jury, who would not like this attitude. Still, I knew it wasn't much. But I badly wanted him on the stand. And I wanted Katherine's counsel to grill him until he was burned black.

Katherine looked me directly in the eye.

'OK, Harry, let's discuss Amelia's evidence first.'

'Right.'

'There isn't any.'

Katherine paused to let this sink in.

'Dream recollection is not evidence. Period. I can do nothing with her testimony, you have to understand that, Harry.'

'But surely it must count as corroboration.'

'No,' Katherine said firmly. 'It counts for nothing.'

So I'm down to two, I thought.

'We have a problem with Lucy too, her testimony is just not

clear enough. We have lots of probable inappropriate touching. That is indecent, of course, but we need to prove it. In a case of his word against hers, this can be explained away and I don't doubt his counsel will prepare Uncle Richard until he knows just how to phrase his denial.'

I broke eye contact and looked to the side, at my hand on the table, and fidgeted with an imaginary speck of dust.

'Harry, I believe the testimony you've got from her utterly, it's not that, we just need more than words.'

I stayed silent. Katherine ploughed on.

'The incidents are a decade old. Lucy wasn't raped or penetrated. And, I'm not blaming you here, but we need a more coherent recollection. She's not going to say under oath that she's 100 per cent sure about exactly what he did.'

So I'm down to one, I thought, preparing myself for the final blow.

Katherine sensed my disappointment. She softened her stare, uncrossed her legs and leaned forward as she spoke.

'Harry, I believe the girls, I believe that he is a child molester, but what I believe and what I can realistically prove beyond all reasonable doubt are two different things. I can only put this man on trial if these match up. It's the same with Emma. We're looking at several "minor" indecent assaults. Harry, you know I only use the word "minor" in terms of evidence and not impact, don't you? I know that the three girls have been left deeply affected by their uncle's behaviour.'

I nodded, smiled a tight-lipped smile and looked back at Katherine.

'I've sent this to my counsel and he agrees,' she said. 'I'm sorry. That's why I wanted to meet you today to explain why in person. Emails can sound so terribly cold, can't they?'

'OK. Thank you, Katherine. I appreciate and understand where you're coming from.'

Up to this point, this had been a fairly typical meeting where a case of hard-to-prove historical abuse had been shot down in flames. But then something extraordinary happened.

Katherine sat back and looked at me for a long moment; her eyes narrowed slightly. I was just about to ask her what the matter was when she spoke.

'Do you though, Harry? Really? Your eyes are giving me another answer. You want this man convicted, don't you?'

'Of course.'

'Well, that's why I wanted to meet. I wanted to tell you that despite what I've told you today, this case is not dead.'

'What do you mean?'

'I need the others. Find them, Harry. There must have been others in the decade since he left the three girls. Find them. If I charge him now, all will be lost. But if I wait and you put on your detective's hat and dig, then who knows what you will find. I know you have a million and one other cases but you know as well as I do that other children need to be saved from Uncle Richard. We have the monster right here in front of us, ripe for the picking, all for the sake of a little evidence, some better witnesses. Find it and I will convict him. Will you do that, Harry?'

I was dumbfounded. I'd never heard a CPS solicitor talk like this before. It was like listening to a young JFK about to take on the Mafia. In fact, there was something of the politician about the way she spoke.

I thought it was very easy for her to say these words from her secure office-based existence. It was quite another thing for me to head out into the sunlight to hunt for a paedophile without a shred of evidence or knowing where to start. But hey, I wanted the guy punished, didn't I? Wouldn't I feel better giving the same speech to the three sisters? That there's hope? That I might yet turn up a piece of evidence so good that this passionate and ambitious young solicitor would jump on it and put this man away?

'All right,' I said finally. 'I will. Thank you. I wish we had a few more like you.'

Katherine smiled. 'Unfortunately for our budgetary accountants, I have big ideas about justice and criminal investigation and am very persuasive.'

She cast me a large smile to prove it and I imagined an accountant signing away a huge cut of the CPS budget for Katherine's exclusive use. I wondered whether she would end up in politics, or perhaps as a judge. If it was the latter, I hoped I'd still be in the police to see it.

'If you want me to meet the girls I will. I'll explain why we can't do anything now but also why we believe them utterly and what we plan to do. This is only about level of evidence and reasonable doubt. It is not about belief.'

'That's very good of you,' I said. 'I'll offer it, but I'm sure it'll be unnecessary. I can explain.'

'Great!' Katherine exclaimed and stood up. 'Thanks, Harry, I know we'll get there. Look, stay and come with me to the canteen for a steak sandwich or something, my treat, OK?'

I was about to accept when my phone buzzed. A text from Ella.

It said: 'Alec is at Jades'.

'Christ!'

'Some other time, perhaps?' Katherine called after me as I ran for the stairs.

CHAPTER TWENTY-ONE

THE SECRET IN HER EYES

Ella walked in and sat down on the sofa as Jade got up to leave the room. Jade turned to stare at this most unexpected visitor as she passed by.

Ella's every instinct told her that a terrible secret lay behind those eyes, that this little girl was screaming for help. Jade was unable to say what it was because she was frightened, because she was frightened of – of what exactly?

'You've got it wrong,' Louise snapped suddenly, folding her large arms, standing self-righteously, trying to tower over Ella.

'Got what wrong?'

'My Alec's done nothing wrong, it's a stupid misunderstanding and your bloody interfering is making our lives a nightmare.'

'But once such serious allegations have been made, we have to investigate them, surely you must see that.'

'My Alec is a brilliant dad to Jade. She loves him and he would never do something like that to her, or any little girl. I told you I talked to him already about it when I heard. You don't think I'd know when he was lying? I know all right.'

'All we're asking is access to check Jade's medical records and

for a doctor to examine her, just to make certain that Jade is
OK.'

Louise looked at Ella in indignant silence.

Fair enough, Louise is in shock, Ella thought, but surely there
was a maternal instinct in there somewhere? Some small part of
her that needed our official reassurance? So that she didn't have
to rely on Alec's word alone?

'What did you say to Alec when you found out?' Ella asked.

'I said to him, "Tell me it isn't true." I knew it wasn't true
anyway.'

Louise had confronted Alec in the worst possible way. Instead
of asking for an explanation of the facts, she'd pleaded with him.
She didn't want him to confirm what Jade had told her.

In some ways it's difficult to blame her. After all, Louise wasn't
a solicitor or police officer; she was a mum (although in my
experience mums often prove to be extremely incisive inquisi-
tors) who simply wanted to stop her world from falling apart.

'What did Alec say?' Ella asked.

'He looked me straight in the eye and told me he loved me,'
Louise said confidently. 'Then he said how much he loved Jade.'

Alec knew which tune to sing, giving Louise the reassurance
she'd requested. Her concerns had melted away with Alec's
words of love and compassion. No explanations necessary. In
one way this could be seen as a fine example of love and trust but
in another way, Louise's focus was all wrong. Her six-year-old
daughter had told her that her stepdad Alec had sexually abused
her. Kids can't make this kind of thing up.

'And that was enough for you, was it?' Ella asked.

'What else could I ask for? A bloody DNA test?'

Ella shrugged. 'All I'm saying is let us look at Jade's medical
records, perform an examination and if nothing's wrong we'll
vanish from your life.'

We would never have known about Jade if she hadn't

repeated the allegation – two months later – to a friend in the playground and a parent overheard.

Playground talk is often undervalued. Parents and teachers often think that if they tell us something they've overheard in the playground then we'll storm the school and raid the family home, arresting everyone while shouting out the name of the child.

In child protection we are, of course, sensitive. We don't mind having our time wasted. We approach these sorts of cases cautiously. We know that children say funny things and sometimes muddle meanings. We have no objection to speaking to a hundred parents and children, especially if we end up rescuing a child from abuse.

All too often, parents and children fear what the police or social services will do, thanks to TV drama shows and the bad police news that always finds its way, quite rightly, into the media. Unfortunately this doesn't help us when people are debating whether to confide in us over something that is highly sensitive. In this case, of course, the parent did the right thing and talked to a teacher, and the teacher called us.

The fear that had gripped Ella the moment she'd walked into the flat had stayed with her but she couldn't understand why. OK, so Jade might be scared and Louise was angry and hostile, but that was to be expected. No one wants to face the fact that the person they love and share a bed with has a sexual interest in children.

No, it wasn't this. It was the shadow, the shadow in the kitchen. That had unnerved her and that feeling hadn't gone away. Ella thought she felt movement behind her. She turned and looked at the doorway to the lounge. No one there. But she was now certain Alec was somewhere in the flat.

If he was, then he was breaking the law.

Ella rummaged in her large handbag and pulled out the forms. She then rummaged some more. 'Can't find my pen,' she muttered. But she was looking for her phone. When she found it, her nimble thumbs typed 'Alec is at Jades', knowing I'd understand.

Louise had given me exactly the same treatment when I'd first spoken to her at the school, so I'd wasted no time and gone straight for the jugular: either Alec goes or Jade does.

You have to be very careful about using this sort of threat. Once made, it has to be followed through and you can suddenly find yourself removing a child you really weren't expecting to.

Luckily, Louise quickly gave in and called Alec. He agreed to leave the flat and stay at his mum's for a few days and not to see Jade until we'd completed our investigation. He had little choice. If Alec was guilty, all he could do was hope that Jade wouldn't disclose during the interview. If he was innocent, then he'd want to cooperate so we could clear his name as quickly as possible.

'In these sorts of cases,' Rob told me during my early days, 'always bear in mind that the accused might just be innocent. To be wrongly accused of child abuse can surely be one of the most tragic and cruel situations a decent man can find himself in. The distress is incalculable.'

With this in mind, the faster the investigation moved the better. Letting a case like this drag would be a crime, so Ella's offer of help had been greatly appreciated.

'Is Alec here?' Ella asked, trying and failing to keep a slight tremor out of her voice.

'No!' Louise said.

'Louise, I know there's someone else here.'

'OK, look, yes but –'

Ella pulled out her phone from her bag, ready to call, and stood up.

'It's not Alec! But Alec can't know.'

'What do you mean?'

'It's another man, he's married and I don't want Jade to know, yet. If Alec is guilty, I don't want him back.'

Ella looked back over her shoulder again and then back at Louise. She didn't believe her for a moment.

'Then you'll want to sign the forms then.'

'Jesus H. Christ. You don't give up, do you? All right, give them over.'

As Louise bent over the papers and signed in the box, Ella wondered what her next move should be.

She'd seen my reply. 'On my way. Called 999 and office.'

Even though she was scared and wanted nothing more than to walk out of the front door and into the sunshine, Ella couldn't bring herself to leave Jade in the flat as long as she thought Alec was there too.

'Here,' Louise said, handing the papers back.

'Thanks,' Ella said. 'We'll arrange for Jade to be interviewed and to have a medical as soon as possible.' She was trying to think of a reason to stay a bit longer but was rapidly realising that she was going to simply have to demand to see the 'other man'.

'So you can go now,' Louise said, crossing her arms.

'I could murder a cup of tea.'

Louise's mouth fell open. 'I ain't got time to stand here all day and chat! I've done what you asked so you can bloody well go.'

'No. I can't leave until I'm satisfied Alec isn't here.'

This time there really was a sound behind her. Ella span.

She jumped in shock. A man was blocking the doorway. He was stocky and a bit below average height, balding with a pot-belly and big arms. He looked at Louise in disgust.

'Alec, no!' Louise said.

'Aw, you stupid cow,' he said. 'She's never laid eyes on me before, how'd she know who I was? And why the fuck did you sign them forms anyway?'

Ella still held the papers in her hands. Alec eyed them desperately.

'If you try and take these from me,' she said, 'you'll be prosecuted for assault and then,' here Ella looked back at Louise, 'Jade will definitely be removed. Louise, you shouldn't have let him back in.'

Louise was crying. 'But I love him. My Alec ain't hurt Jade. He never would.'

'You should listen to her,' Alec said with a sneer.

'And you've broken the terms of our agreement.'

'No!' Louise said. 'Don't take my Jade, you can't take her. I won't let you!'

Alec had come to see Jade, to turn her against us and to coach her on exactly what she should say. The bastard was as guilty as hell. There was no way Ella could leave with Alec still there. The moment she did, Jade would be in danger.

Anger flowed through Ella, giving her the strength to stand up to Alec, a common thug, the lowest form of humanity, a paedophile, every child's real-life nightmare, the sort of man she'd devoted her life to protecting children from.

'I'm not leaving,' Ella said, sounding like a cross primary school teacher. 'Alec, you have to go now.'

'Why? You going to call the cops, are you?'

Ella immediately called his bluff and pressed the call button, reminding herself that all bullies were cowards.

'You stupid interfering bitch!' he snarled, stepping forward.

I was doing my best to race through the City in my unmarked car. Getting to Hackney Downs in the next five minutes – and still in one piece – in this traffic was asking too much of my faithful Fiesta. The motor whined complainingly each time I floored the accelerator.

Craig, on the other hand, was just around the corner when I called. I just hoped there was a patrol car nearby. Ella was certainly in the right area, armed units liked to hang out in Hackney, especially near the Downs Park Estate, where she was, as there'd been a few shootings in recent weeks. If there was any chance of action, then this was the place.

My phone started to ring. Rob, who always complained I was never quick enough to pick up my phone, had badgered me until I'd finally installed a hands-free set in the car. Problem was, I had left in such a rush I hadn't attached my phone; it was somewhere in my bag on the bag seat, rolling around with Amelia's dream diary.

'Dammit!'

I skidded to a halt at a set of red lights, reached around, tore my bag apart and shoved the phone into the slot just as it stopped ringing. Missed call from Ella.

'Fuck!'

I called her back and span my wheels in the direction of Hackney.

'I've already called them,' Ella said quickly. Alec stopped. 'I sent them a text, look.'

She broke the connection and held the screen with the text message towards Alec, who squinted at it, mouth hanging open.

Without another word he turned and walked quickly down the hall. Ella dropped her shoulders and shut her eyes for a moment. Then her phone started to ring and she answered it.

'Harry? You almost here are you?'

'Ten minutes away. Local uniforms will be there any second, if not Craig.'

'Great, thanks.'

'What the hell's going on?'

'It's OK, slow down, he's just left. I'll tell you everything when you get here.'

'It's OK, Jade,' Ella said. 'You're doing really well, just a few more minutes now.'

Jade was struggling with the interview. I could tell from her body language that it wouldn't be long before she'd give up entirely. There was no eye contact and Sarah often had to repeat the question.

When Jade answered she simply shook her head without saying a word. She looked down, letting her long brown hair fall over her face, and shifted on her seat uncomfortably, breathing noisily through a slightly bunged-up nose.

It was clear to us that something had happened to Jade, but that she wasn't yet ready to release the memories. We wondered whether this was thanks to Alec. I found it impossible to imagine that Alec was innocent or that Jade had made up the accusation of sexual abuse.

'Why won't she talk to us?' Ella asked after we'd finally been forced to give up.

'It may be that Jade simply doesn't trust us,' I said. 'Or even like us enough to open up. I once interviewed a child who told us she'd suffered the most horrible abuse. The strange thing was that she'd been through a memorandum interview a few weeks earlier. When I asked her about the first interview, she said that the detective had been "bossy" and reminded her of a teacher she didn't like at school. She was convinced the officer hated her and was trying to get her in trouble. As a result, she'd said nothing about the rapes she'd endured.'

The case was disintegrating before our eyes. There were serious concerns, but no facts, only a child's claim overheard by a friend's mother that her stepfather had touched her. Although the mother had confirmed this, it didn't help that Louise denied it, as did Alec and, now, Jade.

'I'm really worried, Harry,' Ella said after the interview was over. 'We're going to lose her.'

This was developing into the worst kind of case, where you had to return a child to the source of the abuse.

'Can't we charge Alec with something?' Ella asked.

'What happened in the flat isn't enough for us to do anything significant. OK, so Alec had broken our agreement, but if we have no evidence about Jade, then there's almost nothing to charge him with.'

'Christ,' Ella said in frustration, 'surely there must be something we can do. If we send her home, then *I'll* feel like the abuser. It'd be like lowering a kitten into a tank full of piranhas.'

I sighed. This was another unpleasant first for Ella. 'Yeah, I've been forced to do that a few times. It's extremely nasty. But look, let's not give up yet. I'll tell Louise the result of the interview and then we've still got the medical exam.'

Louise frowned when I told her. 'See, I told you she wouldn't say nothing.'

'Well, it's not enough. It means we still don't know.'

Louise deflated slightly. She wasn't going to hear the words 'Alec is innocent' from me.

Ella and I travelled to the hospital with Jade, still silent in the back of the car, her mum next to her. I could see them both in the rear-view mirror, and noted the similarities in their faces. Jade really was her mother's child. I had a bad feeling about this. Jade had been through so much already and now she was about to undergo the trauma of a medical exam. I looked in the mirror again. Jade was staring out of the window, at the streets soaked in summer rain.

Uncertainty took hold of me. Was my judgement off? Was I reading too much into the situation? Ella seemed convinced, but then she'd stood toe-to-toe with bullyboy Alec, that had been more than enough.

We had already put Jade through so much. We'd removed her from the family home to put her through an unpleasant interview and now, although the doctors are truly wonderful when it comes to child protection cases, Jade was about to undergo an intimate and invasive examination.

When the medical failed to prove anything, it really felt as if we were the abusers.

'We should be celebrating,' Ella said after we'd taken Louise and Jade home. 'All the evidence says Jade is fine. No abuse, nothing. Only what seems to be a mistaken allegation from her.'

I didn't say anything.

'There's no reason for me to visit them again. The home is clean and comfy; compared to many other families in the area, they're living a first-class life.'

I nodded. There was nothing else to say. 'Come on, I'll drop you at your office.'

'No, I'll head back on foot, thanks. I could use the walk.'

As Ella walked, she knew she would never know the secret in Jade's eyes.

CHAPTER TWENTY-TWO

HARRY'S HOLIDAY

God, I needed this. A holiday. Although it didn't feel like one yet. After being slowly shepherded through the dawn chaos at Stansted airport, I found myself concertinaed into a seat designed for someone who was four-foot-six not six-foot-four. I tried to immerse myself in the thriller I'd bought on impulse from Smiths, but I quickly found my mind wandering back to work.

Although I was on my way, I wasn't really on holiday yet. It takes about three days to wind down. Some cases come along with you like uninvited guests and distract you from conversations, from taking in the sights you're supposed to be seeing, or join you at the restaurant table.

I'm sure it's different for every child protection officer but for me, the toddlers and the historic cases had the most impact.

Jade stayed with me, as did Amelia, Lucy and Emma. Katherine's words played around in my mind. I don't think she realised the impact she would have on me. Finding other victims so she could nail Uncle Richard to the prison wall was going to be extremely difficult.

Cases like Jade, where the evidence isn't clear, where something's missing but you don't know what, just nag away at the back of your mind. I worried about getting a call weeks, months or even years later and being told that Jade was badly injured or dead.

The historic cases stayed with me because the strength of the victim is vital. After suffering so much, victims still have to show great stamina and maintain their courage in the months leading up to the trial. Unlike children, they understand what had happened to them and feel the true magnitude of the abuser's betrayal. They relied on our support and I often wondered whether I'd done enough.

Arriving in Amsterdam and being met by relatives proved to be a great distraction. Our kids were back in the UK, staying with grandparents, so Mrs Keeble and I were free to do whatever we liked. After a quick coffee and catch up, it was decided that we should go shopping.

It has to be said that this was not my first choice. I am not a very good shopper. In fact, I am very bad company for a female shopper. As far as clothes go, I walk in, pick up something in my size, pay for it and go home. Whether it looks good on me or not is pot luck.

I couldn't win with Mrs Keeble. She would understandably want my opinion, to make sure I approved of what she had chosen. However quickly I wiped the tired and bored expression from my face and replaced it with a beam of joy as the fitting room curtain was flung back, I always failed. All too often I'd find myself blurting out things like 'Everything looks good on you' or 'That's nice', only to be told off for using the word 'nice' or told 'You're just saying that'. So, when the next option was presented to me, I'd do my best to express a genuine opinion and that always got me into *real* trouble.

When forced into a shopping trip, I usually try to be as complimentary and charming as possible but I've learned the hard way that the safest option is simply to stand outside.

Sure enough, as I was the only male in our group of shoppers and as I didn't want to end up offending our female hosts, I said I'd wait outside. I excused myself, telling them I wanted to people-watch. 'It's every cop's favourite hobby,' I explained, backing out of the doors and wishing them luck.

It was a bright summer's day. The streets were busy with pedestrians and the ubiquitous cyclists. I couldn't see a pavement café, so I found a bench and spent the next twenty minutes watching the locals keenly, absorbing their different faces, clothes and expressions, and listening to the pleasant sing-song sounds of the Dutch language.

When the ladies finally emerged from the shop I stood up.

Great, I thought, coffee time.

But no, they immediately came to a halt outside the lamp shop next door. I had begun to walk towards them, but when I saw them step inside I stopped. Again, decisions about light fittings would be a matter of taste and discussion beyond my comprehension.

I returned to my bench and got back to people-watching. The children on my books had finally left me, at least for now.

'SHTOP! POLITIE!'

Needless to say, this grabbed my attention.

I looked over my left shoulder, in the direction of the shout. A young man in a dark blue puffer jacket and black jeans sprinted past me with a brown leather handbag in his left hand. Behind him a policeman lay on the pavement, clutching his shin.

I stood up as the robber turned a corner and dived into an alleyway, throwing the bag into a pile of rubbish as he went.

What's all this, then? I wondered in the great tradition of the British police officer.

I looked back over my right shoulder at the lamp shop where Mrs Keeble was evidently still busy studying light fittings.

'I'm a foreign police officer, in a foreign country out shopping,'

I told myself. 'In the UK I am duty-bound to react, but not in Holland. And I *am* on holiday, after all. Yes, shopping may not be much fun but I really should ignore this ...'

My legs, however, had other ideas. They were already moving at full pelt. Reason had lost out to instinct and I was in hot pursuit. All thoughts of shopping, child protection and what Mrs Keeble would say and do when she found out were blasted out of my mind.

I sprinted down the alleyway after the perp. I hadn't done this for a while but I knew from having carried out multiple foot chases in and around London that the key to catching a suspect on the run was to keep pace with your target. As soon as he hit an obstacle, that's the moment to speed up and catch him.

He was out the end of the other alleyway and into the next street. I found my rhythm, extended my stride and let the adrenaline do its work, giving me energy I would have found hard to muster if I'd been chasing a football.

The distance between us stabilised. He was young and was good for a mile at least before he started to tire. I'd worn my comfiest trainers for the flight, so dug in.

We turned another corner and, to my great disappointment, entered a long stretch of straight road with a canal to one side. No obstacles. Damn. I pushed myself and ran harder, harder, harder; as I did so I felt the anger and frustration that had been building up inside me in recent weeks rise to the surface; this sudden chase was the physical release I didn't know I was waiting for. This was old-fashioned and uncomplicated policing, pursuing an obviously guilty-as-hell bad guy through the streets. I let everything out through my limbs and lungs and started to close the gap.

I passed some young people riding bikes. They looked on in amazement as I hurtled past, arms and legs pumping. How did it go again?

'SHTOP, POLIZIE?'

It came out in a high-pitched screech and sounded more like a question than an order, but it worked. The people on the bikes proved to be very public-spirited and joined the chase, following about twenty metres behind me.

People shouted; more cyclists joined us and started to gain on me. Three young men on fast-looking road bikes accelerated past yelling something; they obviously had a plan but I had no idea what it was, so I just kept running, digging deep now as my lungs burned.

We were sprinting alongside the canal. The three young men on bikes overtook on the building side of the road before veering in front of the mugger and he was forced to slow; he tried to dance his way around them. I, however, was still going full pelt and had no intention of braking. Fifteen stone of British child protection officer piled into him. We both went flying to the ground, rolling with the momentum over the cobbled street – and towards the canal.

'Nooooo!'

I let go of the robber and threw out my limbs to stop myself going over the edge, rolling to a stop with an arm and a leg hanging over the water.

The thief tumbled to a halt just beside me and before he could strike out with his arms or legs I got hold of him, flipping him roughly on to his back. Thoughts of needles flitted through my mind as I fought to get hold of his arms. I had no idea if he was a junkie but I did know that Amsterdam had more than its fair share of addicts.

Fighting with heroin addicts is every cop's nightmare. With crack addicts you have to fight a lot harder, but at least you won't get 'pricked' and then have to spend a few anxious days praying for the all-clear. I rolled on top of him and used my weight to push his arms down and to the side, palms up, a position from which it was impossible to escape.

I was now surrounded by about forty Dutch people, most of whom seemed to be on bikes. Both the suspect and I were panting and sweating. He had dark brown hair, and brown eyes with a white scar that cut across one eyebrow.

I looked straight into his eyes. 'Are you OK?'

Of course, I wasn't concerned about his health but by asking about his welfare I was saying that I wasn't going to hurt him and that I wasn't about to let him go anywhere.

He nodded, accepting his fate. He looked around with a startled expression, as if seeing the crowd for the first time. There was a lot of excited chatter in Dutch, which of course I didn't understand. Several people were on their mobiles and someone was filming us with their phone.

'Oh no,' I thought, 'please don't put me on YouTube, I'll never hear the end of it.'

I hoped that at least one of them was calling the police. After what felt like an hour but in fact was probably two minutes (try to remember this if you're waiting for the urgent arrival of the cops – the waiting seems far longer than it is) I heard sirens.

A Dutch cop car flew over a bridge and screeched on the cobbles as it pulled up. Two officers leaped out and handcuffed the man while speaking double-Dutch to me at 100mph.

'English?' I asked hopefully.

'No problem,' one of them said.

'I'm a cop from London, I saw where he threw the handbag.'

The cop beamed at me. 'Exshellent,' he said in an accent that immediately reminded me of the laid-back Amsterdam cops as portrayed by comedians Harry Enfield and Paul Whitehouse.

'We were trying to arrest him when he wriggled away. He was very quick on his feet.'

'Will you come with us to the police station?' the other one enquired.

'Sure,' I said.

Thoughts of where I was and what I should have been doing hit me like a thunderclap. Bloody hell, Mrs Keeble.

'May I just call my wife first? She'll be wondering where I've got to.'

'Hello, Harry,' she answered. 'You getting bored out there, are you?'

'Erm. You're still in the lamp shop, aren't you?'

'Yes, why?'

'Ah, well, you see, I was waiting outside when this bloke ran past with a handbag and—'

'Harry! We're supposed to be on holiday. Really! That's the last time I'm leaving you outside on your own.'

Two minutes later, with one red ear, I was in the back of the police car, heading to the station.

'Wife not happy?'

'No, she not happy at all. We're supposed to be on holiday.'

He smiled. 'Don't worry,' he said sympathetically, 'we appreciate you.'

At the station I gave a statement, which was transcribed in Dutch.

'Sign here,' one of the officers said.

'But it's in Dutch.'

'Ach, don't worry, it's fine.'

I shrugged and did as they asked. I wouldn't get away with this in London, but when in Rome ...

Afterwards, it really was off for tea and medals, well, a plaque in fact from the grateful Dutch police, handed to me in the canteen to a smattering of applause.

Red-faced, I sat down and sipped my tea. The lady owner of the handbag was sat at another table and I nodded hello. She frowned at me. She was very young, even younger than the robber, and didn't look at all happy to be there.

Oh well, I'd captured an escaped robber. Hurrah. A pleasant

job for once, a welcome change from a weaselly paedophile or vindictive mother. As I revelled in the glory, a sergeant came in and gave me a bottle of wine and I answered lots of questions about what it was like being a policeman in London. They listened appreciatively. Fantastic.

It got even better when I took out my mobile and rang Rob. As he was my boss I had to let him know I'd gone 'live' while in another country.

'Great work, Harry,' he said. 'You've done the Met proud and for that I can give you the day back for putting yourself out on holiday, so I'll expect you back here a day later than planned, OK?'

Happy days.

Just then a police officer came in and led the victim away.

'Off for another statement is she?' I asked.

'No,' my new cop friend said. 'The "robber" is actually her boyfriend. He took the bag because it has all their ID in it.'

My grip tightened on the bottle of wine.

'They're teenage runaways from Ukraine. They have no visas. She's underage, so it's one for child services.'

Sometimes, no matter where you go, work simply won't let you be.

CHAPTER TWENTY-THREE

THE SNIP

'Morning!' I arrived back at my desk, refreshed and recharged, although I deflated slightly when I saw the files and folders piled exactly where I'd left them, pens, markers, staplers and sticky tape strewn across them.

'Welcome back the conquering hero,' Rob said with a smile. 'Where's your plaque from the Dutch cops?'

'Pride of place on the mantelpiece,' I replied.

'Time for breakfast at Bodrum's?'

'I'd be delighted.'

Twenty minutes later, Rob and I sat back in our plastic chairs in our local Turkish café, having simultaneously demolished two breakfast specials. It sat heavy in my stomach, but as it hadn't been fried I told myself it was healthy.

'How are things, Harry?' Rob asked.

'Good, thanks,' I replied.

'Great. Pleased to hear it. Anything in particular you want to chat about?'

What was he getting at? I wondered. It wasn't like Rob to hold back when he wanted to tell me something.

'You had some tough cases before your holiday, Harry,' he said. 'Not getting to you, are they?'

'No,' I said, appreciating Rob's concern. 'Well, yes, but only on a professional level,' I said. 'The pressure's always there but this is what I want to do. This is what I signed up for. I've been doing this job long enough to handle it, and without losing sight of what we're trying to achieve.'

'Excellent,' Rob replied. 'You know the social worker you were with on Jade's case?'

'Ella? What about her?'

'I've heard she's struggling since Jade.'

'Well, that's understandable,' I said. 'She's new and she's been put through the wringer on a few cases already. She's young and naïve but smart and she's learning fast. But why bring this up with me?'

'As you know, we've been bringing social workers more and more into our world,' Rob said. 'Sitting in on interviews, sometimes leading them, and being part of investigations.'

'Yes and I think it's great,' I said. 'The more we get to see of each other's world the better our understanding and the better for the kids we're trying to protect.'

'I agree,' Rob said. 'Ella's been at the forefront of this. The idea is that if we start the new ones off this way, then this approach will feel natural from day one. I'm a little concerned, however, after speaking to her bosses that she's in danger of being overwhelmed. She seems to have seen you the most since joining this summer, so I just want you to keep an eye on her.'

'No problem,' I said. 'Maybe she's hit some kind of wall with Jade's case but I'm fairly certain she'll come through it.'

'Right then,' Rob said, as the waitress came with the bill. 'I'll get this and then it's back to it.'

*

I made my way back to my desk, sat down and began my morning work routine. First I studied the overnight crimes. This meant reading and understanding each allegation and writing up what actions were required and allocating them to an officer.

I would then do the same with the latest referrals from social services. Once this had been done, it was time to see whether what I'd planned for the day had survived the onslaught of new cases. That morning I was on form and happily ploughed through all the files, batting them expertly off to various members of the team.

Until I reached the last one.

I stopped and re-read the report. Oh no, not again. Why me? And on my first day back, too.

The report was deceptively to the point. I looked across the office. Rob was bent in concentration over a thick file on his desk. There was no way he would let me palm this one off to a junior detective. I could hear his voice: 'Just get on with it, Harry.'

A rabbi's efforts at the circumcision of babies had been criticised. He was, apparently, so inaccurate that a baby had to be taken to casualty.

The report had been written late at night and was full of crossings-out and spelling mistakes. The uniform cop responsible could have been a bad speller, slapdash or, more likely, in a huge hurry after a hectic shift.

I'd been there often enough myself. Meet the complainant to take notes and then head back to the police station to write it up over a cup of tea. Then, on the way back, 'Urgent Assistance' screams over the radio and off you run to the aid of another officer, who's usually rolling around on a Hackney pavement with some idiot who can't take his Stella.

In my uniform days we had two guys on the team who always

liked to take on the 'griefy' calls, one of whom had the wonderful nickname of 'Spoons'. One day Spoons turned up to a domestic only to be stabbed repeatedly in the head. I was around the corner in the middle of taking notes about an aggravated burglary. I left the victim open-mouthed as I ran off to help Spoons, knocking over her Hoover on the way out and leaving her front door wide open.

'What took you so long?' Spoons demanded with a wry smile when I arrived. He was sitting on a garden wall. So much blood was streaming down his face, he could hardly see. Fortunately, the stab wounds hadn't penetrated his skull. The attack earned Spoons a nice collection of scars and a month off work to recover.

I put the report down, brushed my memories aside and thought about how to move this investigation forward in such a way that I would still have my job at the end of it. This could be a straightforward one-off incident, but I knew that it could well head in other directions that would involve – and possibly incense – the local community.

Well, whatever happened, if any child needed our protection, I would go to any length to make them safe, cultural sensibilities be damned. Protect the child and everything else will take care of itself. That was the theory, anyway.

I called Bronwyn at social services for a discussion about our strategy.

'God, Harry, you sure know how to pick 'em,' she said. 'OK, I'm happy for this to be a joint investigation. Ella can join you.'

Ella walked across the car park towards me. After my chat with Rob I studied her carefully. I'd seen her go through a great deal already this summer.

God knows what she was dealing with on a day-to-day basis,

without the horrors I ended up throwing her. I wondered if she would start to associate my smiling mug with the most unpleasant and difficult cases.

'Hi, Harry,' she said brightly as she threw her bag on the back seat, before climbing in beside me. 'Go anywhere good for your holiday?'

'Amsterdam.'

'Really?' Ella looked at me and winked. 'I never had you down as a coffee and hash-cookie kind of guy.'

I was mortified. 'I'm not!' I replied. 'I've got family who live out there.'

Ella laughed. 'Don't worry, I know you're as straight as they come,' adding after a moment's thought, 'and that's a good thing. I'm sick of all the drug addicts in this city. People think it will make their lives more bearable but we spend all of our time mopping up after them.'

'Well, no drugs involved in today's case.'

'And perhaps there should have been. A bit of anaesthetic wouldn't hurt.'

'Very droll.' The informant was the mother of a recently circumcised baby.

'This is pretty rare,' I told Ella. 'I've only investigated two other cases in the Jewish community. They tend to deal with these things internally.' I informed Ella about my previous cases and explained that the 20,000-strong Jewish population based in Stamford Hill, North London, was home to an orthodox and secretive Hasidic Jewish group called the Haredi. They were famous for being just about the most law-abiding citizens in London and even had their own independent systems of justice, health and welfare.

'The Haredi community as a whole tries to avoid contact with modern society,' I said. 'Television is frowned upon. They're very much of another time. The long black coats, tall black hats and white stockings the men wear on the Sabbath goes back to eighteenth-century Eastern Europe.

'They even have their own ambulance service, called *Hatzola* – the Hebrew word for rescue. Now that's impressive.'

Ella stared at me. 'Finished with your lecture of the day, have we?'

'What?'

'Harry, I'm Jewish.'

'Oh, I er, I had, I mean, I didn't know.'

Ella giggled. 'God, you should see yourself. It's OK, Harry, you're not supposed to know automatically. My family is Jewish-lite; in fact you could say I'm a lapsed Jew. But although my family hail from deepest Finchley, I have been in Stamford Hill a couple of times.'

The house was large, almost mansion-sized, and overlooked the wide-open spaces of the Lea Valley, one of the capital's largest and most hidden green areas, home to fields, reservoirs, nature reserves and a world-class centre for water sports.

I rang the doorbell, running through my mental checklist. If her husband wasn't in, the mother might not answer and was unlikely to look directly at me if she did. There was also a good chance she wouldn't shake my hand.

I looked at my reflection in the glass of the door and straightened my tie as a shadow appeared and walked down the hallway towards us. The door opened wide to reveal an attractive dark-haired thirty-something woman dressed in a charcoal pencil skirt and tight cream jumper. She beamed at me.

'Hi there!' she said in a strong American accent. 'How're you doing?' She thrust out her hand. As I took it, I saw Ella was amused by my surprise at the accent and the woman's unexpected forthrightness.

'I'm Mary. Won't you come in?'

I was still a bit shell-shocked when we entered the lounge and sat down. The home was magnificent. The rooms, high-ceilinged and huge, were immaculately furnished in a modern style.

'Thank you so much for coming so soon,' she said. 'Now I have a number of concerns I'd like to tell you about,' and immediately she started dictating a list.

Fast-talking Mary had taken advantage of my flummoxed state. I hadn't been expecting this. In these situations, as the police officer, I'm supposed to control the polite conversation and direct it where I want it to go.

'I've not been in the UK all that long,' Mary said. 'I'm here on a two-year assignment to manage the new London department of my bank. I'd put baby Machion in the care of the local rabbi to be "done", but I am not happy at all. He was clumsy and I had to take my baby to A&E for a stitch to be put in.

'Now, what are we going to do about it?'

Phew. I could tell she was a high-powered manager. She wanted action, which was understandable, but I was feeling very 'managed' and didn't like the fact she was going so fast.

'I think if you would tell us in detail what happened first, that would be very helpful,' I said, taking out my pen and notebook.

'Of course. It was my husband, David, who was keen to get it done. He brought it up just before the birth. He said Machion should look like he did. It was important, he also said, because he was a Jew and Jewish boys are circumcised. I wasn't entirely reconciled with the idea. I mean, we're not orthodox by any stretch and I wasn't sure it was worth putting our baby through the trauma of having his penis cut just so he'd look like his father.

'Anyway, David is very persuasive and he talked me into it. Jewish boys are usually circumcised when they're just eight days old, so we asked a friend to recommend someone and he knew a mohel (someone who performs circumcisions), just up the road in Stamford Hill, so we called him. I didn't know this but some of these guys apparently have no medical training. That can't be legal, can it?'

'What happened next?' I asked. I wanted to bypass Mary's question as I suspected she might turn my answer into a lengthy and distracting debate.

'Two rabbis came to visit the next day. They were two big guys, beard and forelocks, with black silk kaftans, white stockings, polished black shoes and *shtreimels*, you know, the large fur hats. It felt strange having these two very serious men in my house.

'I asked them if it was going to hurt Machion. The rabbi waved his hand, dismissively. "Do not concern yourself with this, he is a baby," he said. "I promise you he will be content as soon as I give him back to you."'

Mary laughed sardonically. 'I wasn't so sure. I mean if someone said they were going to hack at your penis without anaesthetic, how would you feel? I don't think you'd be all sweetness and light, would you?'

I instinctively pushed my legs together at the thought. A friend of mine had had a circumcision as an adult, with anaesthetic. When he woke up a couple of mornings later with an erection, he had to go back to the hospital for more stitches. Ouch.

'Then he gave me a list of things to buy: an unopened bottle of olive oil, gauze swabs, sterile dressings, disposable nappies, a pillow, cotton wool, prayer shawls and a bottle of Kedem Traditional Kiddush wine.

'We held a party on the day of the circumcision with all our family and friends, as is the tradition. When the rabbi and his assistant arrived, they unpacked a small bag of medical bits and pieces, including the beaker my son's foreskin would go in.

'When I brought Machion downstairs, I was already feeling a

bit weak-kneed. It was a relief to pass him to a friend; it's a blessing to help carry the baby at this time so he was passed around. He was as good as gold, looking around, quiet but alert and fascinated by all the attention.

'The rabbi asked for silence and began to pray. As he did so he took a small surgical clip and put it over Machion's foreskin, pulling it forward. As soon as this was done he cut through it with a small knife and it came away. Machion screamed.'

Mary paused and swallowed. She looked pale.

'There was a lot of blood. Then the rabbi sucked the wound.'

'What?'

I couldn't believe what I'd just heard. Mary had said it so matter-of-factly. Suck the wound? What was this? Surely this wasn't normal.

'Harry,' Ella said, stepping in before I could continue. 'It sounds terrible but it's what they do, it's the tradition.'

'She's right,' Mary said. 'There's nothing sexual to it. In the old days it was important to prevent infection. Then he gave the baby a few drops of wine as an anaesthetic.'

Good grief, I thought, without the cultural basis you could argue that Machion had suffered actual bodily harm and an indecent assault and had been forced to drink alcohol.

'The point is,' Mary continued, 'that rabbi lied. Machion cried for a day afterwards. Changing his nappy was a nightmare. We could only bathe him after a week and the dressing came off. His penis was in a real mess. Look, I can show you.'

She'd taken a picture. I tightened my stomach. 'Come on, Harry,' I told myself, 'you've seen worse.'

The photo showed a small bloody and purple penis that looked swollen and definitely painful. But there didn't seem to be any infection.

'How long ago was this picture taken?'

'Yesterday. We took him to the hospital where the doctors

checked him over and gave him a stitch. He's fine now, the bruising's already gone down quite a bit. So,' Mary said, 'where do we go from here?'

Good question. I wasn't sure.

Ella spoke first. 'I understand,' she said. 'Your baby was in pain and you would have given anything for that pain to be yours rather than Machion's. The problem is what you've told us today is similar to what goes on at circumcision ceremonies in general. It sounds to me like the procedure was worse than you imagined.'

'It was barbaric.'

'Yes, well, that remains a matter of opinion, we will need to do a medical. But it may be there was nothing wrong with the way the ceremony was carried out; even though anaesthetic wasn't used, nothing illegal happened. The debate about the rights and wrongs of this are beyond us, I'm afraid.'

'What about the rabbi?' Mary asked.

'Look, you have a concern about his fitness to practise. We have to look into this and we will approach various Jewish organisations with the medical report. They will talk to the rabbi on your behalf.'

Mary kept eye contact and nodded understandingly. Her mother's instinct had fired her into action. She had raised the alarm, we had listened and we had an outcome that, while perhaps not ideal, she could accept.

CHAPTER TWENTY-FOUR

MY FATHER, THE FATHER

'Hello, Chloe,' Mrs Baker said.

Chloe stopped walking but said nothing. She looked down at her feet. It was a sunny lunchtime and the school corridor was empty.

'I just wondered whether you'd done your history homework yet.'

Chloe shook her head.

Mrs Baker, who'd taught Chloe history for a year, was worried. Chloe, who was overweight by quite a large margin, was a model pupil. She'd always handed her homework in on time before, and it was usually excellent. But she was too quiet in class; she never interacted during group discussions. Chloe also seemed much younger than fourteen. Mrs Baker had always been left with a sense that something was wrong and now this, another late homework assignment.

'Chloe, can I have a quick chat with you? You're not in trouble. I'd just like to ask you something in my office.'

Chloe nodded. As Mrs Baker sat down she relaxed her bearing, letting her Head of Year's persona soften and melt away. For the next twenty minutes, she would no longer be Mrs

Baker, Head of Year, she would instead be Sylvia, Chloe's friend.

'Is something the matter, Chloe?' Sylvia asked.

Chloe shrugged and kept her eyes firmly focused on her knees.

As softly as she could manage, Sylvia said, 'Chloe, look at me. I want you to know that you can trust me. I know something is troubling you and I'd very much like to know what it is so I can help.'

Chloe said something but it came out so quietly that Sylvia had to ask her to speak up.

'It's my boyfriend, Miss,' Chloe said. 'He's been really nasty to me.'

Sylvia knew her pupils very well and she could tell when they were lying, or holding something back.

'Is there something else, Chloe?'

'Yes, Miss.' She paused. Sylvia waited patiently for her to break the silence.

'I think I might be pregnant.'

That fear was true, Sylvia realised. She kept calm; she didn't act outraged, surprised or sympathetic.

'Actually, I really am pregnant.'

Sylvia looked more closely at Chloe. She was big, so the pregnancy had been easier to hide.

There was a knock at the door. Sylvia snapped a quick 'Not now!' Whoever it was went away.

Sylvia was worried this interruption had spooked Chloe, who'd just started crying. Sylvia moved her chair closer and gave Chloe a tissue.

'It's all right, there, there. Have a good cry, it's OK.'

'Actually, Miss, it's not my boyfriend. It's my dad,' Chloe said through her tears.

'Your dad? What about him, does he know?'

'Oh no, Miss, I haven't told anyone except you.' She wiped her eyes.

'My dad is the dad.'

Ella and I entered the school. Apart from a couple of stragglers, the kids had all gone home. Cleaners mopped the corridors and tidied the classrooms. The caretaker, jangling his enormous bunch of keys, had started locking up.

The school receptionist slid back the glass window. I stooped while Ella leaned forward. My warrant card did the work and we were quickly led through the maze of corridors, past the artwork tacked to walls, passing teachers on their way home, who looked at us in curiosity.

We reached the door with a 'Head of Year' sign painted gold on a wooden plate. The receptionist knocked and on hearing a decisive 'Yup!' pushed the door open and showed us in.

A woman in her early fifties with a kindly face and greying hair was bent over a file on her desk. She took off her gold-rimmed glasses as we entered and stood up and smiled, thrusting out her hand. She was wearing an expensive-looking white suit.

'Thanks for coming so quickly,' she said.

In the presence of the Head of Year, I found myself slipping into schoolboy mode and introduced myself as Detective Sergeant Keeble.

'Please, first names here. Call me Sylvia.' She looked across at the receptionist who had remained in the doorway. 'Thank you, Hannah.' The receptionist closed the door.

Sylvia began to tell us about the chat she'd had with Chloe that lunchtime.

'It's my first one. I've been teaching for twenty years and this is the first one. I always knew it would happen one day and I wondered how I'd feel when it did, how I would react. I'll never forget it. And do you know something else? I realised from the moment I first laid eyes on Chloe that something wasn't right.

'She wanted to tell me, I think, for some time, but I also think she was scared of my reaction. It came out in bits and pieces really, first telling me it was her boyfriend.'

Sylvia was clearly upset; proof of this came when she pulled a tissue from the box on her desk and dabbed her eyes with it. 'I managed not to cry in front of her at least.'

'How did the talk end?' I asked.

'I told Chloe I wanted to help her, that I would keep her here and make sure she was safe, but she wouldn't stay and ran out of the room. That's when I called you. Actually, she apologised. She said, "Sorry, Miss, I shouldn't have told you." Incredible really, that she should apologise for what she'd been through.'

'Does Chloe have any siblings?' Ella asked.

'Yes, she has a younger sister by two years who's also at the school.'

A double whammy: a rape and two children in danger. I could see that Sylvia, who must have been a very strong person to work in a large school like this, was probably, for the first time in a long time, uncertain whether she had done the right thing by letting Chloe leave. She certainly had no idea what she should do next.

This was where I came in. 'Sylvia, we have to make some urgent decisions, are you OK if we crack on right now?'

'Yes, of course, that's what I want you to do.'

Ella spoke next. 'Sylvia, just before we go any further, we want you to know you've done a great job here. You've correctly identified a serious child protection issue, and recognised that as far as a child's safety is concerned, there is no such thing as confidentiality.'

Ella had said exactly what Sylvia needed to hear. She'd

reassured Sylvia that she'd done exactly the right thing. By doing so, Ella had brought Sylvia back to professional mode, which was incredibly helpful – another reason why joint investigations were so useful.

'Ella's quite right,' I said. 'And at some point we will have to explain to Chloe that you had no choice but to repeat her disclosure. Have you made any notes?'

'Yes, I wrote down everything I could remember.'

'I'll take those, they're important evidence. I take it Chloe is at home?'

'Yes.'

I took a deep breath. 'OK, here we go. We need to decide whether we remove her now or speak to her tomorrow.'

This is where child protection parts company with more traditional police departments. Drug investigations, for example, are run with the intention of getting the biggest haul with the best evidence, so if you have to wait a few days and lose some interim evidence, then that's what you do.

Child protection is the same, but the consequences are far nastier.

'Can't you just remove Chloe and her sister from her home?' Sylvia asked.

'This is one option,' I replied, 'but it's not necessarily the best. I have the power to charge over to Chloe's house and remove both her and her sister immediately, no problem. That way Chloe won't be sexually abused tonight and will go straight into emergency foster care.'

'Pardon me for saying,' Sylvia said, 'but this seems like the obvious thing to do.'

'There's one big problem,' I answered. 'Cooperation. When we are forced to remove a teenager from the family home in a surprise raid they often end up scared or angry, or feel betrayed by the person they've entrusted with their terrible secret. They then refuse to cooperate and have to go home. No evidence means no child protection.

'There's also the chance that Chloe's father would be able to exert his influence over her while she was still in earshot. By waiting, we get to Chloe "clean", before her father can threaten her.'

'But she's pregnant, surely that makes it straightforward.'

'She says she's pregnant. She may be wrong. And perhaps her dad isn't the father. Even if her father's baby is on the way, we might still lose the case. DNA tests can't be performed until a baby is born. This scenario doesn't bear thinking about. Chloe and her sister would remain in the care of their rapist for several more months before we could even think of intervening at this level again.

'In the meantime the father would be able to exert his influence over his children, making sure they would never talk to us.'

I let this sink in for a moment. Sylvia nodded slowly. She understood my reasoning. That didn't mean she had to like it, of course.

'The most effective intervention is here, at the school, first thing tomorrow. I'm certain that with your help we'll get Chloe's cooperation. We will, of course, talk to her sister as well.'

I sounded a lot more certain than I felt. It was on my shoulders. Was I prepared to run the risk of Chloe being raped for the sake of achieving what I thought was the most effective intervention?

Working in child protection can be unpleasant; in cases where abuse has already happened there are no winners, no stunning successes. We're not the Flying Squad, lying in wait for a gang of bank robbers. We arrive after the crime, to pick up the pieces. Our successes are measured in stopping further abuse and helping victims to heal.

We agreed to meet in Sylvia's office first thing and Sylvia

would intercept Chloe as soon as she arrived at school. Ella and I shook hands with Sylvia.

'I don't think I'm going to get much sleep tonight,' Sylvia said.

'None of us are,' Ella replied with a reassuring smile. 'The important thing is that we're all here for Chloe. Just remember, you've done exactly what you should have. Now the responsibility lies with us.'

As we reached my car, Ella stopped and looked at me. 'I've got a bad feeling about this, Harry. Are you sure?'

'You sounded a lot more certain back in the school,' I said. 'What's changed your mind?'

'My mind hasn't changed, I know this approach is our best option. It's what my heart is telling me that I'm most worried about.'

I drove in silence, the same thought revolving through my head, over and over: 'Please, God, leave her alone tonight, please.'

CHAPTER TWENTY-FIVE

A LESSON IN RELATIVITY

I worked late, running the seven different long and detailed searches on the whole family, looking for anything, no matter how subtle, that would tell me to run round to Chloe's house and scoop her up in my arms.

'Come on, Merlin,' I said, looking intently into the screen as the office cleaners worked around me. 'Don't let me down.'

Nothing came up.

I checked again, this time looking at the extended family.

Ella sat in a pub with her friends, not drinking, not talking.

'What's up with you?' one of them asked. 'You never come out these days and when you do you don't say anything.'

'Yeah, this is supposed to take your mind off work,' said another.

'Then why is it all you talk about are your jobs?' Ella was shocked at herself. 'I'm sorry, I shouldn't have said that, I know you're trying to help. I have to go home, sorry.'

As a cop I was well used to waiting, whether for a drugs courier, or for the cry of 'Go, go go!' to raid a crack house, but this was agony.

I sat up in bed. Is it time? I looked over at the clock. 3 a.m.

My eyes were open long before the six o'clock alarm buzzed. I swung my arm, trying to hit the off-button without looking. Kiss FM started playing. If that didn't wake you up, then nothing would. I switched it off, swung my legs off the bed, sat up and yawned.

'You were back late last night,' Mrs Keeble said. 'Difficult case?'

I nodded, yawning again. 'That obvious?' I said eventually.

'God, you look shattered. You'd never think you'd just had a break.'

A commotion erupted downstairs. The boys were up. Whenever Mrs Keeble knew I was in the middle of a 'bad one', she did her best to make sure the boys were only mildly manic throughout breakfast.

I felt as though I was stuck in a trance while the morning's chaos whirled around me at high speed. The builders who were extending the house we were living in showed up early for their morning brew.

The marriages of so many detectives my age had broken under the strain of the job. Many cops I knew, whether working on drugs, robbery, burglary or murder squads, became so absorbed by their work that it took over their life. If anything, working in child protection had helped make my marriage stronger. After nearly twenty years in the job, as I approached forty, I still woke up and thanked the stars that I had three amazing kids and a beautiful, patient wife. I also made sure to treasure every moment I had with them.

That morning, however, I was desperate to get away. Tanked up on coffee, I slipped into the Fiesta and drove straight down to the school, arriving at 8 a.m.

'Goodness, you look worse than I feel,' Ella said, handing me a cup of coffee in a white Styrofoam cup. 'Working man's choice,' she told me with a smile.

I took it gratefully. 'Thanks, Ella.'

Sylvia was waiting for us. She'd cleared her desk so we would have her for the whole day. She was the key. We were relying on her to get Chloe to talk to us, so that we could make her safe.

'Good morning,' she said. 'Hardly slept a wink last night.'

We shook hands. 'Thank you for doing this,' I said.

'It's the least I can do. A teacher on the gate is going to call me as soon as Chloe arrives and then I'll intercept her before she gets to her classroom. If you wait in the meeting room across the hall, I'll call you in when Chloe's ready.'

'Let's hope she'll want to work with us,' Ella said.

'I think she will. She doesn't know what to do about the baby and is very frightened of her father. If she isn't ready, I'll send her back to her class, shall I?'

I didn't want to think about that option but Sylvia was quite right. We couldn't force Chloe to tell us anything if she didn't want to.

'I've told all her teachers, no questions. They know something's up but they don't know the details. That's what you wanted, wasn't it?'

'Perfect,' I said. 'Thank you so much.'

'Not at all. That was the easy part. Now comes the difficult bit.'

Ella and I waited in the small conference room. Nothing to do but wait – and make small talk.

'So, how are things?' I asked, placing my empty coffee cup on the table.

Ella shrugged. 'With work? It's a love-hate relationship at the moment.'

'Any plans to move up the ladder?'

Ella laughed. 'Management? Me? Not a chance! Besides, the fact is it's far too soon, I want to make decisions without thinking about cost and politics. At the moment I can ask for as many foster placements as I want while my manager has to deal with the flak. She's in her office at nine o'clock most nights and always arguing with her bosses over our placement costs. I would hate that.

'Rightly or wrongly, the popular view is that child protection is the most high-status job in social care, so the powers that be watch it very closely. Our managers are under enormous pressure but there are plenty of points to be won by those on the civil service promotional trail.

'I'd welcome the extra money of course, but I know that in the end, it's just not worth it. Management is not for me. There's a man, Gary, who started not long after I did. He's the opposite and has been clearing cases like there's no tomorrow. He thinks about nothing but promotion.'

I smiled. 'A real teacher's pet. We have them in the police too.'

'I don't know how he does it,' Ella continued. 'He's been taking on loads of cases, even the most involved and problematic ones – long-term jobs like Mandy, you remember her?'

'Of course I remember Mandy, the mother with too much love for her male "friends".'

'Gary took her case over from me after you kept tying me up with all these urgent jobs.'

I smiled apologetically.

'Don't worry, it's great working with you, and cops in general. But I think Gary's been to see Mandy just once in two months and has somehow convinced my boss that she doesn't need us any more. My boss is happy. She sees one less file, money saved, gives Gary another gold star. I'm not so sure. I think I should go and see Mandy for myself.'

'Perhaps she's taken the two hundred pounds for the op.'

'Don't even joke about that,' Ella said crossly.

'Any luck with the blind dates yet?' I asked, changing the subject.

'God, no!' Ella exclaimed in a short laugh. 'I don't know how I let them but my friends talked me into trying speed dating.'

'No good?'

'Why is it everyone wants to know what you do, not who you are?'

I shrugged.

'One bloke asked me what I did for a living and so I told him. Completely dried up. Didn't have a clue what to say to me after that. Didn't even pretend. I didn't make it on to any speed dating bachelor's favourite list. Do you have any idea how humiliating that was? I mean, am I really that bad?'

'Not at all,' I said quickly.

The door opened. It was Sylvia.

We got to our feet.

'There's someone who wants to see you,' Sylvia said, breaking into a gentle smile.

The first flood of relief. We've got her. We exchanged grateful glances.

'Thank you, Sylvia,' I said as we crossed the hall.

She nodded. 'Let's just make her safe, right?'

I looked at the door. Behind it was a child whose life was in unimaginable turmoil. I looked at Ella who nodded, ready.

Deep breath. Hand on the handle, twist, open and in we go.

Chloe was sitting on a chair in the middle of the office, hands in her lap. She looked calm. After introducing ourselves and sitting down, I spoke.

'Chloe, do you know why Sylvia called us?'

She nodded. 'Yes.'

'I think you have something to tell us.'

There was a pause as Chloe turned her gaze to the floor.

Another wait. This was an unpleasant lesson in Einstein's Theory of Relativity. Although we didn't have to sit through the night this time, the second hand on the wall clock over the desk ticked loudly and slowly while we waited for Chloe to speak, as if it were encountering unusual resistance.

I waited. I had to be careful. I wanted so much to hear the magic words but I couldn't force Chloe to speak them. Putting words into a child's mouth is like handing their abuser a get-out-of-jail-free card. If Chloe said what I hoped, then I had two questions. Once they'd been answered we'd stop talking and everything else would be done on video.

The air buzzed with tension as we willed Chloe to say the words. Tick, tick, T-ick went the second hand.

Chloe looked up. 'My dad's got me pregnant.' She began to cry.

Sylvia moved her chair close and put her arm around her. Chloe's sobs came with the horror and relief of sharing the reality of her situation with strangers – strangers that were at least in a position to help. Trusting us with this was so brave, but I couldn't say so, not yet.

The tension flowed out from us all. Ella looked like she'd stopped breathing. We shifted and stretched slightly.

There's some debate on what to do next. Some officers would stop there and go straight to a memorandum interview. I can't say who's right or wrong but I have a different view. This was rape, a serious arrestable offence. In my opinion it's in the child's best interest that I do everything to get any forensic evidence as quickly as possible. It might be that I would be able to spare Chloe a trial and protect other children. I always wrote down everything that was said.

We let Chloe cry until she eventually caught her breath.

'All right?' Sylvia said.

Chloe nodded.

I wanted to tell her it was going to be OK, that I was going to make her and her baby safe, find her dad and lock him up. For now I had to keep it straightforward and professional.

As softly as I could, I asked the question we'd lost most sleep over.

'When was the last time it happened?'

Time slowed again.

If it had happened recently, i.e. within seven days, then I needed to grab the evidence and get a forensic strategy going. If Chloe had had sex last night, then her body was a crime scene and I would hate myself for having made her wait.

'About two weeks ago.'

Tension flowed out of us all. I sagged slightly with relief.

One last question: 'Is anyone else at risk?'

'I'm not sure.'

That didn't tell me anything, but as far as this line of questioning was concerned, we were done.

I breathed out. 'Chloe, thank you very much for answering my questions. You have been very, very brave, well done.'

She nodded, staying silent.

I had the facts, now it was time to execute our strategy. Chloe and her sister would be taken into police protection. I hoped to God that her sister hadn't been abused last night. We would find out soon enough. If she had then she'd be a 'scene'.

Ella and I explained what would happen at the interview and the medical exam. What I didn't explain at this point was that if the dad denied it, we wouldn't be able to determine the father of the child until after the birth.

Her father was at work. Perfect. This would give us valuable time to crack on.

Chloe was quiet on the journey to the police station. The end of term was just a week away. My God, that had been close. While other children might be looking forward to family trips to Thorpe Park or Southend, Chloe was about to have an incredibly tough time. We tried to chat, to keep her talking.

'What would you like us to do about your mum?'

'I want to see her. Can she be with me?'

We simply didn't know how her mum would take the news but we would respect Chloe's choice.

'No problem,' I said. 'Is it OK if I go around to your home and talk to her there first?'

Chloe nodded.

Once we were at the suite, Ella and I had a quick word in private.

'If you can show Chloe around the suite, I'll go and fetch Mum. It'll give me a chance to assess her before we let them be together.'

There was a real danger that Chloe's mum would defend her husband and say that Chloe was lying, that it was Chloe's boyfriend or someone else, anyone else, who had got her pregnant.

One wrong word to fragile Chloe and I was certain she would fall apart. She could still easily retract everything she'd told us and if we failed to gather any evidence, then both Chloe and her sister would end up back in the care of their abuser. Mum might even try and warn Dad, giving him a chance to flee or to prepare his story before I got to him. But a little girl wanted her mum. What else could I do? After all, if her mum supported her, then this would be a huge help in getting Chloe through the investigation.

Another hot day. The square, around the corner from Columbia Road's famous flower market, was full of trendy locals reading paperbacks, mums and toddlers and a pair of unemployed older gentlemen enjoying their first strong lager of the morning.

The terraced houses that surrounded the little green square were modest but sold for a small fortune. Two-bed flats on Columbia Road itself went for close to half a million pounds. Not all the families were wealthy though, some had moved here before the insane property boom and wouldn't sell for anything. This was their home.

I found the house. It looked recently redeveloped; the bricks had been repointed and the door still smelled of fresh paint. I pushed the buzzer and stepped back.

A woman opened the door. She was wearing a tracksuit and holding a lit cigarette in her left hand. Her long dark hair was tied up into a pineapple. She crossed her arms and looked me up and down.

'Detective Sergeant Harry Keeble,' I said, showing her my warrant card. 'May I come in?'

She studied it carefully before showing me into the kitchen. OK, here we go. I'm here with the news no mother would ever want to hear. I wanted to soften the blow but I had to be careful. I'd learned from delivering 'death messages' to people as a young constable that if you're too sensitive, you can end up leaving people confused, trying to work out what you mean. You have to be clear, even though it's not easy, especially when you're nervous.

Standing over the table in the small kitchen with a low ceiling, I delivered the message.

'Chloe is at the police station,' I said. 'She's told us that she is pregnant by her father.'

I held my breath, waiting for the response. Her eyes bored into me. I would give her all the time she wanted. Eventually, she broke eye contact, looked down at the ashtray and stubbed out her cigarette, very hard.

'Let's go,' she said quietly.

I just had time to text Ella to alert her that we were on our way. She needed to make sure Chloe didn't see her mum straight away when I brought her into the suite.

Chloe's mum said nothing. A hard look darkened her face. Was she still absorbing what I'd said? Was she in shock? Didn't she want to ask me a question? I decided to let the silence do its work. We arrived ten minutes later and I showed her through to the family room.

'I'll be back in a minute,' I said.

She nodded, her face expressionless.

I joined Ella in the interview room, where Chloe was waiting. I smiled at Chloe, who was staring into a can of coke.

I turned to Ella and said quietly, 'Mum didn't say much. I can't gauge it.'

'I want to see my mum.'

Oh, Christ, here we go, I thought. While it may be in the child's best interests to be with her mum at a time like this, I was still worried about Mum's reaction.

'Let's go, then.'

The family room was just around the corner from the interview room. In twenty seconds I'd know whether the case would collapse, leaving it impossible to manage the safety of Chloe, her baby and her sister.

I nervously pressed down on the door handle to the family room. As the door clicked and opened, I saw Chloe's mum on the sofa.

Chloe followed me into the room.

My mouth was dry.

Mum stood up. I stepped out of the way, but not too much, just in case. One wrong word and I would have to separate them.

Chloe's mum's eyes were firmly fixed on her daughter. She lifted her arms, her face melted into sadness.

'Oh Chloe, my darling,' she cried out, enveloping her daughter in her arms. I stood there, watching, frozen in time as they cried together.

'My precious, darling child, why didn't you tell me?'

*

It was six o'clock on an August evening and the orange light of the sunset was being sliced by the blinds, which threw long shadows across the office. The radio was on, a London station that had been playing mellow summer tunes.

The office was deserted, save for Rob and me. We'd had a chat about Ella and I'd told Rob about her fine performance in recent weeks. 'I really didn't need to be there,' I'd said, referring to our encounter with the Jewish family. 'She had control of the situation and knew exactly which way to steer it. And Chloe's case was one of the toughest Ella has faced so far and she handled it superbly. Of course, I can't tell what's in her mind, though.'

Now Rob was reading yet another lengthy report that needed his approval, and I was battling my way through paperwork, trying to clear as much as possible, so I'd be ready for the fresh batch of children's files that would arrive on my desk in the morning. I stopped writing and shook my hand, trying to ease the constant ache caused by all this sudden penwork. I checked my watch. I had a few more minutes before I had to leave for a family appointment, so bent over the files once again.

My phone started ringing. Damn.

It was Chloe's mum, Margaret.

'Hi, Margaret,' I said warmly, 'how are you? How's Chloe?'

Once she had comforted Chloe, Margaret had opened up to us. There was no question of her not believing her daughter or defending Chloe's dad. She was frank and open about her relationship with her husband, as well as her own feelings of guilt.

Chloe – along with her sister – was safe with grandparents in the Essex countryside. Chloe's sister had not been raped. Dad had been arrested and bailed but banned from visiting the family home until the trial.

Of course, although this was the best possible outcome, Chloe's family were going through hell. It's hard enough for a mum to hear the words, 'I'm pregnant,' from a teenage daughter, let alone to be told she'd been raped and that her husband was the father.

'I just needed to talk,' Margaret said. 'I have these thoughts going around and around my mind and I can't tell anyone. My parents are great but only to a certain point you know? It's like they shut their ears when I want to broach the difficult topics.'

Margaret's initial response had been to tell Chloe to have an abortion. Now she wasn't sure whether by making the decision for Chloe, she had done the right thing. The abortion was due to take place soon.

I didn't have the answers but at least I was able to listen and understand, let Margaret voice the feelings swarming through her mind, achieve a sense of order. By the time we said our good-byes the phone receiver was slightly wet as I realised I'd been pushing it too hard against my ear. I'd been completely immersed.

Rob stared at me over his glasses and smiled. 'In this line of work there's no such thing as answering the phone in passing. And talking of phone behaviour,' he added, 'I do wish you'd learn to answer your mobile more quickly.'

The light had faded, the shadows deepened. I looked at the clock. We'd been talking for an hour.

'Oh no.'

'What is it?' he asked.

'I'm late for my own birthday dinner!' I said, leaving my files where they were as I sprinted out.

CHAPTER TWENTY-SIX

SECOND TIME AROUND

Blood rushed to Dave's head, the buzzing in his ears grew until the room vanished and he was back. Wallpaper from a different decade. A carpet-less floor. The plastic sofa that squeaked every time you moved. No TV, just a record player and radio.

A metallic fumbling, the key rattling against the lock, then dropped. Little Dave, hoping his dad was too drunk to open it. The keys jangling as Dad picked them up, trying again. Mum's terror-filled eyes staring at the door, unable to look away.

And suddenly Dad was in, swearing, grabbing Mum by the arm, punching her in the head. Mum screaming, Dave crying, wetting himself on the sofa in terror, streams of urine flowing off onto the floor, his dad banging Mum's head against the wall, dragging her by the hair into the bedroom.

Ella and I were perched on the edge of a sofa, a couple in their late twenties in front of us. The mum, Charlotte, was red-eyed and wringing her hands. She was a huge woman. Her XXL clothes stretched in desperation to contain her.

Dave, the dad, was smaller but still chubby, balding and

looked like he was on another planet. He stared straight through me with an almost unblinking thousand-yard stare. He seemed so far gone that I wondered whether he was mentally ill.

'It's about this morning isn't it?' Charlotte asked nervously.

Miss Jones was on playground duty. She watched as Charlotte had marched, well, waddled really, up to the school in her pyjamas, five-year-old George and six-year-old Helen struggling to keep up. The other parents, having dropped off their children on time, walked in the opposite direction, looking over their shoulders as Charlotte huffed past; all great material for gossip and giggles later on.

Miss Jones was not amused, however. She'd seen the occasional late parent drop off their children while still in their pyjamas, but from the safety of their car. Charlotte was the first one Miss Jones had seen who had dared to do this on foot.

Miss Jones was a deputy head with extremely high standards. She was very proud of the improvements she'd helped achieve in this once troubled inner-city school. Parents like Charlotte, who had been late many times, needed a firm hand, she believed. Miss Jones had already taken the trouble to warn Charlotte personally the last time this had happened.

Miss Jones watched from the office as Charlotte pushed the school gate's buzzer. She got up and started walking to the gate to let George and Helen in and to quickly lecture Charlotte on her habitual lateness.

George was a nice boy but difficult and easily distracted. Academically, he was bottom of the class. He simply couldn't focus on one thing for more than a minute at a time. Miss Jones had seen it herself when she'd taught his class after the teacher had fallen sick. He'd quickly got bored with the abacus and started throwing paper balls across the classroom before seeing how far he could push his chair back without tipping over.

Moments later he had crashed to the floor, bringing the lesson to a halt.

Miss Jones wished she could stop Charlotte from coming to school. It was embarrassing. She looked ridiculous for a start, dressed like that. What kind of place did Charlotte think the school was? Miss Jones thought all this as she strode across the playground at top speed, as quickly as her knee-length skirt would allow. Everything was forgotten, however, when she heard Charlotte screaming.

'You little bastard!'

Miss Jones was so stunned she missed her stride and almost tripped. She'd never seen anything like it before. Charlotte was hitting George repeatedly on the head. Parents and passers-by had turned and were watching, frozen in shock.

Miss Jones started to run.

A policeman was at the door.

'Is your mum in, son?'

'He's a nice lad,' the copper said when Mum was in the hallway. 'How old?'

'Ten,' Mum said.

'What happened to your face?'

'Fell down the stairs, didn't I?'

'The neighbours called us; said your husband was beating you.'

'Nonsense.'

The copper looked down the hall at Dave.

'Think of the boy,' he said. 'You might be able to take it but he won't.'

'Oh yeah, and what are you gonna do? Lock him up like you said you were the last time? You want to know what happened when he got back?'

'Listen, we can help.'

'If word gets back that you've – look, are we done here?'

The door closed. The policeman's shadow hovered for a moment, then vanished.

'I was really stressed, you know?' Charlotte said. 'It's my time of the month. And Georgie's been diagnosed with ADHD but Dave and me didn't want him taking pills.

'He'd been playing up all morning; he didn't wanna get dressed, screaming about his cereal, fighting with his sister. I just hadn't had time to get dressed. I'd been warned so often about being late for school I just got them ready and went as I was. I didn't want to risk the school refusing us in future. It's a good place, hard to get into and we really appreciate it, don't we, Dave?'

Dave grunted.

'I know what the other mums think of me, no makeup, overweight, in a mess, a pyjama parent. I know they take the mick but I'm at me wits' end, I really am. I feel like I've given up, let meself go completely. I wasn't always this size, was I, Dave?'

Another grunt.

'It's only a short walk but I was already late and I had to practically drag Georgie the whole way. He kicked, cried and teased his sis. Then when I got there, walking past all the mums, I heard one of them whisper, "What's the matter with her?" By the time I was at the school gate I was sweating. We was out of paracetamol so I was in agony. I just stared dead ahead and focused on the gate. Just get them in and go, was all I could think.'

Charlotte paused.

'And then what happened?' Ella asked.

We knew the answer to this, of course; the school had been our first port of call after Miss Jones reported the crime.

'The gate was locked. I couldn't believe I was late, after all that. I was a wreck. I saw the deputy head, Miss Jones. I knew her from last time; she made me feel like a five-year-old, reminded me of my old English teacher, she did.'

Tears started to fall.

'Then Georgie kicked Helen and she started crying. I'd just got her cleaned up after the last fight. Then Georgie kicked me. That's when I flipped. I just lost control, I'm sorry, I'm so, so sorry. I love my baby so much.'

Charlotte, clearly ashamed, knowing she was in serious trouble, ran away before Miss Jones reached the gate.

We knew she hadn't hit Georgie hard, he had no injuries, no bruising and Charlotte and her family weren't known to us. Of course, the problem was that she might have been lying. For all we knew she might have beaten Georgie every day and this would explain his erratic school behaviour; that the diagnosis of Attention Deficit Hyperactivity Disorder was a smoke-screen.

I glanced at Ella. We needed to talk about this in private. We should interview Georgie and Helen. It would be an intrusion, an upsetting experience, but vital for us to help make sure the kids were safe.

In the meantime, Dave was now really staring at me. What was his problem? A silence had fallen as Charlotte finished her story and fought to control her crying. There'd been no comfort from Dave, no arm round the shoulder, offer of tea, a fag or a tissue, just a cold hard stare, which was now directed at me.

It was tempting to ask him directly what his problem was, but I knew the value of silence. Some cops can't stand it and fill the void with any old nonsense, thinking that if the witness or suspect isn't talking then they're not doing a good job. Silence draws people out into the open. Someone has to fill it. The trick is not to be the first. I kept quiet, letting the pressure build.

Obviously Ella, being new, wasn't aware of this tactic. Would she be able to read the situation, I wondered? I let the silence roll on, the pressure increasing with each passing second.

Still nobody spoke. Still Dave stared.

I looked back at him, waiting.

Dave snapped. He leaped to his feet and thrust out his arm, pointing straight at me.

'Where the fuck were you?'

I stayed perfectly still. Ella looked at me in surprise. I had no idea what Dave was talking about, so stayed silent.

'Where the fuck *were* you?' Louder this time, Dave's face was red and full of hatred.

Charlotte reached up towards him. 'Dave ... not now ...'

He batted her hand away.

'Where the fuck were you when Mum was having her head bashed against the wall? Where the fuck were you when my dad dragged her up the stairs and fucking raped her? I had to listen to him doing that over and over again, week after week. Where the fuck were you?'

Dave was shaking with rage. He repeated the sentence, pausing after each word. 'Where – the – fuck – were – you?'

Judgement time. Was I about to be smacked in the mouth? Or was Dave, now he'd said his piece, simply going to sit down again? Or was he about to have a total breakdown?

I'd made pre-emptive strikes in the past; it's impossible to get it right every time. Although we are 'trained and allowed' to do this, most cops are reluctant to try anything pre-emptive these days. This is partly thanks to the tragic death of Ian Tomlinson, the 47-year-old newspaper seller who collapsed and died minutes after being struck with a baton and pushed to the ground by a PC during the G20 protests in 2010.

Even if you make a wrong decision, it doesn't necessarily mean that it was a bad decision. The worst thing is to make no decision at all. I searched Dave's face, looking for micro-expressions that might suggest he was about to get physical. I looked into his eyes and saw the terror of a little boy. I had done something to bring out a past trauma.

'Dave, it's OK,' I said calmly. 'Tell me what happened.'

'The neighbours called you. At first Mum denied it was happening. Then, when the beatings got worse, she called you, many times. And what did you fuckers do? Nothing. Fuck all! For three years I watched my mum get battered and you did nothing, now you're all over us for this shit. George is a nightmare, but we love him, very much, but it's hard you know, really hard.'

Dave sat down, put his head in his hands and started to weep. Charlotte put a heavy arm across his shoulders.

'OK,' I said, getting up. 'Ella and I need to have a word in private.'

'That was pretty intense,' Ella said. 'You've just been used as an emotional punchbag. My turn to ask you for once. Are you OK?'

I let out a long breath and tried to relax my neck and shoulders.

'Yes, thank you. I'm just glad I made the right call and didn't arrest him before he'd finished.'

I needed to recover quickly so we could move things on. The police's failure to protect Dave had left him scarred and full of hatred. OK, so we didn't punch and kick his mother, and she had resisted the police's help, but we clearly didn't do enough for Dave.

Detectives today often find themselves paying for the past crimes of their police forebears. Our slip-ups, mistakes, abuses always come back to us in the end, whether it's a young man falsely arrested for drug dealing, or someone on the receiving end of racism or verbal abuse, or someone whose cries for help were ignored.

One of the worst cases of paying for the past I knew of was that of a teenage boy who lived in Broadwater Farm during the time of the riots. Along with five others, he was arrested for the murder of PC Keith Blakelock. He was held for days without access to parents or solicitors and his treatment gave the judge, Mr Justice Hodgson, 'sleepless nights'. With no evidence, apart from officers' shaky testimony, the teenager was freed without any charge.[1]

He went on to become one of London's most violent drug dealers whose speciality was torturing rivals until they told him where their stash and cash was hidden. Although he may have been no angel to start with, his alleged abuse at the hands of the police and the resulting media outcry only helped to push him into the life of an outlaw.

'So, what next?' Ella said.

'We open two investigations,' I said.

'Two?'

'Yes. We're going to interview Georgie. My gut is telling me that Charlotte is telling the truth, but we have to be certain.'

'Agreed,' Ella said, 'and the second?'

'I'm going to ask Dave if he'd like to come in and talk about what happened to him,' I said. 'Perhaps it's too late; the damage has certainly been done, but if I take him seriously now, perhaps he'll be able to move on with his life.

'I think that because of what's happened to him he's afraid to discipline Georgie or deal with his wife's problems. Call me an optimistic fool, but I've seen this approach work before. Perhaps it will help Dave become a more attentive father and husband, and help Charlotte with Georgie.'

Ella nodded.

'And Dave's done me a favour,' I added ruefully.

'What's that?'

'He's reminded me of something,' I said, 'or rather someone. Someone who deserves a visit.'

*

'Why didn't I speak to her sooner?' Sylvia asked.

Because Chloe and her sister hadn't been abused the night we decided to wait, Ella and I had escaped the guilt. Sylvia, on the other hand, hadn't.

'Chloe was in my class two weeks ago, the day after she said she was last raped. I should have picked up on it.'

Dealing with Dave had made me think of Sylvia. Her trauma was different but the emotions were similar. Feelings of helplessness and hopelessness, coupled with guilt and anger – anger at herself, at Chloe's father and at us for putting her through the unexpected agony of becoming a tool in our investigation.

'I keep asking myself: why didn't I do something sooner? It had been going on for months. I knew something was wrong. And yet I let Chloe be. I don't know why.'

There was no answer. Sylvia had done all that she should have. We certainly couldn't have asked for more but Sylvia expected more of herself, as would I, if I were in her position.

I had come to see Sylvia, not only to check that she was OK, but to update her on Chloe's case. Summer term had ended and the kids were on holiday but, as the Head of Year, Sylvia still had plenty on her plate. She'd agreed to see me late in the afternoon. She stirred her freshly sugared tea as I told her that our decisions had paid off. Chloe and her sister were safe.

'Will Chloe be able to return to this school?' she asked.

I shrugged. 'I don't know. It looks unlikely. She's certainly going to need a lot of time out while all this is dealt with. But don't worry too much. She's young and smart, she can get through this. Apart from her mum and sister, there will be people on hand to help her rebuild her life.'

'I wish I could tell her I was sorry,' Sylvia said. 'For not helping sooner. It's made me wonder how many others I've missed over the years. I've been revisiting classrooms from the past, looking for children like Chloe.'

'Self-torture really isn't the way forward,' I said.

By the time I left I wasn't sure if my visit had been useful or not. We walked past empty classrooms, paintings and school projects still pinned to various walls and positioned on display tables in the corridors.

'Another year done,' Sylvia said with a sigh. 'I remember them all, but this one's definitely going to take prominence.'

'Remember it for the right reasons, Sylvia,' I said. 'Chloe opened up to you because she trusted you and no one else. You saved Chloe from more abuse. God knows what she would have gone through at home if her father had found out. I know there are no winners in this sort of situation but, as far as I can see, you're bloody good at what you do and this shouldn't stop you from continuing to do an amazing job.'

Sylvia smiled. 'You're right of course. The head says one thing but the heart says another, though, doesn't it?'

I smiled back and shook her hand. 'Promise me you'll enjoy the summer break.'

'All right, thanks, Harry.'

'You too, Sylvia. See you.'

I climbed into my oven-hot car, performed the usual frantic routine of winding down the windows as quickly as possible and drove back to the office in the late afternoon sun.

CHAPTER TWENTY-SEVEN

MOTHER NATURE'S DAY OFF

Rob frowned at me.

'What's wrong?' I asked.

'You're tidying up your desk, putting pens into the pen pot, staples into your stapler and those folders look like they're in order. Almost.'

'And?'

'You never tidy up. What's wrong?'

Word had reached me that Leigh was downstairs and that Sarah was looking after her.

Certain cases stay with us. They fade over time but every now and then the memories return; sometimes they're like a kick in the stomach. It was the end of the day. Time to head home. But I was anxious not to meet Leigh again.

I shrugged at Rob. 'Even I have to tidy up sometimes.'

Rob looked at me disbelievingly. His phone rang. He left me to my pointless tasks, until I thought Leigh must have finished and it was safe to leave. I took the lift down to the ground floor but instead of taking the shortest route, which was through our suite, I went via the canteen.

Many of the tables were full. Most of the officers were simply on their 'grub' breaks, making for a jolly atmosphere. A group of detectives just starting their late shift were eating all-day breakfasts while debating what to do with all the prisoners that were in the 'bin'. Uniformed officers were snatching a quick Coke and ham roll while writing up arrest notes for their 'body' while several civilian staff flicked through magazines, reports or files.

I looked through the canteen's large windows. It was another beautiful late summer's evening. The muggy London heat was fading and the sun, sinking fast through the horizon's smog, cast a soft golden light on the streets outside, making Stoke Newington look, well, *almost* pretty.

A female uniformed officer burst out laughing. A pulse of jealousy passed through me. I can't do that, I thought. I am a cop, just like her, but I can't do that.

I reached the other side of the canteen, left the building and hurried across the car park, preoccupied with my thoughts. I hurried towards the gate, keen to get into open space, away from the station, perhaps crossing the park, some breathing space. I twisted the silver handle on the huge green security gate, pushed it open a crack, slipped through and turned right down Victoria Grove. Ahead was the park and then my car. Sanctuary.

Leigh's daughter, Nicola, was fourteen when her stepfather, Terry, had started abusing her. Although not strictly a paedophile, as Nicola was fourteen, he had taken the textbook approach in the lead-up to the abuse.

First, he identified a vulnerability. Nicola's mum didn't know her daughter smoked. Terry caught her when he turned up early to collect Nicola from a party. He knew Nicola would be scared about her mother's reaction and he used this fear, pushed it as far as he could, and when her fear was at its height, he 'rescued' her.

He wouldn't tell.

He was a friend.

He could be trusted.

Terry kept looking for another opportunity, a lever with which he could ease Nicola towards his evil aim. He searched her handbag and went through her phone whenever she was in the shower. It took him about two months to find it.

A pack of three.

Terry's delight must have been almost uncontrollable. His patience had been rewarded with a huge prize. He put the condoms back. Terry then picked up the home phone and rang Nicola's mobile, just once. The unanswered number unknown; a record for all to see.

Nicola was coming down the hall when she saw her stepfather, screwdriver in hand, at her doorway. She was wrapped up in a towel, a second towel coiled around her head and her clothes bundled up in her arms. When she saw Terry she jumped in surprise and awkwardly pushed her knickers out of sight. She was simply embarrassed, not threatened.

'We need to talk,' Terry told her, stepping into her room.

Nicola followed him.

'I was going to fix your curtain rail when your phone rang, I went to answer it for you, but I saw these. I'm shocked, Nicola.'

'I haven't actually—'

Before she could explain, Terry released a wave of understanding and empathy, quickly followed by a statement of the 'trouble' she'd be in if her mum found out. Terry took Nicola up and down on a roller coaster of fear and uncertainty as he 'agonised' about what he should do, before he proved once again that he was a friend, who really understood her, supported her and was there to see her through the dangers ahead.

Terry began to exploit his prize over the next few weeks. As per the manual of child abuse, he started with small infractions of personal space, before 'accidental' touching, then friendly purposeful touching and finally inappropriate stroking. To Nicola, this progression was barely obvious until Terry became overtly sexual.

She pushed away the thoughts that told her she was being sexually abused. She did not, would not, believe it was happening. But she couldn't push away the fear, which was forever present and never more so than when Terry was climbing the stairs to the bedroom. Somehow Nicola lived with the fear and struggled through each day.

The longer the abuse went on, as the times Terry climbed the stairs with sex on his mind multiplied into a countless blur, Nicola found it more and more difficult to tell someone what was happening.

She worried that her mum wouldn't believe her, that Mum would say she had gone to bed willingly with Terry, that Nicola was the villain for stealing her mum's boyfriend.

The fact that Nicola was only fourteen and completely innocent didn't enter her mind. Not many fourteen-year-olds think of themselves as a 'child'. They yearn for adulthood; this yearning can have an unpleasant side effect.

Nicola lived a lie; an existence that left her constantly sick with anxiety. Sick with disgust and sick with the fear of her mother blaming her, and sick of life. The symptoms were seen by her mother, her friends and her teachers but were dismissed as being the result of 'hormones' or 'being a teenager'.

Nicola didn't start drinking or self-harming. Instead she found the courage to step forward. One evening she called the National Society for the Prevention of Cruelty to Children, who met up with her the following lunchtime.

By 3 p.m. she was sitting in our memorandum suite at Stoke Newington Police Station, her mum at her side. Leigh left more of an impression on me than her daughter. She was well presented, articulate, intelligent and movie-star beautiful. Her subtle designer clothes were matched with just a touch of makeup. She said all the right things.

'Tell them everything that happened, darling,' she encouraged.

While readers of a transcript of the interview would nominate Leigh for Mum-of-the-Year, something was missing in real life.

Something which, to me at least, was plain.

Disbelief.

Leigh was behaving like a professional. She knew what she needed to say and what we needed to hear, based on what her daughter was saying. She was doing what she had to do, so it would be over as soon as possible and we could all go home.

There was a coldness in Leigh, which I was certain would be missed by most people. Of most concern to me was whether Nicola would pick up on it. A mother–daughter bond has depths that no professional can reach. Daughters know better than anyone when their mothers say one thing but mean something quite different.

If I could feel it, so surely must Nicola, I thought.

I wasn't able to put my opinion into any police report. The police officer's 'hunch', which was once a useful police tool – when your unconscious analyses your entire history in an instant and screams at you not to believe a victim's statement, or to look under the hi-fi for the stash, or to grab someone's arm before a punch has been thrown – has no place in the modern world.

There was nothing I could do.

Nicola was wringing her hands. No eye contact. Almost from the moment the interview began, Nicola was overwhelmed with emotion and she was soon unable to continue.

Tears made talking impossible. A second attempt the following day also ended in failure. Although Nicola had found the strength to come forward, she couldn't sustain it.

Leigh didn't express a single doubt in her daughter. It came in her body language, the almost unnoticeable coolness. That had been enough to undermine her daughter. Our actions were limited by the failure of the memorandum interview, so we asked Terry to leave the family home, which he did, singing denial all the way.

With no evidence to keep him away, Terry was back soon enough. Nicola, let down by her mum and the police, felt as if her life was in ruins. She moved in with her aunt. Nicola's younger sister Jackie was left behind.

Now Leigh had come back to the police. With Jackie.

The story was the same. This time, however, the mother's belief was genuine.

So why didn't I want to face Leigh? I honestly didn't know. She wasn't the abuser. I would never put my suspicions to her. How could I? What good would it do now? My faith in maternal instinct had taken another hit. We rely too heavily on this instinct. It is supposedly unassailable but sometimes, too often I feel, it fails.

I reached my car and climbed inside. Although it was now evening, my little tin box had as usual trapped the midday heat. I wound down the windows and was about to put on the radio when my phone started to ring. It was Craig.

'Good news, Harry,' he said.

'What is it?'

'We've found Jordan, Demaine's dad. You're going to have to move fast though.'

I started the engine.

'I'm on my way.'

CHAPTER TWENTY-EIGHT

FINDING JORDAN

The monster was in the rear-view mirror. His muscular body, framed in the glass, reminded me of the scarred body map of his four-year-old son.

I tightened my grip on the wheel, turning my knuckles white.

Jordan had parked his BMW around the corner, a tactic used by experienced drug dealers. Cars – particularly sports cars or four-by-fours with personalised number plates – are a major giveaway. A dealer who needs to sweep the scene for cops and rivals parks a street away from the address they're about to visit.

Sure enough, Jordan's streetwise eyes scanned the area; he glanced repeatedly over his shoulder, to the sides, ahead. I stayed perfectly still. He was too tall to see my silhouette through the dirty back window of my run-of-the-mill old grey Fiesta. He drew closer, his reflection no longer fitting the mirror. His designer shirt was ironed and his jeans were hanging low.

I'd arrested dozens like him when I'd led a small drugs squad in Haringey. These men, often raised in Jamaican slums, had fought their way out, terrorising their peers and winning the support of drug lords, before seizing the chance to try their methods in the

UK. Once arrested, many of them were surprisingly pleasant to deal with. Of course, dealing Class-A drugs is reprehensible but a hard life in Jamaica does not necessarily equate to being a hardened criminal – or an idiot. Most of them understood the rules of the game and played along.

That didn't mean they gave up without a fight. They usually resisted arrest and if they were able to escape, they vanished, collected a false passport and jumped on a plane home. I had a feeling that Jordan would not be one of the pleasant ones.

Ten yards. I could see his jewelled watch swinging loosely on his wrist.

Five yards. There was nothing in our intelligence to suggest he was armed, hence my hastily arranged arrest, but the thought he might be carrying skittered across my mind.

Three yards. Now or never.

I threw open the door.

Ella stepped from the street, over the border into the Kinsgmead Estate and walked quickly to Mandy's block. This was an unannounced visit.

Ella had taken a quick look at Mandy's file and had seen that there were no further planned visits from social services. She wanted to double-check, to be certain that Mandy was OK, but had a hard time convincing Siobhan, her manager, who said that Ella had enough to be getting on with.

Ella saw the kids in the stairwell, looked back fearlessly and smiled as she hurried up the steps, one floor, then two, out on to the landing. She found the brown door, tagged in black marker. It was ajar, just like last time. She pushed it open.

'Mandy?'

I leaped out, quickly stretching to my full height. Jordan came to a halt right in front of me, drawing up in surprise. Time slows in these moments and, as our eyes locked, my peripheral vision went into overdrive, watching his hands; will it be fight or flight?

He dropped to his left, away from the car, knees bending, ready to run.

This man was no father. Children were not there to be nurtured, but were simply an extension of his 'pride'. He'd meted out gratuitous violence on his little boy, violence he saw as important to his education as mathematics.

I had my hand on his shoulder before he'd fully turned. I placed a foot behind his right knee and he went down. As he fell and started to struggle, I pulled out my cuffs.

'What the hell is this?' Jordan yelled. 'I got nothin' on me! I ain't done nothin'!'

'My name is Detective Sergeant Harry Keeble from Hackney Child Protection—'

'Child protection?' he shrieked, interrupting me, speaking at a hundred miles an hour. 'What you talking about man? I never hurt my kids? What the fuck?'

I continued, ignoring him, struggling to get the cuffs on. 'I am arresting you for—'

'OI!'

I turned at the shout and saw a tall, thin West Indian man with long dreadlocks jogging towards us.

'What's going on?' he demanded.

I could see a group of men following him across the street. A small crowd had stepped out from a 7–11 and a barber's to see what was going on.

'Oh, great,' I thought.

The people of Hackney generally have two responses to police action. The first is to ignore it, no matter what it is. We could be landing a helicopter in the street and people will still cross the road under it to go to the shop for a packet of biscuits. The second is to immediately get involved as much as humanly possible.

'I'm a police officer and I'm arresting this man. Please stand back.'

'What's he done?' the Rastafarian demanded.

I wasn't about to share that information but Jordan didn't know that. Panic flickered across his eyes. He knew what I wanted him for. He was as guilty as hell. If I explained, then it wouldn't only be his rep that would take a beating.

If I didn't tell them, however, then they might start shouting harassment. Then I'd be in trouble.

'Nah, man,' Jordan said quietly, relaxing enough so I could get the handcuffs on. I helped him up. He turned and looked the Rastafarian in the eye as he spoke. 'It's OK, man, I'll sort it, just go.'

'Mandy?'

Ella stepped into the hall. It was too quiet. Where were the kids? All their stuff was here. The mess was just as it always was. The kitchen still looked like a rampaging bull had cooked dinner. There was still that certain smell.

Ella had a bad feeling.

One hinge on the lounge door had gone and it was propped open wide. Ella walked slowly forward, silent now. She turned the corner.

'Mandy? You there?'

Ella's eyes scanned the lounge, looking for life. Nothing.

The front door slammed.

'Jesus!' she cried, springing forward and turning around all in one movement.

Mandy was there. With all her kids; all noise and action, laughing and yelling. Ella's smile of relief faded when she looked more closely at Mandy.

'Oh, Mandy,' she said despairingly, 'not again.'

*

I whistled a merry tune as I crossed the office and picked up the phone.

'Somebody's in a good mood,' Clara said with a smile.

'Well, Clara,' I said, 'today has had its ups and downs but it's only five o'clock and Jordan's in the bin. And now, before the day is done, I'm going to deal with these.'

I had been locked in battle with the local parking authority over a whole stack of tickets I'd collected in the line of duty and was determined to get them sorted once and for all. Twenty frustrating minutes later, I was on hold and regretting my decision when the line went dead.

'Hello? Hello?' I asked. 'What the hell – those bastards hung up on me!'

Then I turned and saw Clara. Her finger was resting on the connection.

'Oh,' I said, too surprised to say anything else. 'What's up?'

'Someone wants to see you about one of your cases, Harry,' she said quietly. Her expression told me this was important, something game-changing, something I'd been hoping for.

'What about?' I asked, almost in a whisper.

'Uncle Richard.'

Ella's final visit of the day. She pressed the bell, which emitted a happy ding-dong. The house was a pleasant-looking semi on the eastern edge of Hackney, close to Victoria Park.

Michael, the foster father, answered. He was in his forties, dressed in a loose-fitting white T-shirt and dirty blue jeans. He was also covered in sawdust.

'Sorry,' he said with a chuckle, 'I'm attempting a little DIY. She's in her room,' he said. 'Go straight up.'

'Thanks. How is she?'

'She's sad, lonely, but she's a great kid. At the moment she's not been part of normal life long enough to feel that she

belongs here, in London. But after what's happened to her I think she feels that she doesn't belong at home any more either.'

Ella climbed the wooden stairs and stood for a moment in front of the white painted door.

She tapped on the wood.

'Jemi?'

Ella pushed the door open.

Jemi was sitting on the edge of her bed. She was reading *Alice's Adventures in Wonderland*.

'Hi, Jemi, how are you?'

'Fine, thank you,' she replied quietly. Her throat had healed perfectly. Her West African accent made the words sound soft.

Ella reached in her bag and took out the papers that had granted Jemi amnesty. She was innocent, of course, but her entry had been illegal. With her amnesty, Jemi's mother would be able to come and see her daughter. Or, if Jemi wished, she could return to Sierra Leone. It took a while for Ella to explain, so that Jemi first understood and then, secondly, believed her.

Suddenly Jemi was the girl in the picture again. Except this time there were tears of happiness in her eyes.

The end of a court case can sometimes be anticlimactic. Months of preparation, gathering and sorting files, listing and supplying evidence and statements, preparing for cross-examinations, arguments; studying pleas and letting the court's schedule rule your diary and then, in just one short moment, the jury pronounces the result, the judge gives sentence, everyone leaves the courtroom and it's time to box the evidence while wondering whether justice has really been done.

Not today.

Uncle Richard's most recent victim had come forward after Craig and I found and talked to his latest girlfriend, another single mum, about our concerns. When she approached her daughter the truth burst out of her like a river through a broken dam. They came to see us straight away, interrupting my battle with the parking authority.

The abuse was recent enough for forensics to be useful, and Uncle Richard had repeated the modus operandi he'd used on his stepdaughters Amelia, Lucy and Emma to the letter.

And now, here we were, in the Old Bailey.

Compared to the three sisters, Uncle Richard's testimony sounded both fake and weak. When Katherine's carefully selected counsel got him on the stand, it wasn't long before he started sweating.

The counsel played with times, dates, places, actions before unleashing several other questions, questions Uncle Richard couldn't find the answers to, but not because he didn't know what had happened.

Katherine had to fight to keep her courtroom composure once the foreman of the jury had spoken. Her lips wobbled, threatening to reveal her trademark giant smile. When the judge put on his glasses to read his statement and give sentence, she couldn't hold it back and beamed. It was a smile of triumph, satisfaction and relief. Uncle Richard would lose his freedom for twelve years.

Amelia, Lucy and Emma were in shock, the best kind; disbelief that they'd not only had their day in court, but that the court had believed them.

Maybe there aren't any winners in child protection, but it felt damn close that day.

Afterwards, in a private room for witnesses, deep inside the Old Bailey, Katherine and the three girls hugged, their victory tinged by the trauma that had brought them there.

Katherine handed Amelia her dream diary.

'I'll never forget this,' Katherine said, smiling. 'It was an inspiration. I don't think I could have argued as well as I did without it.'

'I don't need it any more,' Amelia said. 'It's in the past now.'

CHAPTER TWENTY-NINE

THE PRESENT MOMENT

I start to fill in the sticky label. It's routine, automatic: date, time, place, etc.

Craig is sitting next to me. A young and attractive solicitor is on the chair opposite. She's uncomfortable.

Mark is next to her. His hands are clasped tightly together; he stares intently as I write. Halfway through I look up at him. Our eyes meet and lock. I take in his pallid white skin and pencil-thin moustache. I manage a weak smile, but only just.

The solicitor, Rebecca, is uncomfortable. Of course, it's strictly formal in front of her client, so no first names. Today we're Ms Downs and DS Keeble. She's not a real solicitor. She's a legal representative, working her way up to solicitor. Few qualified legal eagles will turn out at random hours through the day and night to sit at police station counters with paedophiles, rapists, drug dealers, addicts and drunks.

Come the weekend, if she's not on call, no doubt she'll be downing shots with her upwardly mobile friends, talking about their careers, business trips and deals, how they had a difficult encounter with a client, or what went wrong with their media strategy.

Is Rebecca going to tell them she's helped a guilty child molestor escape prison? Of course not. Perhaps she'll eventually confide in her best friend or in her mum but I suspect not. Rebecca's job requires her to ignore her maternal and moral instincts in the interests of justice. To that extent, she is able to provide her advice with professional pride but personal disgust.

Mark is slowly and gently squeezing his clasped hands together.

'Sign here, please.' I push my pen and exhibit label across. The exhibit label is for the tape.

He unclasps his hands to take the pen and paper. I see the blood return, the whiteness fading. He wipes his palms down on the desk before picking up the pen. The sweat marks on the table evaporate as he signs. He is signing to acknowledge the tapes are his. Two hours of Mark saying nothing but his name and 'No comment'.

Bastard.

He knows. He is on top, in the lead.

I watch him sign. His hand shakes. I want to believe doubt is still in his mind. He cannot be sure my evidence is mortally weak. Can he?

I need to achieve something. Two victims and their mother have to get something from this. If he ever expresses remorse, I won't believe it. Paedophiles love what they do. They believe it is right and 'normal' to have sex with children, even if they're handicapped.

Mark is waiting for me to say the magic words: 'You will be bailed to come back to this police station.' Then Rebecca will nod to him, satisfied that this is proof of our weakness. I can see them talking before the interview. 'Their case is weak,' Rebecca is saying. 'If you say anything it will only help them because they have nothing. Answer every question "No comment" and they won't charge you.'

The irony is that two hours of 'No comments' means he's

guilty. We all know it. Innocent people facing child sexual abuse charges not only talk, they plead with undeniable earnestness; they are sickened by the accusation.

Yes, he's guilty all right, yet, here we are, about to release him back into the community.

I don't say what Mark wants to hear yet. But the moment is drawing near. After that, I will sit down with a mum and her two handicapped girls, who have learning disabilities, to try and explain this. I will dress it up a bit but the message will be clear: 'The man who sexually assaulted you will never be brought to justice.' I'll explain about the 'quality' of the evidence to the mother, but what can I tell the girls?

A man has sexually assaulted them. He will not be punished. What else can they think other than that it's because they don't matter? That they're not important? Mark's sexual intrusion into their lives has already affected their perception of sex; they're uncertain where the boundaries lie.

Mark is making me sick. I've dealt with hundreds of paedophiles who fit the stereotypical model and whom I despise. Nonetheless, I can deal with them in a perfectly professional and friendly manner. But I'm struggling with Mark. The fact we've shared a pen and that I've made him a cup of tea only adds to my nausea.

I feel Craig looking at me. I know it's time to go. I don't trust my stomach. I don't want to make eye contact with anyone. I want to be on my own.

A minute later I'm standing in front of the custody officer, Mark beside me. I force out the words.

'Please can we bail Mark for six weeks for further enquiries?'

Mark is emotionless. I try not to look at him, but can't help it. I feel as though he's taunting me with his lack of interaction. He is resting his hands on the tops of his jeans pockets. He is doing everything the custody officer is asking, but I'm not hearing. I am not even angry. I just feel very, very sick.

'Harry?'

I look up. The desk sergeant is waiting. They all are.

'Right,' I say. 'This way then.'

I show them to the door. I thank Rebecca. I catch her eye. Her look tells me all I need to know. It's not her fault. We are agents of Justice. I nod. She turns, steps out of the door without a goodbye.

I need to take a walk, anywhere. I tell Craig I am off to the cash point.

I step into a sunny Stoke Newington high street, heading towards Church Street. The sun is bright and I squint at the faces of people walking towards me, trying to force my thoughts away from Mark, just for the moment, just for a little while, just until the sickness goes away.

I walk past the first cash machine and keep going, towards Stamford Hill. I feel as though I can keep going for ever, walking, walking, walking, blocking everything out. As long as I keep moving then somehow, everything will be OK.

The tarmac is hot, sticky. Soon I am sweating. People's shadows are harsh, black. The sun ricochets off car and shop windows. I can't stop. I feel as though I'm on a hill and a heavy and unsteady load is sitting on a barrow behind me, pushing me on, down the street. I ease myself into a loop and start curling back. I pass the Volvo garage where the Hasidic Jews buy their cars; Safeways where drug-addicted shoplifters wait for collection; then the Stamford Hill Estate.

I stop. I'm standing in the street, looking across Hackney.

Ella emerges from a newsagents; she's opening a pack of cigarettes. She rummages in her bag and pulls out a plastic lighter.

'Still smoking, then?'

'Oh! Christ, you made me jump. And you sound like my mum. Yes, I'm still smoking. I've just been to see Mandy.'

'How is she?'

'Pregnant.'

'You're joking!'

'Welcome to child protection.'

I smile at the memory of the exact same words I'd said to Ella upon our first meeting and shake my head in despair at Mandy's pregnancy. Ella takes a long drag of her cigarette.

'Did you get Jordan?'

'Yup. Hopefully, now he's locked up, Demaine will forget and stop trying to emulate him.'

'What about all the others we've seen this summer?'

'What do you mean?'

'Aren't you curious? Don't you want to know what happened to your cases? The children we've seen together?'

'I suppose I've become used to the fast pace. I often don't get to find out the ending, what happens once the dust has settled.'

'That's where we come in, while you dash off to the next emergency.'

In many ways this is a blessing, I think to myself. Not all endings are happy ones.

'Well?'

I look at the estate, kids playing in the park in the sunshine, and then back at Ella.

'Of course.'

And she tells me.

Anthony is beginning a new life, perhaps his ultimate future is uncertain, but he is at least safe, while his mother receives treatment in prison for her warped maternal instinct.

After her second 'holiday' in Holloway, Samantha – the woman who left her children home alone – is out with a second chance with Nadia and Aisha.

Cheryl is alone, without alcoholic Sean, whether for good or not, nobody knows. But at least Billy is safe for now.

Jemi the slave-girl is waiting for her flight home. Just a visit. She has dreams of being an English police officer.

Rachel is easing back into her non-virtual world. Mum Melanie is finally paying her attention again, not expecting her to be Mummy's princess.

Chloe is at Grandma's, going on long walks in the country with Mum, her father's child aborted. She is moving on. Her father is a strong but fading memory.

Dave and Charlotte are doing their best with Georgie, which is not brilliant, but at least Miss Jones hasn't witnessed any more pyjama parenting, or felt the need to call us again.

Life isn't perfect. But sometimes, things are better than you think.

Ella drops her cigarette butt and squashes it with her toe. We say goodbye and I start walking. The fever starts to ease; I start coming back down, back to normal with each step.

I see the gleaming glass-fronted building of my police station. Rob is there. Our rock, leading us without fear or prejudice. Clara is sorting our chaotic duty rotas while dealing with half a dozen urgent phone calls. In my mind's eye I see Craig and Sarah standing by the fax machine, new cases rolling through.

I feel as though I've just climbed out of a roller coaster, drained but glad to be safe. The station stands like a comforting parent above me. Its permanence is reassuring. The station isn't going anywhere. Neither are the people inside. Whatever I have to do in my job, I know I can do it.

I smile.

I'm going to go and see the mother and her two children. I will give them all the time they need. I will do everything I can to make things better for them. Then I will go home and be with my family.

I take a deep breath and start to walk again, confidently this time, with purpose.

ACKNOWLEDGEMENTS

I hope that I have done justice to the stories of the abused children featured in this book. Their bravery, along with those adult victims who have confronted their traumatic past, cannot be praised enough.

The UK's social workers have long been given a rough ride by the British media but in my experience Child Social Services have proven, in the main, to be professional, courageous and compassionate – not easy in this line of work.

The Crown Prosecution Service is vital in our never-ending quest for justice. They did a fantastic job supporting many victims and our officers throughout the difficult trials described in this book.

And of course, I salute, as ever, Metropolitan Police Child Protection Teams who perform their difficult and outstanding work every single day of the year.

I have encountered a great many teachers and foster carers who truly are the unsung heroes of child protection. Teachers, who sometimes know their pupils better than anyone, pluck many children at risk straight from the classroom, while foster carers do an incredible job providing these unlucky children with love, security and a chance to heal.

Andrew Lownie, the hardest-working literary agent in the business – andrewlownie.co.uk – is as deserving as always of a special mention for his unstinting and enthusiastic support, counsel and friendship.

Finally, I would like to acknowledge the editorial wizardry and behind-the-scenes work of Kerri Sharp and her team at Simon & Schuster who have, as ever, steered this book through the editorial process with much aplomb.

For those who wish to contact me to discuss any issues raised in this book, then I am available via email: harrykeeble@btinternet.com

END NOTE

If you have been the victim of sexual abuse, whether yesterday or twenty years ago, it's vital to report it. Even if you don't want to follow it up with a police investigation, you hold valuable criminal intelligence that could be used to help protect other children. Also, by coming forward, you will have taken the first step on the road to achieving some kind of closure.

You can do this by contacting your local police (alternatively, this can be done anonymously by calling Crimestoppers), local social services and various voluntary organisations.

You are also more than welcome to approach me directly via my website: harrykeeble.com or via email: harrykeeble@btinternet.com

Crimestoppers: crimestoppers-uk.org, telephone 0800 555 111

Help and information for adults can be found via the National Society for the Prevention of Cruelty to Children (NSPCC): www.nspcc.org.uk, telephone 0808 800 5000

For children see ChildLine: childline.org.uk, telephone 0800 11 11

If you'd like to work in child protection then visit my website: harrykeeble.com

Please support my Facebook campaign: Save our Social Workers

REFERENCES

CHAPTER ONE – WEST IS EAST

1. 'Afghanistan: When Women Set Themselves on Fire', by Abigail Hauslohner, *Time Magazine*, 7 July 2010.

CHAPTER TWO – OPEN HOUSE

1. 'Cooke: The predatory paedophile', BBC News Online, 17 December 1999,
   http://news.bbc.co.uk/1/hi/uk/570385.stm
2. 'Sidney Cooke Exclusive: "British Fritzl" strikes up prison friendship with reviled paedophile', by Jeremy Armstrong, *Daily Mirror*, 15 January 2009.
3. *Out of Sight: NSPCC Report on Child Deaths from Abuse 1973 to 2000*, (Editor) C. Cloke, 2000, p. 73.
4. 'Drug addict sterilised for cash – but can Barbara Harris save our babies?' by Jon Swaine, *Telegraph*, 19 October 2010.

CHAPTER FIVE – NEW YEAR'S HONOURS

1. For an excellent study on interview techniques see: *A Guide to Interviewing Children: essential skills for counsellors, police, lawyers and social workers*, J. Clare Wilson and Martine Powell, Routledge, 2001.

CHAPTER EIGHT – CRUEL AND UNUSUAL

1. *The Best Kept Secret: Mother–Daughter Sexual Abuse*, Julie Brand, M.S., CAPER Consulting, Child Abuse Prevention, Education and Recovery, 2009.
2. *Female Sexual Abusers: Facts and Fiction*, Sherry Ashfield, Lucy Faithfull Foundation, 2011.
3. 'Maternal abusers: underlying concerns for children', J. Turton, *Essex Human Rights Review*, (7) 2010.
4. 'Understanding the Prevalence of Female Interpreted Sexual Abuse and the Impact of That Abuse on Victims', by Jacqui Saradjian, in *Female Sexual Offenders: Theory, Assessment, and Treatment*, Dr Theresa A. Gannon (Editor), Franca Cortoni (Editor), Wiley Blackwell, 2010.
5. *Female Sexual Offenders: Theory, Assessment, and Treatment*, Dr Theresa A. Gannon (Editor), Franca Cortoni (Editor), Wiley Blackwell, 2010, p. 19.
6. Ibid., p. 47.

CHAPTER TWELVE – HOME SCHOOLED

1. 'Teachers "beat and abuse" Muslim children in British Koran classes', by Richard Kerbaj, *Times*, 10 December 2008.

CHAPTER THIRTEEN – A DETECTIVE CALLS

1. 'Britain's "invisible army" of African slaves, by Emily Dugan, *Independent*, 13 August 2007.
2. 'Pastor jailed for trafficking African child "slaves"', BBC News Online, 18 March 2011, http://www.bbc.co.uk/news/uk-england-london-12789690

CHAPTER FOURTEEN – HERE'S TO YOU, MRS ROBINSON

1. Dr Pat Sikes, education lecturer at Sheffield University, has studied interviews between teachers and pupils over a 25-year period and has estimated that as many as 1,500 sexual relationships

could be taking place every year. That would be one in every two or three schools. Sikes has stated that some students are the instigators of these relationships and that in 40 per cent of cases the teacher is a woman.

2. 'Pupil sex row deepens', BBC News Online, 6 February 1999, http://news.bbc.co.uk/1/hi/education/273662.stm
3. 'Dance teacher seduced boy, 15. Jail threat to woman who lured pupil away from his school lessons for visits to the pub and sex', by Tosin Sumaiman, 2 June 2005, and 'Teacher who seduced schoolboy put on sex register', by Simon Freeman, 22 June 2005, both *Times* Online.

CHAPTER SIXTEEN – THE SOCIAL NETWORK

1. 'IPCC launch Ashleigh investigation', by Robin Perrie, *Sun*, 9 March 2010.
2. 'The Predator Fear, Growing Up Online', *Frontline*, PBS, 22 January 2008, http://www.pbs.org/wgbh/pages/frontline/kid-sonline/safe/predator.html
3. 'MSN shuts down its chatrooms', BBC News Online, 24 September 2003,
http://news.bbc.co.uk/1/hi/technology/3133192.stm
4. 'MySpace removes 90,000 sex offenders ... but paedophiles may be turning to Facebook instead', *Daily Mail*, 5 February 2009.

CHAPTER EIGHTEEN – THE ESTATE WE'RE IN

1. *Chavs*, Owen Jones, Verso, 2011, p. 207.
2. *Poor Kids*, BBC1 documentary, 7 June 2011, http://www.bbc.co.uk/programmes/b011vnls#broadcasts
3. 'What children think and feel about growing up poor', BBC News Online, 7 June 2011,
http://www.bbc.co.uk/news/education-13632856
4. 'Single parents, equal families: fact file', Gingerbread, http://www.gingerbread.org.uk/content/365/Gingerbread-Factfile

The poverty line used here is 60 per cent of the median UK income after housing costs have been paid. Below this amount, a household is described as living in income poverty. The poverty line is adjusted to take into account how expenditure needs differ between types of households; 11,615,000 people, or 23 per cent of the English population, live below the poverty line. See Child Poverty Action Group: http://www.cpag.org.uk/povertyfacts/

5. *From Pain to Violence: the traumatic roots of destructiveness*, Felicity de Zulueta, Wiley-Blackwell, 2006, page 228.

6. '"Single parents: you're brilliant" says national charity', 23 September 2010, http://www.gingerbread.org.uk/news/76/Youre-Brilliant

7. 'The single mother's manifesto', by J.K. Rowling, *Times*, 14 April 2010.

8. 'Single parents, equal families: fact file', Gingerbread, http://www.gingerbread.org.uk/content/365/Gingerbread-Factfile

9. 'Transforming Broadwater Farm', by Chirag Trivedi, BBC News Online, October 2005, http://news.bbc.co.uk/1/hi/england/london/4308018.stm

CHAPTER NINETEEN – A DIFFERENT ME

1. **Heshu Yones:**
'Where's the honour in this?' by Rebecca Allison, *Guardian*, 3 October 2003.
'The crimewave that shames the world', by Robert Fisk, *Independent*, 7 September 2010.
'Execute me, pleads Muslim who killed his daughter over her Western lifestyle', by Terri Judd, *Independent*, 30 September 2003.
'Heshu's boyfriend tells of loss', by Rebecca Smith, *Evening Standard*, 30 September 2003.

2. **Caneze Riaz:**
'Father killed family for being too western', by Nigel Bunyan, *Telegraph*, 21 February 2007.

Murder in the Name of Honour: The True Story of One Woman's Heroic Fight Against an Unbelievable Crime, Rana Husseini Oneworld Publications, 2009, Chapter 12, 'Love Honour and Obey'.

3. 'Fears over forced marriage levels', BBC News Online, 11 March 2008, http://news.bbc.co.uk/1/hi/uk/7288952.stm

4. 'Special Report: For family honor, she had to die', *Chicago Tribune*, 17 November 2005, http://www.kwrw.org/kwahk/index.asp?id=69

5. 'The in-laws lured my sister like an animal and had her killed', by Nikki Watkins, *Sun*, 30 December 2009, http://www.thesun.co.uk/sol/homepage/woman/2787725/12-so-called-honour-killings-in-UK-every-year.html

6. 'Impunity for domestic violence, "honour killings" cannot continue', UN official, UN News Centre Press Release, 4 March 2010, http://www.un.org/apps/news/story.asp?NewsID=33971&Cr=violence+against+women&Cr1

7. 'Police delve into "honour killings"', BBC News Online, 30 September 2003, http://news.bbc.co.uk/1/hi/uk/3151898.stm and 'Special Report: For family honor, she had to die', *Chicago Tribune*, 17 November 2005, http://www.kwrw.org/kwahk/index.asp?id=69

8. *Murder in the Name of Honour: The True Story of One Woman's Heroic Fight Against an Unbelievable Crime*, Rana Husseini, Oneworld Publications, 2009, Chapter 12, 'Love Honour and Obey'.

9. See note 4 (above).

10. 'Five-year-olds to be taught about domestic violence and forced marriages', by Martin Beckford, *Telegraph*, 12 June 2008.

CHAPTER TWENTY-SIX – SECOND TIME AROUND

1. 'They created Winston Silcott, the beast of Broadwater Farm. And they won't let this creation lie down and die', by David Rose, *Observer*, 18 January 2004.